FIFTY YEARS
IN WALL STREET

INTRODUCING WILEY INVESTMENT CLASSICS

There are certain books that have redefined the way we see the worlds of finance and investing—books that deserve a place on every investor's shelf. *Wiley Investment Classics* will introduce you to these memorable books, which are just as relevant and vital today as when they were first published. Open a *Wiley Investment Classic* and rediscover the proven strategies, market philosophies, and definitive techniques that continue to stand the test of time.

FIFTY YEARS IN WALL STREET

HENRY CLEWS

Foreword by Victor Niederhoffer

JOHN WILEY & SONS, INC.

Published by John Wiley & Sons, Inc., Hoboken, New Jersey.
Published simultaneously in Canada.
Full version originally published in 1908 by Irving Publishing Company.

For general information on our other products and services or for technical support, please contact our Customer Care Department within the United States at (800) 762-2974, outside the United States at (317) 572-3993 or fax (317) 572-4002.

Wiley also publishes its books in a variety of electronic formats. Some content that appears in print may not be available in electronic books. For more information about Wiley products, visit our web site at www.wiley.com.

Library of Congress Cataloging-in-Publication

Clews, Henry, 1836–1923.
    Fifty years in Wall Street / Henry Clews ; foreword by Victor Niederhoffer.
      p.   cm. — (Wiley investment classics)
    ISBN-13: 978-0-471-77203-3 (pbk.)
    ISBN-10: 0-471-77203-8 (pbk.)
    1. Wall Street (New York, NY) 2. Speculation. 3. Capitalists and financiers—United States. I. Title. II. Series.
    HG4572.C6 2005
    332.64'2309034—dc22

                              2005052935

Printed in the United States of America

10 9 8 7 6 5 4 3 2 1

CONTENTS

CONTENTS

PUBLISHER'S NOTE

Fifty Years on Wall Street by Henry Clews received extraordinary reviews upon its publication in 1908. Stretching out to more than 1000 pages, the work was lauded for its unique perspective on the historical, political and financial events of the last half of the nineteenth century. As we read the book today, it serves to remind us of the vital role Wall Street played in United States history. This was the Gilded Age—a period of economic, territorial, and population expansion; a period when tremendous individual fortunes were made and labor unions were borne; and a period when Wall Street and Washington D.C. worked hand-in-hand. Written with the authority of an active participant and in a literate and erudite style befitting the times, *Fifty Years on Wall Street* preserves both the historic record and the individualistic spirit of this amazing period of American history.

We discovered *Fifty Years on Wall Street* through Victor Niederhoffer, who recommended that we re-issue the book as part of our Investments Classics line. Author of the acclaimed *Education of a Speculator* and a collector of investment books, Mr. Niederhoffer owned one of the few remaining copies of *Fifty Years on Wall Street*. Mr. Niederhoffer allowed us to borrow his copy to evaluate. We happily accepted his kind offer because, at the time, the book was selling for $3500 on the Internet.

As we began reading, *Fifty Years on Wall Street,* we quickly realized that the book would make an excellent addition to our line of investment classics. We think this book will stand the test of time, in the same manner as other Wiley Investment Classics, such as *Reminiscences of a Stock Operator* and *Where Are the Customers Yachts.* However, as enthusiastic as we were, the book presented a problem: it was simply too long. While some contemporary readers undoubtedly would embrace a 1000 page book on Wall Street history, we felt many more would be put off by the length. We decided to edit the book down to a more manageable size.

To reflect the breadth of the book, we felt we needed to include sections which cumulatively touched on all of the following themes:

- The characteristics of winning and losing speculators
- Wall Street during periods of war
- How operators attempted to "corner" the markets for individual stocks
- The causes and consequences of Wall Street panics
- The influence of Wall Street on national politics
- How individuals like Jay Gould, Daniel Drew, and Commodore Vanderbilt made their fortunes.

We attempted to capture the most interesting and important elements of the book and to do justice to Mr. Clews wide-ranging experiences and expansive sensibility. While some may differ on our selections, we feel confident that contemporary readers will find the new edition of *Fifty Years on Wall Street* a worthy addition to *Wiley's Investment Classics* line.

We hope Mr. Clews would be pleased.

FOREWORD

Dear Reader:

You are holding in your hand a horn of plenty overflowing with stories about the legends of Wall Street, century-old methods for making money, and ideas for predicting the current market. Ostensibly a recounting of the leading events and personalities that affected the career of a prominent investment manager during the 100 years leading up to the Panic of 1907, *Fifty Years in Wall Street* grows and grows in a fashion similar to Don Quixote, until the noble, rich, and expansive tapestry of nineteenth-century financial life uplifts you into a quixotic fervor and hope for today.

Henry Clews was born in 1836 in Staffordshire, England, on a sheep farm. His father, James, was a potter. Henry married Lucy Madison Worthington, a descendant of President James Madison, and she received her PhD in sociology from Columbia University in 1899. They had two sons, John and Henry, Henry being a renowned sculptor whose mansion in Cannes is still a tourist attraction. A daughter, Elsie, wrote a book that recommended trial marriages. During their fifty years of marriage, Henry and Lucy were lions of New York society, earning reprimands from such muckrakers as Matthew Josephson in the *Robber Barons* and other agrarian reformers of the day and fray.

Henry Clews occupied the same position of prominence in Wall Street that Robert Rubin does today. He came to America in 1853 and started out as a clerk in a firm of wool importers. His initial efforts to gain admittance to Wall Street's inner circle were snubbed until 1857, when fears of excessive trade deficits, caused a panic "during which the average stock dropped 50% in a few days." The chilling effect of this panic, the "Western Blizzard," opened up the closed club to young blood. Clews subsequently became one of the "Three Musketeers" who were mainly responsible for the marketing of United States debt during the Civil War. The reward for the financial marketing and political advice that he gave General Ulysses S. Grant during his campaigns was the traditional one: He was offered the office of Secretary of the Treasury. Unlike Robert Rubin, he turned it down; but like Robert Rubin, he did accept the job of "Fiscal Agent for the United States Government in all foreign countries in place of Baring Brothers." Regrettably, the profits from this exclusive club were not enough for him to avoid bankruptcy himself. In 1873, the Credit Mobilier crisis caused his firm to go under and led to the loss of funds for all clients, including such distant entities as the City of San Diego.

He reemerged in business in 1877, paid his debts and formed Henry Clews & Co., eventually taking over the entire space of the Mills Building on Wall Street and Broad opposite the stock exchange, an edifice that still exists today. He prospered there as an investment banker and adviser, and was known, like Warren Buffett today, as "The Sage of Wall Street." He and his business played a prominent part in all Wall Street and city events until his death at the ripe old age of 87 in 1923.

Here are some of my favorite sections of *Fifty Years in Wall Street,* as fresh and resonant today as the day they happened in the 1800s.

CHAPTER 1: MY DEBUT IN WALL STREET

Clews began his Wall Street career during the Panic of 1857. As in the panics of recent times, the infrastructure of Wall Street was shaken up enough to let an outsider into that exclusive and very profitable club.

CHAPTER 2: HOW TO MAKE MONEY IN WALL STREET

Timeless advice, good as gold during the nineteenth century and even better during the last 100 years.

Yes, cane investing. Get ready to hobble to the full extent of your wherewithal.

Chapter 4: Wall Street During the War

The heroic and patriotic role played by Wall Street in providing the capital necessary for the expansion of businesses and the survival of our country during the Revolutionary and Civil wars.

Chapter 7: "Corners" and Their Effect on Values

Why scarcity would develop if speculators were precluded from their natural inclination to squeeze the weak while simultaneously telescoping prices through time.

Chapter 8: The Commodore's "Corners"

The illustrious career of Cornelius Jeremiah Vanderbilt; how his ample reserves and fearless campaigns overcame the poor bears who constantly tried to water him down.

Chapter 10: Panics—Their Causes— How Far Preventable

The causes, prevalence, and violence of panics; the importance of interest rates in creating and ending them. Note that Chairman Greenspan apparently was aware of the salubrious impact of interest rates in his command to open up the throttle of liquidity to full speed after the October 1987 panic.

Chapter 11: Old Time Panics

The history of the New York Stock Exchange, starting with their patriotic agreement never to cut rates—a patriotism which is even stronger today than the day in 1792 that they first agreed to restrain competition.

Chapter 14: Booms in Wall Street

A portrait of the greatest operator of the nineteenth century and a depiction of his methods. Like Soros in our day, he was fol-

lowed by everyone and the mere mention that he and his followers were involved in an issue, usually transportation or chemi-
cals-based, was enough to lift the stock to the stratosphere. "The
beauty of their methods is the quiet and lack of ostentation with
which they carry it on. Their influence is as irresistible as the
laws of gravitation." But unlike Soros, John D. Rockefeller,
the richest man in human history up to the end of the nineteenth century, was a chronic bull. His quiet purchases of stocks
built a foundation of prosperity that "reaches clear to the bowels
of the earth."

CHAPTER 16: THE UPS AND DOWNS OF WALL STREET

The careers of great operators that have "generally gone up like
a rocket and come down like a stick." At last, we meet a bear,
Jacob Little, who was more bearish than Alan Abelson and David
Tice combined. He was short of stock during the panic of 1837.
"That panic swept the whole United States with the besom of
destruction, and sent prices down to zero." Like his modern
counterparts, that left him more bearish and more distrustful
than ever. It is hoped that his fate of being wiped out "and submerged" after the outbreak of the Civil War will not be visited
upon the chronic bears of today, who as relentlessly as Jacob
Little and the other bears portrayed in the chapter, have fought
the 1.5 million-percent-a-century rise in stocks.

CHAPTER 18: THE TWEED RING, AND THE COMMITTEE OF SEVENTY

How the Boss manipulated the money markets and conspired to
create panics. Lives there a government official—present, former, or prospective—who would not envy and learn from the
Boss's connections and profits from the government—Wall Street
interface?

Great books are not only distinguished for their content but for
their wonderful language. It would be remiss not to point out

some of the evocative expressions you will find throughout Clews' masterful work.

Dedication to Veterans

Aught—"I have also endeavored to refrain from setting down aught in malice."

My Debut in Wall Street

Foot up—"It was there that Jacob Little made and lost his nine fortunes. It was there that Anthony Morse, the lightning calculator, operated. He could foot up four columns of figures as easily as the ordinary accountant could run up one."

Old Fogyism—"This crisis sounded the death knell of old fogyism in the 'street.'"

Wall Street as a Civilizer

Bone and Sinew—"He has no right to set himself up as a censor, a public detractor, and a public libeler upon a set of men and merchants who are the bone and sinew of the commercial and industrial interests and prosperity of the country."

Mountebank—"Talmadge has employed his flash wit and mountebank eloquence to bring financial disgrace on the business methods of the whole country by the manner in which he has ignorantly vilified Wall Street."

More War Reminiscences— British and Napoleonic Designs

Fair Soil—"He made a bold attempt to plant that blood-stained foot on this fair soil, in open defiance of the Monroe doctrine, and to crush the liberties that his immortal uncle, even in the full flush of his great conquests, dared not attack and was forced to respect."

Foreign Intrigues Against
American Liberty

Copper—"The conclusion was manifest to European statesmen, who, unlike Wall Street men, never 'copper' the points given by spies."

Secretary Chase and the Treasury

Gilroy's Kite—"The height which Gilroy's kite attained would have been nowhere in point of altitude to that which I should have reached had I not had the good luck to have cleared my decks as I did, and in the nick of time."

Table Tapping—"I do not indulge in any table tapping or dark seances like the elder Vanderbilt, but this strange, peculiar and admonitory influence clings to me in times of approaching squalls more tenaciously than at any ordinary junctures."

Corners

Dotage—"The members thought he must be mad, or at least in his dotage."

Dressing Down—"John, don't them fellows need dressing down?"

Mooted—When a compromise was mooted to him, the Commodore replied, "Put it up to a thousand."

Threescore and Ten—"He was then threescore and ten, the Scriptural limit of human days."

Whist—"It was virtually, at first, a silent game of whist, at which the Commodore was a noted player."

Daniel Drew

Drover—"He dressed like a drover, having originally been employed in that capacity."

Ennobling—"Another motive, however less ennobling to man's nature, seemed to be the true one."

Andrew Johnson's Vargies

Ribaldry—"These jests were taken seriously by the President, whose hot Southern blood became so aroused that he forgot the dignity of his office and station and condescended to bandy words, and exchange terms of ribaldry with people in the crowd."

Hon. Samuel J. Tilden

Propitious—"He did not wait until the tide began to ebb, but, like an able seaman, set his sail at the propitious moment to catch the prosperous breeze as well as the tide."

Notice that several of the chapters deal with case studies of the havoc and opportunity found in panics. The timeless method that Henry Clews recommends for making money on Wall Street is to buy stocks below intrinsic value during the two or three squalls that occur during every year. "It is at these times that wealthy old veterans of the street emerge from the repose of their comfortable homes, and in times of panic, which recur sometimes oftener than once a year, these old fellows will be seen in Wall Street, hobbling down on their canes to their brokers' offices."

"Then they always buy good stocks to the extent of their bank balances. When the panic has spent its force, these old fellows, who have been resting judiciously on their oars in expectation of the inevitable event, which usually returns with the regularity of the seasons, quickly realize, deposit their profits with their bankers, or the overplus thereof, after purchasing more real estate that is on the up grade and retire for another season to the quietude of their splendid homes and the bosoms of their happy families."

But is it true? The least that a poor speculator can do, some 150 years after Clews shared his timeless advice, is to test it. Using daily Dow Jones Industrial Average prices from year-end 1899, Mr. Tom Downing and I ran a number of tests. Here is a typical

FOREWORD

result. The table shows what follows a decline of more than 10% over a five-day period, close to close.

Date	5-Day Move	Price	Price [t+200]	Subsequent 200 Day Return
5/9/1901	−10.4%	67.38	65.27	−3.1%
12/12/1904	−10.2%	65.77	80.92	23.0%
3/14/1907	−11.9%	76.23	58.65	−23.1%
7/30/1914	−11.3%	71.42	89.90	25.9%
5/10/1915	−10.8%	62.06	94.35	52.0%
2/2/1917	−10.6%	87.01	72.95	−16.2%
10/24/1929	−12.4%	299.47	221.08	−26.2%
6/17/1930	−11.2%	228.57	167.03	−26.9%
12/16/1930	−10.8%	157.51	96.61	−38.7%
9/18/1931	−10.3%	115.08	41.22	−64.2%
12/14/1931	−14.3%	77.22	71.53	−7.4%
4/6/1932	−13.9%	66.46	61.46	−7.5%
6/27/1932	−10.2%	42.93	72.64	69.2%
9/14/1932	−17.6%	65.88	105.04	59.4%
11/30/1932	−10.8%	56.35	93.18	65.4%
2/27/1933	−11.0%	50.16	98.87	97.1%
7/21/1933	−15.5%	88.71	93.91	5.9%
10/19/1933	−14.6%	84.38	88.97	5.4%
7/26/1934	−12.1%	85.51	116.58	36.3%
10/18/1937	−12.7%	125.73	141.73	12.7%
3/28/1938	−10.8%	107.25	148.26	38.2%
5/14/1940	−13.2%	128.27	120.88	−5.8%
5/28/1962	−11.0%	576.93	673.73	16.8%
10/19/1987	−29.6%	1730.74	2134.07	22.7%
8/31/1998	−12.0%	7539.06	10490.51	39.1%
9/20/2001	−12.8%	8376.21	9096.09	8.6%

Mean 13.8%

Note that since 1932, the average move was about 30% in the next 200 trading days, with one decline of 6% out of 14 occurrences. Mr. Downing and I systematically looked at numerous other definitions of a panic, varying the extent of the decline and the duration—for example, a decline of 5% in three days. The results are qualitatively similar: much regret and potential lodging on the Bowery in the first third of the twentieth century, and much valuable real estate stashed away for the rainy days thereafter. All things considered, the old-time advice on what to do in panics holds up quite well.

In closing, the speculator would do well to recall Clews' sage guidance that "the common delusion, that expert knowledge is not required in speculation, has wrecked many fortunes and reputations in Wall Street, and is still very influential in its pernicious and illusory achievements."

Victor Niederhoffer
Weston, Connecticut
September 2005

15 TO 17 BROAD STREET
NEW YORK.

To My Readers:

The following pages are intended to throw some light on imperfectly known events connected with Wall Street speculations and investments, and also upon the condition and progress of the country from a financial standpoint, during the fifty years which I have experienced in the great money center.

The theme is worthy of an abler pen, but in the absence of other contributors to this branch of our National history, I venture the plain narrative of an active participator in the financial events of the time in which I have lived.

I have also made a brief retrospect of the history of Wall Street, and financial affairs connected therewith since the origin of the Stock Exchange in New York City.

In sketching the men and events of Wall Street, I have freely employed the vernacular of the speculative fraternity as being best adapted to a true picture of their characteristics, although probably not most consonant with literary propriety.

I have simply attempted to unfold a plain, unvarnished tale, drawing my material from experience and the records of reliable narrators.

HENRY CLEWS.

NEW YORK, March 31, 1908.

FIFTY YEARS
IN WALL STREET

CHAPTER 1

MY DEBUT
IN WALL STREET

MY advent in Wall Street was on the heels of the panic of 1857. That panic was known as the "Western blizzard." It was entitled to the name, as its destructive power and chilling effects had surpassed all other financial gales that had swept over Wall Street. The first serious result of its fatal force was the failure of the Ohio Life and Trust Company, a concern of gigantic dimensions in those days.

The Company had an office in Wall Street, and on the announcement of the collapse, business became completely paralyzed. This failure was immediately followed by the suspension of many large firms that had withstood the shock of all ordinary collisions and had successfully weathered many financial storms.

The panic was due in part to excessive importations of foreign goods, and also to the rapid construction of railroads, to a large extent on borrowed capital. There were other contributing causes. The crops were bad that year, and the country was unable to pay for its imports in produce, and coin was brought to the exporting point. In October, the New York City banks suspended payments, and their example was followed throughout the country. Bank credits had been unduly expanded everywhere, and the time had naturally arrived for contraction. It came with a bound, and financial disaster spread like a whirlwind, becoming general.

The Stock Exchange bad been a moderately growing concern for the ten years previous to this calamity, and the securities there dealt in had been rapidly accumulating in number

1

and appreciating in value. Its members were wealthy and conservative, with a strong infusion of Knickerbocker blood, an admixture of the Southern element and a sprinkling of Englishmen and other foreigners.

The effect of the crisis on the majority of Stock Exchange properties was ruinous. Prices fell fifty per cent. in a few days, and a large proportion of the Board of Brokers were obliged to go into involuntary liquidation. There was a great shaking up all around.

Then came the work of rehabilitation and reorganization. Confidence gradually returned. The Young Republic had great recuperative powers, and they were thoroughly exerted in the work of resuming business. Much of the old conservative element had fallen in the general upheaval, to rise no more. This element was eliminated, and its place supplied by better material, and with young blood, and in December the banks resumed business.

This panic and its immediate results created an entire revolution in the methods of doing business in Wall Street. Prior to this time, the antique element had ruled in things financial, speculative and commercial. This crisis sounded the death knell of old fogyism in the "street." A younger race of financiers arose and filled the places of the old conservative leaders.

The change was a fine exemplification of the survival of the fittest, and proved that there was a law of natural selection in financial affairs that superseded old conservatism and sealed its doom.

Until that time, the general idea prevailed that those engaged in financial matters must be people well advanced in years, even to the verge of infirmity. It is the same idea that has been handed down, as if by divine right, from old world prejudices, especially in the learned professions. No doctor was considered a safe prescriber unless his hoary locks, bald head and wrinkled brow proclaimed that he had almost passed the period of exercising human sympathy. The same rule of judgment was applied to the lawyer and the clergyman.

These unworthy prejudices were fostered by the character of the Government of the old country, and nurtured by the surroundings of the venerable monarchies of Europe, where they exist largely even to the present day. So tenacious of life are these old-fashioned ideas, that many of them were found in full vigor, dominating Wall Street affairs up to the crash of 1857, fostering the antique element and choking off salutary enterprise.

Hence the process of decay of these archaic notions and our gradual development.

This struggle for new life in Wall Street was not successfully developed without a serious effort to attain it. The old potentates of the street fought hard to prolong their obstructive power, and their tenacious vitality was hard to smother, reminding one of the nine lives attributed to the feline species. The efforts of the young and enterprising men to gain an entrance to the Stock Exchange were regarded by the older members as an impertinent intrusion on the natural rights of the senior members. It was next to impossible for a young man, without powerful and wealthy patrons, to obtain membership in the New York Stock Exchange at the time of which I speak.

The old fellows were united together in a mutual admiration league, and fought the young men tooth and nail, contesting every inch of ground when a young man sought entrance to their sacred circle.

The idea then struck me that there was a chance for young men to come to the front in Wall Street. I was then engaged in the dry goods importing trade, in which I received my early training. I had been kept out of the Exchange for several years by the methods to which I have alluded. My fate was similar to that of many others. It was only by an enterprising effort, and by changing the base of my operations, that I finally succeeded.

The commissions charged at that time were an eighth of one per cent. for buying and selling, respectively.

After numerous efforts to gain admission to the Exchange, without success, I finally made up my mind to force it. I at once inserted an advertisement in the newspapers, and proposed to buy and sell stocks at a sixteenth of one per cent.

each way. This was such a bombshell in the camp of these old fogies that they were almost paralyzed. What rendered it more distasteful to them still was the fact that, while they lost customers, I steadily gained them. The result was that they felt compelled to admit me to their ranks, so that I could be kept amenable to their rules and do business only in their own conventional fashion. My membership cost me, in all, initiation fee and other trifling expenses in connection therewith, $500. This presents a striking contrast to the recent price of a seat, $35,000, but though this difference seems very large, yet the changes in every other respect connected with Wall Street affairs have been in similar proportion. Among some of the old members of that day were Jacob Little, John Ward, David Clarkson and others whose names may be found in the archives of the Stock Exchange.

As an instance of the way in which membership was then appreciated, it may be mentioned that speculators frequently offered $100 a week, or ten times the cost of membership, for the privilege of listening at the keyhole during the calls.

Although the prostration growing out of this panic was very great and of long continuance throughout the country, general confidence being shaken to its very foundation, yet, on the whole, it was a great gain, and marked an era of financial and speculative progress. It was the chief cause in drawing out the young element in the business of Wall Street, which might have lain dormant for a much longer period without this sudden and somewhat rude awakening. It not only brought Young America to the front in speculation, commerce and general business, but it imparted an impetus of genuine enterprise to every department of trade and industry, from the good effects of which the country has never since receded.

This new element, emanating from the throes of one of the greatest business revolutions that any country has ever experienced, has continued to grow and thrive with marvellous rapidity. It is now getting so large that the Exchange will soon require a whole block instead of a basement as at its origin for its head-quarters. The Governing Committee of the

Stock Exchange are now looking forward to arrangements for this consummation. How the ancient fathers of my early days in Wall Street would have been shocked at the bare idea of such amazing progress!

It is not the least singular phase of this evolution in Wall Street, that the youthful element to which I have referred stands alone as compared with the progress achieved by the same class of men in any other nation. In America only does the youthful element predominate in financial affairs; and results have justified the selection, which perhaps in no other nation is possible. Thanks to the freedom of our Republican institutions, which, in spite of some individual deductions and the occasional obstructions of "crankdom," make way for that progress, in the wake of which the other nations of the world are emulous to follow.

The Exchange was at this time situated on William Street between Beaver Street and Exchange Place. That place is rich in speculative reminiscences. It was there that Jacob Little made and lost his nine fortunes. It was there that Anthony Morse, the lightning calculator, operated. He could foot up four columns of figures as easily as the ordinary accountant could run up one. He had been a clerk, and having saved seven hundred dollars by close economy, began to deal in stocks. His career at that time was more marvellous even than that of Keene of a recent date. Morse made a fortune of several millions in a year, and became bankrupt during the same period, without any available assets to speak of. It was all honorably lost, however. There was no Ferdinand Ward game connected with it.

Youthful speculators had not then learned the "crooked" methods of the young idea of modern times. It was there also that Daniel Drew began to accumulate those millions that afterward were subject to such a rude scattering. It was there that the celebrated "corners" in Rock Island, Prarie du Chien and Harlem were concocted. It was there that the wealth was accumulated which built twenty thousand miles of Western railroads, causing many millions of acres, that would other-wise have been a wilderness, to blossom like the rose, in spite of Mr. Powderly's opinion that no material good can come out of speculation, and thus adding immense wealth in real estate to the country, besides conferring incalculable benefits on trade and commerce, and preparing comfortable homes not only for the pioneers and surplus population of the Eastern States, but a teeming soil that has attracted the downtrodden of every nation to come and partake of the blessings of freedom and prosperity.

One of Jacob Little's speculative ventures has been rendered historically famous through the rule of limitation of sixty days for option contracts. The necessity for this limit was brought about by one of his celebrated attempts to manipulate the market. He was one of the most prominent speculators in Erie in the early days of Drew's transactions with that property and its stocks. Mr. Little had been selling large blocks of Erie on seller's option, to run from six to twelve months. This was in the early history of "corners," before the method of managing them scientifically had been fully developed and while "blind pools" were yet in embryo.

The leading members of the Erie Board formed a pool to "corner" Mr. Little, and ran Erie shares up to a considerable height. They imagined that he was in blissful ignorance of their purpose, and had everything arranged for a *coup d'etat* which was to reach its crisis at two o'clock on a certain day, when Little was to be completely overwhelmed and hopelessly ruined. An hour prior to the time appointed by the clique for his disaster he walked into the Erie office, opened a bag filled with convertible bonds, and requested an exchange of stock for the same. He had purchased the bonds in London and had them safely locked up for the emergency, which he promptly met on its arrival. He got the stock, settled his contracts, broke the "corner," and came out triumphantly.

The option limit of sixty days was afterwards adopted in order to prevent similar triumphs in manipulation on the "short" side.

As will be illustrated more fully in subsequent chapters, Mr. Little's convertible bond trick was used with signal advantage by his speculative successors in Erie, who practically demonstrated on several occasions that there were millions in it.

Mr. Little was generous and liberal to a fault with his brother speculators who had experienced misfortune. He used to say that he could paper his private office with notes he had forgiven to the members of the Board. He was also remarkable for his great memory. He could easily remember all the operations he made in the course of a day without making a note or a mistake.

Like Drew, he was careless in his attire, wearing a hat like that of a farmer, and not a very prosperous one, but he had no compeer in his day at calculating ahead in a speculative venture.

CHAPTER 2

HOW TO MAKE MONEY
IN WALL STREET

How to take Advantage of Periodical Panics in
Order to Make Money. — Wholesome Advice to
Young Speculators. — Alleged "Points" from Big
Speculators End in Loss or Disaster. — Professional
Advice the Surest and Cheapest, and How and
Where to Obtain It.

BUT few gain sufficient experience in Wall Street to command success until they reach that period of life in which they have one foot in the grave. When this time comes these old veterans of the Street usually spend long intervals of repose at their comfortable homes, and in times of panic, which recur sometimes oftener than once a year, these old fellows will be seen in Wall Street, hobbling down on their canes to their brokers' offices.

Then they always buy good stocks to the extent of their bank balances, which have been permitted to accumulate for just such an emergency. The panic usually rages until enough of these cash purchases of stock is made to afford a big "rake in." When the panic has spent its force, these old fellows, who have been resting judiciously on their oars in expectation of the inevitable event, which usually returns with the regularity of the seasons, quickly realize, deposit their profits with their bankers, or the overplus thereof, after purchasing more real estate that is on the up grade, for permanent investment, and

9

retire for another season to the quietude of their splendid homes and the bosoms of their happy families.

If young men had only the patience to watch the speculative signs of the times, as manifested in the periodical egress of these old prophetic speculators from their shells of security, they would make more money at these intervals than by following up the slippery "tips" of the professional "pointers" of the Stock Exchange all the year round, and they would feel no necessity for hanging at the coat tails, around the hotels, of those specious frauds, who pretend to be deep in the councils of the big operators and of all the new "pools" in process of formation. I say to the young speculators, therefore, watch the ominous visits to the Street of these old men. They are as certain to be seen on the eve of a panic as spiders creeping stealthily and noiselessly from their cobwebs just before rain. If you only wait to see them purchase, then put up a fair margin for yourselves, keep out of the "bucket shops" as well as the "sample rooms," and only visit Delmonico's for light lunch in business hours, you can hardly fail to realize handsome profits on your ventures.

The habit of following points which are supposed to emanate from the big operators, nearly always ends in loss and sometimes in disaster to young speculators. The latter become slavish in their methods of thought, having their minds entirely subjected to others, who are presumed to do the thinking for them, and they consequently fail to cultivate the self-reliance that is indispensable to the success of any kind of business.

To the question often put, especially by men outside of Wall Street, "How can I make money in Wall Street?" there is probably no better answer than the one given by old Meyer Rothschild to a person who asked him a similar question. He said, "I buys 'sheep' and sells 'dear.'"

Those who follow this method always succeed. There has hardly been a year within my recollection, going back nearly thirty years, when there have not been two or three squalls in "the Street," during the year, when it was possible to purchase stocks below their intrinsic value. The squall usually passes over in a few days, and then the lucky buyers of stocks at panic prices come in for their ranging from five to ten per cent. on the entire venture.

The question of making money, then, becomes a mere matter of calculation, depending on the number of the squalls that may occur during any particular year.

If the venture is made at the right time—at the lucky moment, so to speak—and each successive venture is fortunate, as happens often to those who use their judgment in the best way, it is possible to realize a net gain of fifty per cent. per annum on the aggregate of the year's investments.

In this way it is easy to see how the rich will get richer, and the poor poorer.

Sometimes men make money in Wall Street by strange turns in their fortunes that appear like having been governed by a special Providence, and this sometimes occurs when men appear to be utter wrecks.

One of the strangest examples of this kind, in my personal experience, occurred in the summer of 1885.

A man called at my office utterly broken down in spirit, but with a few hundred dollars left out of many thousands that he had possessed a few months previously.

"I read your letter of the third of July," he said, "and had some mind to act on the advice which it contained, but was unfortunately dissuaded therefrom by reading an article in a city paper by a very able writer, who had got the bearish mania, then prevalent, on the brain, and who, I am informed, is now, like myself, almost ruined."

"I hardly know what to do," he continued. "I have a few hundred dollars left, which I will leave with you, and you can use your pleasure with it. I am going out to the country for the remainder of the summer. I will leave my address with you, and, if there is any good result, you can let me know of it. I really don't hope for much, and of course, I need hardly tell you that, in the event of being 'wiped out,' you need not apply to me for more margin. Let this go with the rest," he added, in a despairing tone.

The man walked sadly out, and I did not see him again for months. I invested his pittance on the *carte blanche* order which he had given me, to the best of my judgment. The result was favorable, and his account began to accumulate. He was duly advised, according to our business methods, of his good luck, but I did not hear anything from him personally for several months.

One day, a portly gentleman, with rosy health beaming in his face, stepped into my private office, and was quite profuse in his thanks for me.

"Well," I said; "I have but a hazy recollection of your acquaintance, if I know you at all."

"Don't you recollect," he said, "the time I went to the country for the summer, when I told you my case, and how I had been unfortunate in speculation?"

"And are you the man who went to the country in despair to die?" I asked, in surprise at his changed appearance.

"I am," he replied, "And I owe the wonderful change which you now see to your timely advice. I staked almost my last dollar on that counsel, and now I am comfortably fixed through your management of the small fund placed at your disposal."

Now, this was an example of a man who did make money simply by taking the advice that was freely tendered him.

There are others who lose, in spite of all that the most honest judgment can do to prevent them.

Some men, when they have money, are so fearfully perverse that all attempts to get them to do the right thing only have the opposite effect, and they prefer to follow every wild rumor.

One day, for instance, a man gave me an order to buy a thousand shares of Erie without limit. The order was executed at 94. I had no sooner brought it than the stock went down.

My customer returned in a short time and ordered the stock to be sold. It was then 92$\frac{1}{2}$.

In half an afterwards he returned again and ordered it bought back again, without any limit as before. It was bought back at 95.

After consulting with other friends for some time he ordered it sold again. The market by that time was 90.

He then came back the fifth time, and said: "I first saw one man who told me to buy, and then another who told me to sell. I understand one is called a 'bull' and the other a 'bear.' About these names I don't know much, but I do know now that I am a _____ jackass."

This affords a good illustration of the way the average speculator is managed and perplexed in Wall Street. There is a means of avoiding such a peck of trouble, however, if he would only take a little wholesome advice, wait patiently for a proper opportunity, and not rush headlong to purchase on the "tips" of the delusive rumor mongers. He would then begin to learn how to make money in Wall Street.

As I have pointed out in another chapter, speculation is a business that must be studied as a specialty, and though it is popularly believed that any man who has money can speculate, yet the ordinary man, without special training in the business, is liable to make as great a mistake in this attempt, as the man who thinks he can act as his own lawyer, and who is said "to have a fool for a client."

The common delusion, that expert knowledge is not required in speculation, has wrecked many fortunes and reputations in Wall Street, and is still very influential in its pernicious and illusory achievements.

When a man wants correct advice in law he goes to a professional lawyer in good standing, one who has made a reputation in the courts, and who has afforded other evidence to the public that he is thoroughly reliable. No man of average common sense would trust a case in law to a bar room "bummer" who would assert that he was well acquainted with Aaron J. Vanderpoel, Roscoe Conkling, and Wm. M. Evarts, and had got all the inside "tips" from these legal lights on the law relating to the case in question. The fellow would be laughed at, and, in all probability, if he persisted in this kind of talk, would be handed over to the city physician to be examined in relation to his sanity, but in Wall Street affairs men can every day make similar pretensions and pass for embodiments of speculative wisdom.

If speculators are caught and fleeced by following such counsel, the professional brokers who are members of the Stock Exchange, are no more to blame than the eminent lawyers to whom I have referred would be for the upshot of a case that had been taken into court on the advice which some irresponsible person had pretended to receive from these celebrities of the New York Bar.

Professional advice in Wall Street, as in legal affairs, is worth paying for, and cost far less in the end than the cheap "points" that are distributed profusely around the Street, thick as autumn leaves in Vallombrosa, and which only allure the innocent speculator to put his money where he is almost certain to lose it.

My advice to speculators who wish to make money in Wall Street, therefore, is to ignore the counsel of the back-room "tippers" and "tipplers," turn their backs on "bucket shops," and when they want "points" to purchase, let them go to those who have established a reputation for giving sound advice in such manners, and who have ample resources for furnishing correct information on financial topics, as well as a personal interest in making all the money they can for their clients.

There is no difficulty in finding out such reliable men and firms in the vicinity of Wall Street, if speculators will only read the newspapers, or make inquiry of the first messenger boy they may happen to meet.

CHAPTER 3

CAUSES OF LOSS
IN SPECULATION

INADEQUATE INFORMATION.—FALSE INFORMATION.—
DEFECTS OF NEWS AGENCIES.—INSUFFICIENCY OF
MARGINS.—DANGERS OF PERSONAL IDIOSYNCRASIES.—
OPERATING IN SEASON AND OUT OF SEASON.—NECESSITY
OF INTELLIGENCE, JUDGMENT AND NERVE.—AN IDEAL
STANDARD.—WHAT MAKE A KING AMONG SPECULATORS?

A S there is always the chance of speculators whose operations, in the long run, leave a net result of loss rather
than profit, it may not be amiss if I state what experience has
taught me as to the causes of this want of success.

Undoubtedly, many who enter the arena of speculation are
in every way unfitted to take the risks against such wily
opponents as they must encounter. They are either too ignorant or too wise, too timid or too bold, too pessimistic or too
sanguine, too slow or too hasty, too diffident or too conceited,
too confiding or too incredulous. These are constitutional
defects, any one of which may easily cost an operator a fortune. And yet self-knowledge, with self-control, may prevent
these natural disqualifications from seriously interfering with
success. There is no mental discipline more severe and exacting than that of speculation. There is no pursuit in which a
man can less afford to indulge in whims, or prejudices, or pet
theories, than that of stacking his money against the prospective changes in financial values. He must be as calm and as
impartial as a judge, not less in respect to the risks he incurs

than in regard to the integrity of his own judgment. I should lay it down as the first rule necessary to success, that the judgment be not warped by any natural idiosyncrasies; this being secured, a man may succeed in spite of his constitutional defects.

Singular as it may seem, there are no advantages beset with greater dangers than information—the one thing most largely sought after and most highly prized. Very naturally, most men object to taking a risk without possessing some knowledge of the conditions that determine the risk; and yet how few take care that their knowledge is adequate enough or certain enough for the formation of a safe judgment. In some cases, knowledge is unattainable and the operation must be a leap in the dark; and in such instances a man is unwise to step in unless his experience satisfies him that he is uncommonly sagacious in guessing.

Many speculators lose because the information on which they base their operations is *insufficient;* more because it is *false;* and others because, while their information is correct, they do *not know how to turn it to account.*

Between one or other of these difficulties in the use of information must be distributed a very large proportion of the losses incurred in speculation. Incomplete or insufficient information is especially dangerous. One-sided knowledge is nowhere so deceiving as here. A railroad, for instance, may report an increase of gross earnings which is construed as making its stock worth two or three per cent. more than its current price; but the improvement may be due to transient special causes, and the road's current expenses may be growing at a rate which makes the net increase show a decrease. A financially embarrassed company may announce an assessment of its stockholders, upon which there is a rush to sell the stock; a little further explanation shows that the proceeds of the assessment will so improve the facilities of the company, or so enable it to reduce its fixed charges, as to make the stock intrinsically far more valuable then it was before; this discovery causes a sharp advance in the shares, and the "short" sellers have to cover their sales at a loss. A stock is bought up freely at New York because London is taking large amounts of it; a day or two later, the deliveries show that large holders connected with the management are unloading on the foreign market upon the knowledge of facts damaging to the prospects of the property; the late buyers then rush to realize, and pocket a loss instead of a profit. Every day furnishes new instances of speculations undertaking on this incomplete kind of information, and which end disastrously because the operators did not wait to be informed on all sides of the case, but were satisfied to take a pound of assumption with but an ounce of fact.

One of the strongest anomalies of speculation is in the facility with which man are induced to take large risks on false information and manufactured "points." Considering the readiness with which a numerous class of "outside" operators buy or sell on sensational rumors, it is not surprising that the professional operators should keep the market well supplied with such decoys; and it is not easy to say which most deserves condemnation—the heedless credulity of the dupes, or the deliberate lies of the canard-makers. There is, however, a third party not less blameable than either of the foregoing. I refer to those who make it a part of their business to circulate false information. Principal among those caterers are the financial news agencies and the morning Wall Street news sheet, both specially devoted to the speculative interests that centre at the Stock Exchange. The object of these agencies is a useful one; but the public have a right to expect that when they subscribe for information upon which immense transactions may be undertaken, the utmost caution, scrutiny and fidelity should be exercised in the procurement and publication of the news. Anything that falls short of this is something worse than bad service and bad faith with subscribers; it is dishonest and mischievous. And yet it cannot be denied that much of the so-called news that reaches the public through these instrumentalities must come under this condemnation. The "points," and "puffs," the alarms and the canards, put out expressly to deceive and mislead, find a wide circulation through these mediums, with an ease which admits of no possible justification. How far these lapses are due to the haste inseparable from the compilation of news of such a character, how far to a lack of proper sifting and caution, and how far to less culpable reasons, I do not pretend to decide; but this will be admitted by every observer, that the circulation of pseudo news is the frequent cause of incalculable losses. Nor is it alone in the matter of circulating false information that these news venders are at fault. The habit of retailing "points" in the interest of cliques, the volunteering of advice as to what people should buy and what they should sell, the strong speculative bias that runs through their editorial opinions, these things appear to most people a revolting abuse of the true functions of journalism. But patent as these things are to those educated in the ways of Wall Street, there is a large class who accept such effusions as gospel, and are easily led by them into the clutches of the sharks. It is but just, however, to acknowledge that with these very serious drawbacks, both these classes of news agencies render valuable service to Wall Street interests, and it is to be hoped that experience will convince them that their enterprises would attain a higher success through emulating a higher standard

Another source of losses in speculation lies in the speculator not holding back a cash reserve sufficient to protect him against an adverse course of prices. Ordinarily, the man who speculates is of a sanguine temperament, and apt to take risks without sufficient provision against contingencies. Hence, it is common with inexperienced operators to use all their available resources in their original margin The result is that, if prices go against them, they are liable to be closed out and saddled with a loss they can ill afford. Such persons should never pledge more than one-half of their available means at the beginning of a transaction; the remaining half should be kept as a guarantee against their being "sold out," or to enable them to duplicate the transaction at the changed price, so as to make an average likely to yield a profit. The violation of this rule creates a class of weak holders, who offer a constant inducement to "room-traders" to raid the market; knowing, as they do, that when they have impaired these unsupported margins, there is sure to be a rush of selling orders calculated to break down prices. It is safe to say that if better provisions were made for keeping margins good, the power of the "bears" and the wreckers would be broken; one-half of the losses of "outside" operators would be obviated, and one-half the risks of speculation would be obliterated.

Another class especially exposed to losses are those who always operate in the same direction. Wall Street has its optimists and pessimists; they are such from a constitutional bent; and they are "bull" or "bear" in season and out of season. As a rule, those that follow a natural disposition, rather than the course of the market and the conditions that mould it, are sure to bankrupt themselves sooner or later. I do not mean to maintain that there is no chance for an operator who clings continuously to one side of the market; for in times when conditions favor higher prices there is always some profitable work to be done by the "bear" in checking excesses of a rise; and, when events favor decline, the "bull" may find his chances in intervals of excessive decline. But the man who can thus successfully steer his craft against the winds and the tides must be a thoroughly trained navigator, cool in temperment, capable of reining his natural proclivities, and above all, the possessor of means large enough to control, if necessary, the course of the market by sheer money power. It is needless to say that nine-tenths of this stereotyped class are devoid of these requisites to success. One cannot but pity the man with sallow face and sluggish gait so suggestive of the blue pill, who, when everybody else is feeling the happy impulse of a common prosperity, persists in believing that the country is going to the dogs, and steadily sells stocks while everybody else is buying them. He is simply ruining himself through unconsciousness that he views everything through bilious spectacles. Equally is the man to be commiserated who, from a constitutional intoxication hope, keeps on buying and holding when it is manifest that the country has passed the summit of an era of prosperity and is destined to a general reaction in trade and values. Of course, such men never remain long in Wall Street; their pockets are soon emptied, and they retire to reflect on the folly of refusing to appreciate and to follow the natural drift of the conditions that regulate values.

A minor source of losses lies in operating at times when the market is so evenly balanced between opposing forces that there is no chance for making profits. At such times, operators get disgusted at the sluggishness of the market; they change their holdings from day to day, with no advantage except to their broker; and their monthly statement shows a heavy list of charges for interest and commissions with no offset of profits. These intervals of stagnancy sometimes run for weeks, sometimes for months; and at such times a wise speculator would take care to keep out of the market and hold himself in readiness for anything that may turn up.

It is necessary to the avoidance of loss that the operator should maintain an intelligent watch upon the influences that control the market. Those influences are two-fold—such as are intrinsic to the market, and such as are external to it. Of the former class are those that relate to the spirit and tone of the market; the position and disposition of the cliques; the action of the large operators; the over-loaded or over-sold state of the market, as indicated by the loaning rates for stocks; the influence exerted by the upward or downward movements in stocks which at the moment are specially active; the possibility of closing out holders on "stop orders" or on the impairment of margins; the unloading of influential cliques and the covering of important lines of short saloo, &c., &c. Influences of this kind are very frequently sufficient of themselves to control the market for a considerable period in direct opposition to the tendency indicated by external conditions. It is, however, no easy matter to form a correct conclusion as to the drift resulting from this set of factors. They are so concealed and so changeful, and the symptoms are so vague, that it requires long experience, added to unusual sagacity, to determine what may be the tendency resulting from the complex action and counteraction of this set of conditions. Some exceptional operators enjoy an instinctive faculty for weighing these shadowy indications with almost unerring certainty. Such men usually care little about outside influences, except so far as they may affect the market for the moment. From the nature of the case, their transactions are apt to be brief ones, and follow quickly the momentary course of the market. They are reckoned among the most sagacious speculators, and are usually very successful. But their success is the result of a special natural gift, and therefore cannot be won by others.

The second class of influences above alluded to as external to the market are of a very broad and varied character. They embrace almost everything that affects the welfare of the country. Those, however, which are most potent are, the state of the crops; the condition of manufacturing industries; the state and prospects of trade; the earnings of the transportation companies; the course of the imports and exports; the attitude of the foreign markets towards American securities; the movements of the precious metals; the condition of the London and Continental money markets; the position of the New York banks and the course of currency movements; the action of Congress, of the Legislatures and of the Courts on matters affecting the value of investments; the acts of labor unions and the drift of labor agitations, and the course of political and social issues. This may be considered a rather startling list of topics for a man to keep himself well informed upon, but there is not one of them which may not any day become a controlling factor in the condition of the stock market. For a man, therefore, who aims to keep his knowledge abreast with his business, it is necessary that he should be a close observer of events. Undoubtedly few possess this breadth of information, and most men think it sufficient to get their knowledge as best they may when the events happen. The misfortune in such cases is, that those better informed utilize the event while the others are "getting posted." Considering how many half-informed or wholly ignorant persons engage in speculation with more or less success, it cannot be pretended that to keep informed on the foregoing set of conditions is essential to a fair degree of success. But it must be maintained that such knowledge is of incalculable value and that a man who has it is in a position to act with more intelligence, assurance and success than one without it. To those who desire to turn to account all coming changes, and to stand always prepared for the good or evil events of the future, this intelligent comprehension of the status of all the forces that make or unmake values is absolutely indispensable. And yet it is one thing to possess this information; another to know how to draw correct conclusions from it, and yet another to know how best to use it in the area of speculation. Failure at any one of these points may be fatal to success and result in disaster.

I conclude, then, that for a man to be a thoroughly equipped speculator, it is necessary that he be possessed of extraordinary parts and attainments. He must be an unceasing and intelligent observer of events at large, and a sagacious interpreter of symptoms on the Exchange; his judgment must be sound, not only as to existing conditions, but as to coming tendencies, and he must possess the calmness and nerve to face unflinchingly whatever emergencies may arise. Whoever enjoys these qualities in the highest degree must be the King of Speculators. As to others, their rank must correspond to the degree of their conformity to this ideal standard.

CHAPTER 4

WALL STREET DURING THE WAR

THE FINANCIERS OF WALL STREET ASSIST THE GOVERNMENT IN THE HOUR OF THE COUNTRY'S PERIL. — THE ISSUE OF THE TREASURY NOTES. — JAY COOKE'S NORTHERN PACIFIC SCHEME PRECIPITATES THE PANIC OF 1873. — WALL STREET HAS PLAYED A PROMINENT PART IN THE GREAT EVOLUTION AND PROGRESS OF THE PRESENT AGE.

WALL Street came to the rescue of the country when the war broke out. The Government then did not have money enough to pay the interest on the debt, and was sorely embarrassed for a time. The Hon. S.P. Chase, Secretary of the Treasury, sent word to Mr. Cisco, the Sub-Treasurer in New York, to do everything in his power to raise the money required to sustain the nation's credit.

Mr. Cisco apprised the "Street" of the instructions he had received from Washington concerning the empty condition of the Treasury. He showed a number of the leading operators and financiers that within a few days the interest on the accruing obligations would have to be paid, or the Government paper should go to protest. It was clearly demonstrated that if funds could not be raised the Government should be placed in a perplexing position, that would, in all probability, greatly complicate and prolong the struggle for national existence. It was one of the most critical moments in the whole history of the Republic, and the emergency required clear, decisive judgment, and promptitude of action.

Wall Street men perceived the gravity of the situation at a glance. If the Government's credit should collapse, it was feared that the whole framework of our political system would be endangered.

The foundation of all securities was threatened with a destructive upheaval, and most serious consequences were likely to ensue, menacing a contraction of all values. The prospect was very dark. Not a ray of hope shone through the sombre clouds that hung dismally over the Union. The internal dissensions of our people, and the apparent destruction of our national life, were watched with the deepest interest by European friends and foes—the latter being then largely in the majority, and only waiting a favorable opportunity to pounce upon what they considered their destined prey.

Manifest destiny seemed to have leagued all her forces in opposition to us. The stoutest hearts quailed at the prospect of our dissolution as a nation.

At this momentous juncture, when there was no eye to pity, and when no other arm seemed mighty enough to save, the Wall Street men were equal to the occasion. They put their heads together, came to the front, and resolved to extricate the Government from its perilous position. It is true that they were well paid for it. They charged twelve per cent. for the loan, but that was nothing when the risk is taken into account. It was then almost impossible to get a loan at any rate of interest. By some of the great nations of Europe the risk then involved in such a loan was regarded in about the same light as the people of this country now estimate the present chances for realizing on Confederate paper money, or Georgia bonds of the old issue.

In this state of public feeling, Lombard Street was not in a favorable mood to negotiate loans with this country, and, the whole fraternity of the Rothschilds shut their fists on their shining shekels and shook their heads negatively and ominously at the bare mention of advancing money to the once great but now doomed Republic.

Money was dear at the time, and the Government was only obliged to pay what could have been obtained in other quarters. Curiously enough, private property then was considered better security than the Government endorsement, on the principle—which was not a very patriotic one, though in reality true—that the country could survive its form of government. That form, however, the best the world has yet seen, survived the shock and maintained its autonomy. That it did so was in a large measure due to the prompt action of Wall Street men in raising the sinews of war at the incipient stage of the rebellion. Had they failed to do so, it is not improbable that the repulse at Bull Run might have proved a decisive blow to the Union, and plunged the country into a state of anarchy from which nothing but a despotism almost as bad could have retrieved it.

The negotiation of this loan brought out the twelve per cent. Treasury notes. After this issue the rates fell. Then came the 11 and the 10¾ per cent. issues, and subsequently the well-known and long to be remembered 7 3-10 Treasury notes.

After this issue had been popularized, successfully disposed of, and finally taken up at maturity by the 5-20 loan, Jay Cooke was quick to issue, after their pattern, his famous 7 3-10 Northern Pacific Railroad bonds. Evidently he had a patent for negotiating that famous 7 3-10 per cent. railroad loan, as almost every clergyman, Sunday-school teacher and public benefactor were found to have invested in them, when the crash came, and although the road was the means of his financial downfall, with the ruin of an innumerable number of others besides, who were dragged into the same speculative whirlpool, this unfortunate event was not entirely an unmixed evil.

It is true that this was the main and visible cause of precipitating the panic of 1873, of which I shall speak more fully in another chapter, but the Pacific road was the great pioneer in opening up the Far West, and developing its material resources, the great artery of the Western railroad system, conveying vigorous and durable vitality to the industrial life of the expansive regions beyond the Rockies.

Thus, in taking a retrospect of my twenty-eight years in Wall Street, I find that what sometimes appeared to be great evils have been succeeded by compensating good, fate counter-balancing fate, as the Latin poet has it. It was so, as I have previously observed, after the panic of 1857. It was so after the convulsion of 1873, and though I have only historic evidence to guide me in regard to the earlier history of the Street, I find it as so after 1837. So, the maxim that history repeats itself has been fully verified in Wall Street.

So, now that I have relapsed into a reflective mood on this subject, a host of important associations connected with the main issue rush upon me. The prominent idea that stands out in bold relief is the rapid and wonderful progress made in Wall Street during the period that I have undertaken to chronicle. And not only so, but the rapid strides that have been made in everything, almost universally, during that time, present a vast theme for consideration. The part that Wall Street men have taken in this mighty evolution is the topic that concerns me most at present. As an attempt to progress with my subject, I observe this division of it becoming more expansive, so that I find myself in the position of the Irishman when he ascended to the top of the mountain. After recovering from the first effects of his surprise, he exclaimed: "I never thought the world was so large!"

So it is with me. I never thought that Wall Street was so big, nor that Wall Street affairs were so extensive, until I began to write about them. They expand, as well as improve, surprisingly on closer acquaintance. I only hope I shall be able to impress this idea more vividly on the minds of my clerical friends, and others who have been misguided in this respect, chiefly on hearsay and irresponsible evidence, and who, I am sorry to say, have been the well-meaning but over-zealous instruments of misleading others.

To come to an approximate deduction of facts, then, it is, I think, a fair estimate of the general progress of humanity to say that there has been greater material advance in everything that relates to a higher civilization, and the greatest good to the greatest number, during the last thirty years, than in all the previous time that has elapsed since the period that the father of history, old Herodotus, began to chronicle, in his racy style, the real and imaginary events of the human family.

The part that Wall Street has played in this amazing progress has been comparatively large, and would, if thoroughly investigated and fully discussed, make a larger book than I have time to write at present.

I can only glance at the prominent topics and leading events in the extensive and somewhat sensational history of Wall Street, and sketch briefly the conspicuous features in the lives of certain celebrities who have been conspicuous in the history of speculation, and of those who have been prominent in the financial affairs of the country.

CHAPTER 5

MY PART IN MARKETING
THE UNITED STATES
CIVIL WAR LOANS

TO a very large majority of Americans now living the great
Civil War—waged from 1861 to 1865—between the North
and the South is only known as a matter of history. But it
was the greatest war the world ever witnessed, involving the
loss of nearly a million of men, and I have a vivid recollection
of it, for I was an actor in it, from its beginning to its end, to
the extent of providing some of the sinews of war for the
United States Government, without which it could not have
defeated the armies of secession, and preserved the Union.

From the time that Abraham Lincoln was elected to
the Presidency of the United States, in November, 1860, the
South began to prepare for secession from the North, peace-
ably if the North consented, but by war if it resisted. It was
bent on this course because it foresaw in a Republican administration at Washington its practical loss of control of
Congress and the spoils of office—in fact, of the Government
itself—that it had so long enjoyed under Democratic adminis-
trations. James Buchanan's term as President having expired
on March 4, 1861, Abraham Lincoln was then inaugurated as
his successor. It angered the South to see a Republican succeed a Democrat in the White House, and it precipitated the
tremendous conflict that followed, by seizing Fort Moultrie, in
Charleston harbor, and firing on Fort Sumter. Fort Moultrie's
guns awoke the North to action, and made it a determined

unit in defense of the flag that had been fired upon, and its cry was, "The Union must and shall be preserved!"

As this was the most eventful and critical period in our national history since 1776, and so many know it only by what they have read of it, I will give a general idea of its salient features bearing upon the Government finances and the war loans.

When, after the bombardment of Fort Sumter by Fort Moultrie, on April 14, 1861, Major Robert Anderson, the Union commander, accepted, under the stern necessities of the situation, General Beauregard's terms of evacuation, the die was cast.

The North picked up the gauntlet of war with patriotic enthusiasm, and the great conflict had begun. But when our troops marched out of that dismantled stronghold of the Union, with drums beating and colors flying, it is safe to say that few or none, either in the North or the South, foresaw the long and mighty struggle that would, for four eventful years, follow the bombardment of Fort Sumter, during which gold would become demonetized before the end of the year. It did so on December 30, 1861, and in the darkest days of the conflict commanded a premium as high as one hundred and eighty-five per cent. over United States legal tender notes, making these worth only 54 1/20 cents in gold, while United States bonds were selling for about 60 cents on the dollar in gold.

When the New York Clearing House agreed, on the date named, to suspend specie payments, the example was at once followed by all the banks in the country, and gold immedi ately began to command a small premium. None supposed then that the suspension would continue for eighteen years.

In England, during the long suspension from 1797 to 1821—through the Napoleonic wars—the premium on gold never rose above forty-one per cent., and that was in 1814, the year before the end of hostilities. This was owing to the policy of William Pitt and his successors in the management of the British finances. They raised all the money needed for war purposes by taxation and loans, thus restricting the paper money issues, so as to prevent currency inflation, whereas we pursued the opposite course.

When Fort Sumter was fired upon, my firm—Livermore, Clews & Co.—was already prominent in Wall Street, and I immediately began to devise ways and means to help the Government to raise the money that I saw would be necessary to prosecute the war for the Union which this bombardment made inevitable. Fort Moultrie's guns had united the North in a call to arms, and men by tens of thousands left the farm, the loom, the office, and the store, from Maine to Indiana, to join the Union army.

Money, therefore, was needed by the United States Government, and very large amounts of it, to equip troops and purchase munitions of war.

As James Buchanan was then President, and, like a long line of his predecessors, a Democrat, he had several Southerners in his Cabinet. These promptly resigned their places and went South, including the Secretary of the Treasury, Howell Cobb, who left with surprising suddenness, and the office was filled for a brief period by General John A. Dix, as acting Secretary.

But before leaving, Howell Cobb had offered and sold to Wall Street bankers $20,000,000 of United States five per cent. bonds at 105, authorized, of course, by an old law. Owing, however, to the heavy decline in securities, and general depression following the outbreak of the war, only about one-quarter of these bonds were taken and paid for by those who had subscribed for them; and nothing was done by the Government to enforce the completion of the purchase by those who had defaulted under the severe stress of the times.

Their default was a serious matter for the Government at that time, as it left the funds in the Treasury in a very depleted condition, and interest payments on the public debt were about to fall due, which it had no money in its vaults to provide for. At this crisis John J. Cisco, the United States Sub-treasurer in New York, was instructed, from Washington, to call a meeting of the principal Wall Street bankers at the Sub-treasury, and after stating the situation to them, to ask for an emergency loan on one-year United States notes, and let them fix the rate of interest themselves to correspond with the state of the money market.

Money was then loaning at about twelve per cent. per annum in Wall Street. So when the bankers who responded to Mr. Cisco's call, myself among the number, assembled at the Sub-treasury, they, after full discussion, agreed to take the amount of notes offered, and at this rate of interest. It was a very high rate for the Government to pay, too high under ordinary circumstances, but the emergency justified it; and Mr. Cisco approved of it, in view of the market rate and the notes running for one year only. My firm took a considerable amount of them and induced others to do so also, and we did so, presumably like the rest of the buyers, not merely because the rate agreed upon was so high, but because we felt it a duty to help the Government; and at all times thereafter during that critical period we worked no less diligently to uphold the public credit.

The Government recognized that a default in its interest payments would have been disastrous to the public credit, and a stumbling block in the way of raising money to prosecute the war, besides causing general depression of business. It therefore had to be prevented at all hazards.

Had these notes not been taken, the Treasury would undoubtedly have been left without the means of paying this interest when due. Consequently, it gratified me to feel that I had been instrumental in inducing others to subscribe for a part of this urgently needed loan.

Soon afterwards Mr. Salmon P. Chase was appointed Secretary of the Treasury by President Lincoln.

Not long afterwards Secretary Chase came to the Sub-treasury and invited bids for $20,000,000 of six per cent. United States bonds maturing in 1884. These were authorized by an old law. He accepted all bids at 94 and over, but rejected all under 94, the result of which was that considerably more than a third of the 1884's remained unsold. This was to be regretted, because the Treasury was in great need of money. I therefore quickly bestirred myself to form a combination to purchase the unsold bonds of 1884 at 94, my firm being willing to take a liberal share of them, and I succeeded in getting subscriptions from banks and capitalists who had not bought any of those sold, for the unsold amount, subject to my own discretion as to the advisability of taking the bonds, after going to Washington and conferring with Secretary Chase.

So I immediately went there by night train and saw the Secretary early in the morning at the Treasury, and told him I had come on behalf of the combination I had formed, to make him a direct offer at his own price—94—for the unsold 1884 bonds. He was evidently pleased and surprised by the apparent improvement in the demand for them. He said, however, with a fine sense of probity, and consideration for the rights of others, that while he was glad I had come to Washington, and made the proposition to take the balance, he did not think it would be fair to those who had bid and whose bids were thrown out, to sell the rest of the issue without first notifying them of the new offer, and giving them the option of taking what they wanted at the price I offered—94.

He asked me to call again the next morning, after he had given the matter further consideration, and I did so. But meanwhile I had talked with many Southern politicians and officeholders, Peter G. Washington, one of the Virginia Washingtons, among them, and seen so much of the extensive war preparations which were being made in and about Washington, that I came to the conclusion that a long and very bitter war lay before us, notwithstanding that Mr. Chase had the day previously assured me that it would all blow over, with peace restored, within sixty days, a prediction that was echoed by Secretary of State Seward a little later. I was particularly impressed by what Mr. Washington, himself a prominent Government official, had told me of Southern sentiment and Southern determination to fight till all was lost or gained, and by his and other Southerners' absolute but mistaken confidence that the South would establish its own Confederacy, however long a war it might take to do it. The

South in seceding from the Union expected to be able to establish a slave oligarchy, for in Lincoln's election it foresaw the doom of slavery, as both he and the Republican party were pledged to work for its abolition. Yancey and the other leading Southern "fire eaters" were responsible for this false view.

When I made my second call upon Mr. Chase, I said: "Since I saw you yesterday, Mr. Secretary, I have heard so much in conversation with Southern politicians and office-holders at the hotels, and seen and heard so much of the extensive war preparations on both sides, that I am convinced the war will be a long one, and I fear we shall see much lower prices for Government bonds and securities of all kinds. Feeling as I do, therefore, in justice to those I represent and who have given me full power to use my own discretion in the matter, I must withdraw the offer I made you yesterday. Had you accepted my offer at the time, of course I would have considered the transaction closed, and taken the bonds without question, but as it is, you will admit I am under no obligation, and free to retire."

"Oh, certainly," said Mr. Chase, "but I think you are making a mistake, for the war will be over in sixty days and these bonds will go to par!"

But my sober second thought and foresight, based upon what I had seen and heard, and the information I had gleaned in Washington, served me well, and my associates in the combination had reason to thank me for my sagacious action, as the bonds soon afterwards declined to 84; and the Union disaster at the battle of Bull Run, fought at Manassas on July 21, 1861, aroused the North to a realization of the gravity and vastness of the conflict far more than any of the warfare that had preceded it had done; at the same time it made it more determined than before to prosecute the war till the South was conquered into submission to the Union forces.

Mr. Chase's second act, in replenishing the Treasury's funds, was to offer for subscription six per cent. United States notes, receivable for all payments, including customs duties, authority to issue which already existed. He found difficulties in the way, however, and, after conferring with the Sub-treasurer, Mr. John J. Cisco, who recommended the appointment of three Wall Street banking houses to act as Government agents for their sale, on commission, namely, Morris Ketchum & Co., Read, Drexel & Van Vleck, and Livermore, Clews & Co., he appointed them. These were the first and sole Government agents for the sale of its securities that had been thus far selected, and they all appreciated the compliment, and did their work well, for they promptly sold all the notes, of this issue, the Secretary had offered.

Mr. Chase throughout made strenuous efforts to supply the Government with the means for carrying on the war, and he was loyally aided by the banking interests of New York, a fact which he recognized and acknowledged to me and others in appreciative terms.

On a subsequent memorable occasion, in the summer of 1861, Secretary Chase appeared at the Sub-treasury after Sub-treasurer John J. Cisco had called, at his request, a number of leading bankers and capitalists to meet and confer with him. When we assembled there he said to us, in his stately and impressive manner, "Gentlemen, the Government needs and must have fifty millions of dollars, and it wants it at once to meet war expenses. For this I am prepared to issue that amount of Treasury notes of the two hundred and fifty million issue just authorized by Congress—by the act of July 17, 1861—bearing interest at 7 3/10 per cent. I am no financier, so I cannot tell you how to raise the money, but you distinguished leaders in the world of finance well know what means to adopt to get it. So I leave it in your hands entirely. All I need say further is to repeat that the Government must have fifty millions of dollars, and I leave it to you to find the way to procure it."

Then Mr. Chase sat down, and all of us who were present compared notes with each other in conversation about the room; that is, we talked the matter over for nearly twenty minutes. The result of the conference was then announced by our spokesman, Moses Taylor, who said, addressing Mr. Chase:

"Mr. Secretary, we have decided to subscribe for the fifty millions of United States Government securities that you offer, and to place that amount at your disposal immediately! So you can begin to draw against it to-morrow!"

A general clapping of hands followed this prompt announcement, and Mr. Chase responded by saying:

"Gentlemen, I thank you on behalf of the Government for your public spirit in helping it so generously and so promptly in this emergency."

The whole scene was of rare and stirring interest, and momentous consequences hinged upon its result. As a drama drawn from real life it would have been effective if represented on the stage, with the large and portly form and massive head of Secretary Chase as its leading feature.

This was the first lot, or installment, of the $250,000,000 issue of 7-30 Treasury notes put on the market.

Of these, the Secretary had the privilege of issuing $50,000,000, payable in coin at the Sub-treasuries in New York, Boston, and Philadelphia, without interest, to be used as currency.

After disposing of the first 50,000,000 of 7-30 notes, as I have described, Secretary Chase communicated with the banks concerning the sale of the remainder, with the view chiefly of saving the payment of commission to the agents. But he was unable in that way to make sales on satisfactory terms to them. So he added to the three Government agents originally appointed for the sale of its securities, Fisk & Hatch, and Vermilye & Co., of New York, and Jay Cooke & Co., of Philadelphia, and told them the "7-30" notes would be delivered to them as fast as called for at the New York Sub-treasury.

Thereupon the New York agents held a meeting, at which it was agreed that Jay Cooke, of Philadelphia, should be at the head of the agency system and take charge of the advertising of the 7-30 loan, or, in other words, that Jay Cooke should act as Chairman of the agency system. The agreement also specified the commission rates and other details for the purpose of avoiding cutting, or clashing, between the agents. To this organization and agreement Mr. Chase assented; and all the agents made strenuous efforts to make sales from the word go.

Jay Cooke & Co. had no office in New York at that time, nor did they establish one till after the end of the war. This really led to their designation as the head of the agency system, as the selection of a New York firm would have created jealousy among the New York firms.

After all the 7-30s authorized to be issued were sold, came the 5-20 loans, which were sold through the same Government agency system, and the 5-20s were as successful as the 7-30s had been.

Mr. Munson B. Field, Assistant Secretary of the Treasury under Salmon P. Chase, had an examination made of the books at Washington, at my request, to see which individual firm of the Government agents sold the most United States 7-30s and 5-20s, and he reported that Livermore, Clews & Co. had the highest record. But I am willing that the credit should be shared equally by the four United States war loan banking firms, viz.: Jay Cooke & Co.; Livermore, Clews & Co.; Vermilye & Co., and Fisk & Hatch, as all did equally good and earnest work in financing the Government during the Civil War. Certainly the four firms are entitled to equal credit, and no one to a greater extent than the others. There was sufficient glory achieved by the magnificently patriotic work done by these four firms to admit of dividing the honors, so that I do not hesitate to say that they did immensely valuable service to the Nation, and made for themselves a proud National record, which should be always greatly appreciated by the American people, as it was at the time by the Government authorities in Washington. The Government was thus enabled to clothe and feed a million of soldiers in arms on the battlefield, fighting for the salvation of the Nation, and these finally brought the war to a victorious end, thus perpetuating the best form of government known to man.

I may here mention that Secretary Chase said:

"If it had not been for Jay Cooke and Henry Clew; I should never have been able to sell enough of the 7-30 notes and 5-20 bonds to carry on the war."

This remark of his was generally published at the time in the newspapers.

The Government had sold through its agents $150,000,000 of the 7-30 notes before the suspension of specie payments, an event that was hastened by the Secretary's 'withdrawal' from the banks into the Sub-treasuries of most of the proceeds of the sales, his call for payment from the agents to the Treasury being in three installments: on August 19th, October 1st, and November 2d. Moreover, the hoarding and exportation of gold were largely stimulated by the anticipation of specie suspension, and, after it occurred, gold suddenly disappeared from circulation.

This obviously involved a corresponding ·contraction of the circulating medium, and Mr. Chase, to neutralize it, and supply the place of the demonetized coin, issued the $50,000,000 of non-interest-bearing notes, which were called United States Demand Notes. He did this also to obviate the necessity of the State Banks issuing more of their own notes, as well as to raise money to meet the rapidly increasing demands of the Treasury.

Congress, seeing that this contraction tended to produce stringency in the money market, and handicapped the Government's agents in the sale of its securities, had, on August 5, 1861, suspended the act of August 6, 1846, "providing for the better organization of the Treasury, and for the collection, safe-keeping, and disbursement of the public revenue." It did this so as to permit the Secretary of the Treasury to deposit any of the money obtained on authorized loans in such solvent specie-paying banks as he might select, and, in addition, it expressed this in a resolution. The resolution was promptly acted upon by Secretary Chase, and this, and a later law, governed the policy of the Treasury ever afterwards. Monetary stringency was thus avoided by the Treasury keeping as much of its money in the banks as it could, and so locking up as little as possible in the Treasury and Sub-treasuries. The evil effects of the Sub-treasuries system in locking money out of circulation was thus practically acknowledged and guarded against.

When the sale of the 7-30s had been completed by the Government agents, there was great pressure brought to bear by the banks throughout the country, who were backed by many influential newspapers, in favor of giving the sale of the 5-20s to the banks instead of to the Government agents. The pressure upon Secretary Chase became so great that he concluded to try the experiment, and authorized all the banks throughout the country to sell the 5-20s. After giving them every opportunity to supersede the agency system, as previously adopted with the six per cent. and the 7-30 Treasury notes, the Secretary was finally compelled to abandon the banks and go back again to the agents, who took hold with vigor and made the sale of the 5-20s as brilliant a success as they had previously made that of the 7-30s. We were friendless in Europe, but we overcame this by patriotism and energy at home.

After a time, some of the banks, and there were only State Banks then, threw out the Demand Notes, and so it became necessary to enforce their circulation. To accomplish this, Secretary Chase asked Congress to make them a legal tender for the payment of all debts, public and private, excepting customs duties, and interest on the public debt, payable in coin.

Congress, therefore, on February 25, 1862, remedied the difficulty by passing the Legal Tender Act, making these and all the United States notes lawful money. In the same act it authorized the issue of $150,000,000 of new non-interest-bearing legal tender notes. The provision for the payment in coin of customs duties and interest on the bonded debt was obviously as necessary as it was wise, as customs duties furnished the means for paying the interest in specie; and the fact of its being payable in gold created a demand for our bonds in other countries, as well as at home, which would not have existed on paper money interest.

Before long, the whole of the authorized $250,000,000 of 7-30 notes had been sold to the public through the Government agents; and later, from, time to time, Congress authorized large additional amounts of these till finally they reached their maximum, in August, 1865, when $830,000,000 of them were outstanding.

At the same date, also, the Government bond issues, which had kept pace with the 7-30 note issues, and simultaneously reached their maximum, showed immense totals. There were then outstanding $514,880,500 of 5-20 bonds, and $172,770,100 of 10-40 bonds. Among our own people patriotism and profit combined to make these great United States loans doubly attractive, and the Government agents used their best efforts to stimulate the demand for them both at home and abroad. Livermore, Clews & Co., in particular, sold large amounts of these in England and other foreign countries, where they ultimately proved extremely profitable investments. To meet the demands of the war, we—the Government agents—were as anxious as the Secretary of the Treasury himself, and never were men more successful in accomplishing their object and doing good work than we were. There was patriotism worthy of Patrick Henry, as well as profit, in this, and Wall Street can lay the flattering unction to its soul that it rendered, through the Government agents, the best of good service to the Government in this time of peril to the Union.

As General Grant said long afterwards to me, we were not fighting for the Union as soldiers in the field, but we served it equally well by helping it in its struggle for money to prosecute the war; and I felt proud of the active part I took in thus helping to preserve the Union as one of its army in civil life.

The campaign in Virginia having proved prolific of disaster to the Union army, Congress, on July 11, 1862, authorized the issue of a hundred and fifty millions more of non-interest-bearing United States legal tender notes, and on January 17, 1863, another hundred millions to which it added $50,000,000 on March 3d, in the same year, making $450,000,000 of legal tender notes, or greenbacks, fifty of which were to be held as a Treasury reserve, for the redemption of temporary loan certificates.

This was the maximum issue of non-interest-bearing legal tender notes at any time, and by the act of January 28, 1865 Congress restricted the total to $400,000,000, and there it remained till Hugh McCulloch became Secretary of the Treasury, early in 1865.

Secretary Chase had meanwhile become Chief Justice of the United States Supreme Court, and Thomas Fessenden, who succeeded him as Secretary, had resigned. Mr. McCulloch began to contract the legal tender notes, and had withdrawn $44,000,000 before Congress interfered to prohibit any further contraction. It did this in response to a general protest against any further curtailment of the greenbacks in circulation.

From that time until the panic of 1873 their amount remained at $356,000,000. In the interval Mr. Boutwell had succeeded Mr. McCulloch, and Mr. Richardson had succeeded Mr. Boutwell as Secretary. Mr. Richardson, under diminished customs and revenue receipts, and the stress of the panic, restored to circulation $26,000,000 of the $44,000,000 of legal tender notes that had been withdrawn by Mr. McCulloch, whereupon Congress, on June 22, 1874, provided that the greenbacks in circulation should remain fixed at the then existing total of $382,000,000.

The same law which thus legalized the reissue of the $26,000,000 of legal tender notes by Secretary Boutwell abolished the National Bank reserve, previously required to be kept on bank-note circulation, and for this substituted the provision that the banks were to deposit five per cent. in legal tender notes of the amount of their own note issues with the United States Treasurer at Washington for the redemption of their notes.

This law is still in force, and the establishment of the Redemption Bureau at Washington has resulted, ever since, in daily receipts by it of mutilated bank notes to be replaced by new notes, in addition to the ebb and flow caused by banks increasing or reducing their circulation. The five per cent. in legal tender deposited is counted by them as part of their legal reserve. But the necessity of sending the notes to Washington, and of receiving them therefrom, involves trouble and loss of time to the banks, and also prevents the banks from contracting their circulation when the demand for it is light and increasing it when heavy, as freely and promptly as they would if every Sub-treasury was made a redemption point for National Banks. Congress ought therefore to authorize the equipment of the Sub-treasuries with redemption bureaus for the banks in their respective districts, in order to facilitate this ebb and flow of bank-note issues, and so increase the much needed elasticity of the currency.

In addition to United States legal tender notes, large amounts of interest-bearing legal tender notes were issued during the war. On September 1, 1865, when the currency, like the whole National debt, reached its greatest amount of inflation, the noninterest-bearing legal tender notes and fractional currency stood at $459,505,311, the three years six per cent. compound interest legal tender notes at more than $217,000,000, and the one and two years five per cent. legal tender notes at nearly $34,000,000, the whole aggregating $685,236,269 issued by the Treasury.

There were also outstanding $107,000,000 of temporary loan certificates. These, being payable after ten days' notice, were treated as greenbacks by the banks, and counted as part of their lawful money reserve, while the remainder circulated as currency, and so practically increased the volume of paper money. At the same time the new National Bank law had put in circulation $170,000,000 of National Bank notes; and more than $70,000,000 of State Bank notes were still circulating. The last named were, however, soon taxed out of existence by Congress. The grand total of the issues enumerated was ten hundred and sixty-seven millions of paper money in circulation. Nor was this all, for there were then outstanding $85,000,000 of one-year certificates of indebtedness; and the $830,000,000 of 7-30 notes, called 7-30s, outstanding were extensively used as money, and so tended to increase the inflation of the currency and prices.

It will be seen therefore that the inflation of the currency was really much larger than it appeared to be by the Public Debt statements at that time. But so rapid was the contraction during the eight years following, through the maturity and cancellation of interest-bearing notes and certificates, that it is safe to say we had from sixty to seventy-five per cent. less paper, used as money, in circulation when the panic of 1873 commenced than we had in September, 1865, and to this enormous contraction of our medium of exchange that disastrous panic, the worst this country ever had, was largely due. It was, I repeat, the worst in its effects that this country ever experienced, not excepting the panics of 1837 and 1857, and was aggravated by the Franco-German War, that practically shut American securities out of the European markets, which had previously taken them freely. This was a severe blow to the American bankers who had undertaken to finance the railways then in process of construction in different parts of the country, and who had relied upon finding both home and foreign markets for the sale of the bonds issued against the completed mileage of these railways, and it led to much embarrassment and a number of failures. The depression following this panic of 1873—in which Jay Cooke & Co. failed owing to their having undertaken to finance the Northern Pacific—was prolonged, and prosperity did not really return to us as a Nation till after the resumption of specie payments in 1879. Meanwhile, nearly all the uncompleted railways in the country had been reorganized through foreclosures that wiped out hundreds of millions.

Our National debt, which had increased from $64,000,000 on June 30, 1860, and $88,409,387 on June 30, 1860, to $2,845,907,626 on September 1, 1865, had then been very largely reduced, for it was only $2,140,695,365 on September 1, 1873. The debt and the currency had gone up and down together under the influence of a common cause. Not till specie payments were resumed by the Government and the banks did gold cease to command a premium. With this the Gold Room became a thing of the past.

The great activity and the enormous sales of the Government agents may be inferred from the maximum amounts I have quoted, of the 7-30 notes, and the 5-20 and 10-40 bonds outstanding five months after Lee surrendered to Grant at Appomattox on April 9, 1865.

The total debt on which interest was payable in coin then amounted to $1,116,658,100, while that bearing interest in lawful money was $1,874,478,100, the first calling for $65,001,570 in gold annually, and the other for $72,527,646 of greenback currency.

That great event—Lee's surrender to Grant—that ended the war, was the fitting prelude to General Grant's election to the Presidency. It made it certain that no other Republican candidate for the office of President of the United States would have any chance of success at the next general election, and, of course, no Democratic candidate could be elected. Grant became our great National hero, and the country glorified him for his splendid war record.

But soon after the memorable historical scene at Appomattox, while the country was rejoicing over the advent of peace, with the Union restored, there came that terrible tragedy at Ford's Theater in Washington, when President Lincoln, on April 14, 1865, was assassinated by John Wilkes Booth, and on the following day Vice President Andrew Johnson was sworn in as President.

Then, indeed, the Nation was plunged into mourning, and mourning emblems from ocean to ocean testified to the National grief.

I will not dwell on the stormy career of Andrew Johnson as President, and the impeachment proceedings against him, that for a long time made both branches of Congress seething cauldrons of excitement. But it was a happy relief to the country when his term expired and General Grant succeeded to the Presidency on March 4, 1869, with Schuyler Colfax as Vice President. The Democratic candidates who had run against General Grant in the campaign in which he was elected in November, 1868, were Horatio Seymour and

General Francis P. Blair, Jr. But the popularity of Grant was so overwhelming that his election was a foregone conclusion.

Till within a short time of its final termination the duration of the war was a matter of much uncertainty, and its ultimate result had long been the subject of doubt and gloomy forebodings by many who failed to see that the superior money power and resources of the North were sure to conquer and crown the Union with victory in the end. Our currency, greatly inflated though it was, remained good throughout the trying ordeal, whereas that of the Confederate States became utterly discredited and worthless, thus repeating the history of the French *assignats*.

A new era opened in our history with the ending of the war, and our currency, which, of course, had previously no circulation in the South, began to circulate there. This, of itself, was equivalent to extensive contraction. The currency of one section had now to supply the currency needs of both sections, and for a long time the drain of money from the North to the South was felt in the money market.

The country was somewhat like a sick man accustomed to and dependent on stimulants, to withdraw which suddenly would have been perilous. Many in Congress recognized this danger, for it was a noticeable feature of the debates on the subject that not a few of those who had been strongly opposed to our excessive issues of paper money during the war, and warned the country against them, were among those who opposed violent contraction as being a remedy worse than the disease. The radical contractionists, however, failed to see, or refused to acknowledge, that the arguments which would have applied to the rising tide of the currency while the war continued, and there was danger of indefinite further inflation, did not apply with equal force to the altered condition of affairs.

Although schemes of radical contraction were rejected, even the moderate measure of contraction that was adopted proved too severe to be endured without much complaining from business interests, so hard and painful is the process of contraction, whereas that of inflation is always pleasant and easy.

In later years I became very well acquainted with General Grant, and toward the end of his first term of the Presidency, when a good deal of opposition was manifested to his renomination by the press, including the New York *Evening Post,* I made strenuous efforts to secure his renomination. To that end I organized a public meeting at the Cooper Institute, and induced William F. Dodge to act as Chairman. It was a great popular success, and Grant's renomination was unanimously advocated with immense enthusiasm. The *Evening Post* then said that after such an overwhelming demonstration it was evident that public sentiment was on the side of Grant, and that it was useless to oppose his renomination. He was accordingly renominated by the Republican Party and triumphantly reelected. His second term as President began on March 4, 1873, and he retired from the Presidency four years later.

General Grant was well aware of the part I took at this meeting, which, many said, turned the scale in favor of his renomination when it was doubtful and trembling in the balance, and he also knew of my services in connection with the Government war loans, and in organizing various public meetings to celebrate Union victories and stimulate recruiting for the army. He said that I deserved some public recognition of my public services in supplying the sinews of war, and asked me how I would like to be Secretary of the Treasury, but I said I preferred Wall Street. Therefore, later on, he appointed me Fiscal Agent for the United States Government in all foreign countries, in place of Baring Brothers, of London, who had been its fiscal agents up to that time, since the Bank of England had acted in that capacity.

When it became certain that General Grant's death was very near, I was anxious to see him once more, and also a strong advocate of his burial in the city of New York, where his tomb would be a conspicuous monument, to be seen by all, instead of burying him almost out of sight in Arlington Cemetery or at West Point, which places were strongly urged. The States of Ohio and Illinois also claimed him, as did the city of St. Louis. They all made strenuous efforts to obtain the family's consent, as well as his, through committees sent to Mount McGregor for that purpose.

So I went to Mount McGregor, where he was, and as delicately as possible urged this upon him and his family. All of the members of the family assented, and the General, being unable to speak, nodded his assent also to what I said. Then when he was wheeled out in his chair, on the veranda, on his way to take his regular afternoon sun bath on the mountain side, accompanied by Dr. Douglas, he wrote on a pad that all he demanded was that his wife should be buried by his side when her own time came. Knowing them all well, I remained there two hours, talking with the General and the family, and my visit, when I made its result known, led to the selection of New York as the great soldier's burial place, on the conditions mentioned by him. Within three days after I had seen him, the great General died. I had visited him on a Monday afternoon, and he died on the following Wednesday. His death threw the Nation into mourning.

Incidentally, I may mention that I started the organization of the famous Committee of Seventy, that brought about the overthrow of the corrupt Tweed Ring, that had robbed the city of New York of about a hundred millions of dollars. I nominated sixty-five of its members, and for my instrumentality in forming that Committee of eminent and public-spirited citizens I received many congratulations. That Committee not only drove the thieves out of office, but caused the prosecution of all of them who had not fled the country, and ultimately brought back and convicted Tweed, who died in prison. Meanwhile, it had reorganized the City Departments, and put new men in office, with Andrew H. Green as Comptroller. It purified, and, for a time, virtually ruled the city, through controlling its government.

But above everything else in my business life, I regard with most satisfaction the work I did in marketing the Civil War loans of the Government of this great and glorious country of ours—the United States of America—and in other

ways strengthening the hands of the Government to the best
of my ability and with all my heart and soul, not only as a
banker but a patriotic American citizen; and I felt that I had
my reward when, after the memorable four years' war, peace
came bringing with it Victory for the Union and a reunited
country, a victory which gave permanence to the best government ever known to man—a government "of the people,
for the people, and by the people," which bids fair to be
everlasting.

CHAPTER 6

SECRETARY CHASE
AND THE TREASURY

THE DEPLETED CONDITION OF THE TREASURY WHEN MR. CHASE TOOK OFFICE. — PREPARATIONS FOR WAR AND GREAT EXCITEMENT IN WASHINGTON. — CHIVALROUS SOUTHERNERS IN A FERMENT. — OFFICIALS UP IN ARMS IN DEFENCE OF THEIR MENACED POSITIONS. — MISCALCULATION WITH REGARD TO THE PROBABLE DURATION OF THE WAR. — A VISIT TO WASHINGTON AND AN INTERVIEW WITH SECRETARY CHASE. — DISAPPOINTMENT ABOUT THE SALE OF GOVERNMENT BONDS. — A PANIC PRECIPITATED IN WALL STREET. — MILLIONAIRES REDUCED TO INDIGENCE IN A FEW HOURS. — MIRACULOUSLY SAVED FROM THE WRECK. — HOW IT HAPPENED.

SOON after Mr. Chase came into the Treasury he found that money was seriously needed. In fact the Treasury was empty. The expenditure for the fiscal year ending June, 1861, was 62 millions, and there were only 41 millions of revenue to meet them, and even this amount was threatened with a serious reduction on account of the traitorous and rebellious attitude of the South.

After President Lincoln had called upon Congress to provide for the enlistment of 400,000 men, the expenses of the Government were soon advanced to the enormous amount of a million dollars a day. The Secretary of the Treasury made a calculation, which he submitted to the President, showing that the probable expenditures would amount to 318 millions for the ensuing year. He advised that 80 millions be provided for by taxation, 240 millions by loan, and that 50 millions of Treasury notes, redeemable in coin on demand, should be issued.

The Secretary was authorized by Congress to borrow a sum not exceeding 250 millions, on the credit of the United States, and as a part of this loan he was, in the words of the Act, "to issue in exchange for coin, or pay for salaries or other dues from the United States, not over 50 millions of Treasury notes, bearing no interest, but payable on demand at New York, Philadelphia or Boston."

When Mr. Chase advertised for bids on the bonds known as the 81 issue all bids at 94 and above were accepted, and those under 94 were rejected.

I got up a syndicate immediately to take the entire balance of the loan at 94, and went on to Washington to see the Secretary. This syndicate comprised a number of New York banks and many large capitalists. I called upon Secretary Chase when I arrived, informed him of the object of my visit and made him an offer of 94 for the entire balance of the loan.

He was in favor of the proposition, but requested me to leave the matter open until the following morning for him to consider. It was a question with him whether he ought not to give those whose bids had been rejected an equal opportunity with the parties I represented.

I never can forget the impression I received on my approach to Washington that morning As I looked through the window of the sleeping-car my eye was met by an entire train load of brass cannon. There were at least a dozen platform cars, each having one of those huge guns, all apparently in order to wheel at once against the enemy. I shall always remember the feelings that came over me at that moment. The question of war or no war was vividly presented to my mind, and this was the uppermost thought during my visit at Washington.

I descended from my traveling quarters as soon as the train was announced as having arrived at the capital, and repaired to Willard's, then the principal, if not, in fact, the only hotel for a traveler to go to, and it was an old-fashioned, historic hostelry. I hastened to my room, rapidly performed my ablutions, and then found my way into the dingy breakfast room. On inquiry, I found that ten o'clock was the usual hour for heads of departments, including Mr. Chase, to be at the Treasury. At that hour I went to see him. I sent in my card and was ushered into his presence without delay. He was a man of portly frame and distinguished bearing, and impressed me with the feeling of being in the presence of an individual far above the average standard of humanity in every respect.

I informed the Secretary of my mission, with the result above stated.

About seven-eighths of the people of Washington, at that time, were Southerners. The office-holders were largely composed of the latter, and they were expecting to be suddenly turned out of office. This rendered the place a boiling cauldron of conspiracy and treason.

As I went around collecting information, the sight of those cannon that at first had made such an indescribable impression upon me, continued to haunt my vision wherever I went. The air was filled with rumors of war, and everybody was wound up to the highest pitch of hostile excitement.

As I mingled among the people, the impression was forced upon me that war was inevitable, and that up to the very hilt of the sword. I felt that the contest would be long and bloody.

I sent a dispatch to my firm in New York, conveying my impressions to that effect, and advised them to clear the decks in preparation therefor. I urged them to lose no time in selling off all the mercantile paper on hand, and requested them to communicate to the members of the syndicate, which I had formed for the purchase of bonds, recommending them to withdraw therefrom, as I was convinced that war to the knife was imminent, and that Government bonds must have a serious fall in price in consequence.

I saw Mr. Chase the next morning, and told him that, as I believed, there was going to be a long and bloody war, I could not conscientiously, in the interest of my clients, renew my bid of the previous day.

With regard to my opinion about the probable length of the war, the Secretary took issue with me very firmly.

Mr. Chase, however, afterwards proved to be a warm and most valued friend of mine, and it was largely due to his aid and recognition that I achieved brilliant success in my early Wall Street career during the war period.

The Secretary was of the opinion that the bonds should command par, at least, and they would be worth that and above it very soon, he thought. He made this assertion on the expectation that the impending difficulties would soon be adjusted, and that in less than sixty days all the trouble would be at an end.

It was not so extraordinary as it may seem to some people now, with the light of later events fully before them, that the Secretary was so sanguine of short work being made of the South, because he only shared the opinion of a large number of people, who greatly underestimated Southern durability.

After leaving the Secretary, who treated me with great consideration, as he did every one in his inimitable and dignified manner, which made such a durable and favorable impression on all who came in contact with him, I felt greatly pleased and highly gratified at meeting him. In fact, his fine, magnetic presence was of a character to command the admiration of almost every person who had the honor of an interview. He was a great man for producing good first impressions, and, unlike many impressions of this character, they were generally lasting.

Had I not visited Washington at the time I did, and had I not obtained the correct impression concerning the future of the then impending difficulties, my firm, like many others that invested in Government bonds, mercantile paper, stocks and other fluctuating properties, would have been irretrievably ruined. I have reason to congratulate myself, therefore, on my good fortune in narrowly escaping such a disaster, almost at the beginning of my Wall Street career, and I was thus enabled, at a later stage of the national trouble, to be of considerable service to the Government, through the Treasury, in its efforts to sustain such an army in the field as was calculated to ensure success to the Federal arms.

My first experience in dealing in Government bonds was just prior to the Lincoln administration, when Mr. Cobb was Secretary of the Treasury. He advertised for sale to the highest bidders an issue of U. S. bonds bearing five per cent. interest, having twenty years to run, and my firm bid for $200,000 of them, hoping to make a quick turn, and a small profit thereon. A five per cent. deposit was made, as required by custom.

The loan was all awarded to most of the bids, mine included, and a very large part of it was awarded to Lockwood & Co., who were then regarded the largest and most prosperous Stock Exchange firm in the street.

George S. Robbins & Co., John Thompson, Marie & Kaus, and a few others, whose names I now forget, made also large bids.

Of those mentioned, however, my firm stood alone in taking up the bonds, as the threatening aspect of political affairs came on so soon afterwards as to depreciate Government securities. The original deposit of five per cent. was lost by these subscribers, and the bonds were permitted to remain in *statu quo,* as the Government never forced the claim against the delinquents.

This, in a large measure, accounted for the impoverished condition of the Treasury when Mr. Chase took charge of it, and for which Mr. Cobb has been made an object, not wholly undeserving, of public reproach.

The $200,000 bonds my firm subscribed for at par were sold mostly at 95 and below, but the fact of taking them, and meeting the subscription, without fail, gave my firm an excellent standing with the Government at the beginning of the war, and enured greatly to my firm's advantage thereafter.

At the time I visited Washington my firm was more largely engaged in dealing in mercantile paper than any other branch of Wall Street business.

I had inaugurated the system at the time of my advent to the "Street" of buying merchants' acceptances and receivables out and out, the rate being governed by the prevailing ruling rate for money, with the usual commission added.

It was by this method that my firm soon became the largest dealers in mercantile paper, which business had formerly been controlled by two other firms for at least a quarter of a century, and whose old fogy methods were by my innovations easily eclipsed.

The merchants at that time would go to these discount firms and leave their receivables, bearing their endorsements, on sale there, and only when sold by piecemeal could they obtain the avails thereof.

The more expeditious plan that I adopted, which was to give these negotiators a check at sight, seemed generally to merit their approbation, and enabled me to command the situation in that line of business, very much to the chagrin of my competitors.

In this way my firm had accumulated about five hundred thousand dollars in notes, which were hypothecated with various city and country banks.

After coming to the conclusion above referred to on my visit to Washington, in regard to the certainty of a prolonged and desperate war, I made quick steps back to New York to dispose of my paper. I went vigorously to work, and succeeded in unloading all but ten thousand dollars of short time notes made by Lane, Boyce & Co., and a note of $500 of Edward Lambert & Co.

I had no sooner accomplished this very desirable work of shifting my burden, and distributing it in a more equable manner on the shoulders of others, but at higher rates than I paid, than in less than a week after my return from Washington the exciting news arrived of the firing of the first hostile gun at Fort Sumter.

The announcement of this overt act of war spread like wildfire, and the wildest scenes of excitement and consternation were witnessed in Wall Street and throughout the entire business community. The whole country was panic stricken in an instant.

Stocks went down with a bound to panic prices. Fortunes were lost, and millionaires were reduced to indigence in a few hours. Money was unobtainable, and distrust everywhere was prevalent.

The two firms whose paper I was unable to dispose of were about the first to fail, and before the maturity of any of the balance of the paper which I had successfully negotiated both the drawers and endorsers thereon, without a single exception, all collapsed.

The height which Gilroy's kite attained would have been nowhere in point of altitude to that which I should have reached had I not had the good luck to have cleared my decks as I did, and in the nick of time.

My safety in this instance was due to my inspiration, to which I believe myself more indebted than anything else for the privilege of remaining in Wall Street up to the present date.

I am no spiritualist nor theosophist, but this gift or occasional visitation of Providence, or whatever people may choose to call it, to which I am subject at intervals, has enabled me to take "points" on the market in at one ear and dispose of them through the other without suffering any evil consequences therefrom, and to look upon these kind friends who usually strew these valuable "tips" so lavishly around with the deepest commiseration. My ability to do this, whatever may be its source, whether human or divine, has saved me from being financially shattered at least two or three times annually.

I do not indulge in any table tapping or dark seances like the elder Vanderbilt, but this strange, peculiar and admonitory influence clings to me in times of approaching squalls more tenaciously than at any ordinary junctures.

I have known others who have had these mysterious forebodings but who recklessly disregarded them, and this has been the rock on which they have split in speculative emergencies.

Therefore I say again, beware of "points." They constitute the *ignis fatuus* which lure more unfortunate speculators to their financial doom than all other influences put together.

CHAPTER 7

"CORNERS" AND THEIR EFFECT ON VALUES

THE SENATE COMMITTEE ON "CORNERS" AND "FUTURES."
— SPECULATION BENEFICIAL TO THE COUNTRY AT LARGE. —
A REGULATOR OF VALUES, AND AN IMPORTANT AGENT IN
THE PREVENTION OF PANICS. — "CORNERS" IN ALL KINDS OF
BUSINESS. — HOW A.T. STEWART MADE "CORNERS." — ALL
IMPORTING FIRMS DEAL IN "FUTURES." — LEGISLATIONS
AGAINST "CORNERS" WOULD STOP ENTERPRISE AND CAUSE
STAGNATION IN BUSINESS. — ONLY THE CONSPIRATORS
THEMSELVES GET HURT IN "CORNERS." — THE BLACK
FRIDAY "CORNER." — SPECULATION IN GRAIN BENEFICIAL
TO CONSUMERS.

THE New York Stock Exchange is organized after the same manner as a social club, such as the Union League, the Union or the Manhattan, and not under a special charter from the Legislature. Hence it is protected from the interference of that honorable body.

Although various attempts have been made, from time to time, at Albany, to levy taxes upon the transactions of the Exchange, and to interfere with the business of speculation and investment in many other ways, these legislative designs have hitherto been happily frustrated.

Shortly after the memorable "corner" in Hannibal and St. Jo., in 1881, another attempt was made by the Legislature to

force Wall Street matters under the jurisdiction of Albany lobby-
ists and "scalpers."

The newspaper articles on the subject of the "corner" had
attracted the attention of the Legislature then in session, and
naturally suggested to some of the wiseacres of that dignified
and incorruptible body that the "corner" afforded an excellent
opportunity, when the public mind was excited on the subject,
to raise an outcry against the shocking immorality of such
huge speculations.

A Senate Committee on "corners" and "futures" was therefore appointed, and various Wall Street men were summoned
to appear before it, and give their testimony on this interesting subject. I had the honor of being one of the witnesses
cited. I promptly obeyed the subpoena in preference to taking
the risk of being hauled up for contempt and sent to durance
vile. I appeared before the Committee at the Metropolitan
Hotel, and not only answered all questions put to me, without
any fashionable lapses of memory, after the manner of certain
other financiers, but I regaled the Committee with a little dis-
sertation on the subject of investigation. I had letters from
members of the Legislature afterwards complimenting me for
having made the points very clear. So I can say, "Praise from
Sir Hubert is praise indeed," and therefore I am encouraged
to reproduce that effort in this volume, not so much from an
intense desire to go down to posterity as a successful orator,
as from a disposition to record my approval, in more permanent form, of the soundness of the legislative judgment on
my explanation of "corners."

When the applause had subsided, I spoke as follows:

"Gentlemen of the Committee on Corners and Futures:
Speculation is a method now adopted for adjusting differences of opinion as to future values, whether of products or
securities. This is more common now than in former years
because the facilities for procuring information have increased
with the greater intelligence and celerity with which all business is now conducted, and also from the greater rapidity
with which such information can be transmitted by telegraph
and cable.

"In former years the results of a crop were known only when it came to the market. Now almost everything affecting its future value is known with a fair degree of accuracy before the crop is harvested. This advanced information naturally becomes the subject of speculative transactions which could not have existed in former times.

"Speculation brings into play the best intelligence as to the future of values. It has always two sides. The one that is based principally on the facts and conditions of the situation wins in the end, and the result of the conflict is the nearest possible approach to correct values. The consequences of speculation are thus financially beneficial to the country at large.

"Speculation for a fall in prices is based upon the presumption of an over-supply. If it succeeds, the production of the particular product is checked until prices recover, and in the meantime production is diverted to articles less abundant. Thus speculation proves a regulator both of values and production. Speculation for a rise in prices is based upon a presumption of scarcity or short supply, and its direct effect is to quicken production and restore the equilibrium of prices.

"'Corners' usually come from running speculation to an excessive length, by which the seller becomes responsible for deliveries beyond what he can possibly make. He thereby places himself at the mercy of those with whom he has made the contracts. These exigencies chiefly affect the speculators themselves, and the community at large but little.

"Extreme prices usually grow out of them, but they are only momentary, and have small effect upon regular or cash transactions, which sympathize very remotely with these temporary and artificial quotations.

"Speculation is not to be judged by its occasional excesses, but by the general effects which the foregoing considerations show to be beneficial. It regulates production by instantaneously advancing prices when there is a scarcity, thereby stimulating production, and by depressing prices when there is over-production. It thus becomes one of the most beneficial agents in the business world for the prevention of panics.

"Speculation, moreover, makes a market for securities that otherwise would not exist. It enables railroads to be built through the ready sale of their bonds, thus adding materially to the wealth of the whole country, and opening a more profitable market to labor. In this it becomes the forerunner of enterprise and material prosperity in business.

"There are 'corners' in all kinds of business as well as in Wall Street speculation. Mr. A.T. Stewart, the great dry goods merchant, made more 'corners' during the latter part of his life than half the rest of the business community put together. He did this mainly by contracting for the entire and exclusive production of certain classes of goods, and as such goods could only be bought at his establishment he had a close 'corner' in them, and accordingly put on his own prices.

"The greater portion of all the large mercantile firms do business in the same way. And all the importing firms deal in futures. They sell goods by sample, agreeing to deliver them at a future stated period, varying from thirty days to twelve months. In the meantime the goods have to be manufactured, and in many instances purchasers have to wait until they are grown, and imported thousands of miles.

"If it were not for the support which comes from the 'short' interest in grain and the general activity created thereby in times of depression, which come periodically in this country, it would be in the power of the large speculative grain dealers in Europe to manipulate prices downward, and purchase our products every year, on raids, at prices much under the cost of production.

"When we sell to Europe we must do so at a profit, or our transactions don't help to enrich the country.

"Another curious thing about 'corners' is that the people who organize and manipulate them generally get most hurt in the enterprise. This was the case with the 'corner' referred to in Hannibal and St. Joseph. Mr. John Duff, of Boston, was the man in whose prolific brain that 'corner' originated, and the result to him was financial ruin. The stock ran up to 350, though the short account amounted to only about 1,200 shares, and the 'shorts' had to settle at 280.

"The result was similar in the 'corner' in Northwest in 1872, manipulated by Jay Gould. The stock was started at 80 and it ran up to 280. It then reacted to the former figure. I believe Jay Gould was alone in that deal, and it came pretty near crushing him, in spite of his incomparable capacity for wriggling out of a tight place.

"Patents are 'corners' protected by law. The inventor has a monopoly for seventeen years in his invention against all the world, and this gives him a right to make and sell the article covered by his patent, often at a profit of several hundred per cent. on the original cost, and on the price it would bring if placed in competition in the open market, like railroad stocks and grain.

"If it is the intention of the Legislature of this State to stop enterprise in business, then your Committee is undertaking to accomplish that work in the right way, but I think your success would be a public calamity."

I doubt the expediency of either undertaking to regulate enterprise by law or to choke off competition by the lawmaking power. The result would be woeful stagnation in business. It would crush the motives for commercial activity and depress the creative energies of prosperity.

The law of supply and demand is the best regulator.

Congress attempted to suppress speculation in gold during the war, and as soon as the act was passed prohibiting such dealings, the premium on gold advanced 100 per cent. This so much terrified the wise statesmen who concocted this sweeping measure of financial reform, that they immediately displayed much more wisdom in hastening to have the bill repealed.

The simple reason that such laws will not work in practice is that where there is a will there is generally a way to evade them. This is the case with the very best of such laws that can possibly be framed. Take the usury laws for example. The methods of getting around these are numerous, and there is practically no limit to the rate of interest that can be exacted except the conscience of the lender, which is frequently very elastic. Daniel O'Connell said he could drive a coach and six through any act of Parliament. Jake Sharp was also of opinion that he could run a double-track horse-car railroad through the best act that could be framed by any Albany Legislature. Jake was checked in his career at considerable trouble and expense, but his case illustrated that the rule referred to holds good generally in legislation.

The fact, however, that it seldom happens that anybody gets badly hurt in "corners," except the conspirators themselves, is sufficient protection for the general public, and should set the minds of legislators at rest, if they mean to do legitimate business in their law-making capacity.

The conspirators in "corners" are usually left high and dry without any market for their fictitious values, and the "corner" very frequently has the effect of putting the property out of the speculative market for a long time. The fate of Han. & St. Jo. is a warning to those who manipulate "corners." The stock was seldom quoted for months afterwards.

Take the case of Black Friday for example. It was most disastrous to the parties intimately connected with it. It came near proving Gould's ruin, and he has not got over the moral effect of it yet. The probability is it will be an heirloom in his family, a skeleton in the Gould closet for generations to come. Gould and Black Friday have become synonymous in the minds of many people, and the further from Wall Street the more the distinction becomes confounded.

In making these remarks I have no intention of throwing any reflection upon Mr. George Gould, who seems to be a very promising young man for a rich man's son. His careful education has, no doubt, done much to counteract the drawbacks incident to the sons of wealthy men to which I have referred more fully in another part of this book. His maternal training, I understand, has been of the most exemplary kind. This will go far to offset the disadvantages to a business career, which the accident of his birth in luxurious surroundings, according to my theory, otherwise entails. If his brain is composed of the genuine plastic material out of which the craniums of successful financiers are made, he may learn to forget that he has been nursed in the lap of luxury, and look back with due respect to the hole whence his father was digged and the rock whence he was hewn. He may have brains enough, possibly, to reflect with more pride on that ingenious mousetrap that first brought his father into prominence, than the gew-gaws of the gilded palace in Fifth avenue, the luxuries of the handsome parlors and rich conservatories at Irvington, and the gorgeous trappings of his father's yacht and palace cars. I have, therefore, great hopes that George will be a conspicuous exception to the rule I have propounded elsewhere regarding rich men's sons.

When a large mercantile firm buys up goods in any line so that nobody else has the same goods, it then has a "corner" in these goods.

"Corners" in goods differ from "corners" in Wall Street in regard to their influence on the organizers. They don't act like a boomerang as the Wall Street "corners" mostly do. The "corner" is sometimes sustained during the life of the manipulator, as in the case of Mr. Stewart.

The successors of the great operators sometimes maintain it, but in this instance Judge Hilton made a signal failure, though in some respects he is a far abler man than Stewart was. Yet, he had not the genius, for working "corners," of his eminent predecessor. He is, probably, so well learned in the law that he has too much inclination to go around the "corners."

One thing is certain, very few of these merchants can become wealthy except through the medium of "corners." It is by these peculiar methods that nearly all large fortunes are amassed in their line, and in a perfectly legitimate manner, too, whatever casuists and hair-splitting moralists may say or think about the matter. The tendency to make "corners" seems to be interwoven in our business methods, and to play an important part in the struggle for existence. So I don't see what we are going to do about it without a radical change in that compendium of the best political wisdom that the world has ever seen. I refer to the Constitution of the United States. All the acumen and sophistry which the most astute

Philadelphia lawyer could bring to bear upon it has hitherto failed to show that there is anything in this wonderful document opposed to the liberty of making "corners."

As Mr. Gladstone has truly said: "This document is the most wonderful work ever struck off at a given time by the brain and purpose of man."

I hold there is nothing in the Constitution opposed to the freedom of making "corners," and that all the evils resulting from these speculative inventions can be met and counteracted by business methods, and the laws regulating the ordinary concerns of life without resorting to any or special methods.

To dispose of "corners" or abolish them on the scale to which I have alluded would presume an entire revolution in our social system, and to attack them piecemeal, as the Legislature frequently does, involves a very suspicious kind of discrimination, and is at variance with the spirit of the Constitution. In fact it often amounts to a kind of thinly-disguised blackmail.

The truth is, that it is almost impossible to legislate against "corners" without aiming a fatal blow at speculation itself, which, as I have shown, is a vital principle in the regulation of values, the stability of business, and the prevention of panics.

I believe the men of most experience, not only in Wall Street, but in other departments of finance and commerce, will bear me out in the statement that a market where even values are considerably inflated by speculation, is more desirable than a period of depression. The result, in the long run, is the greatest good to the greatest number. I don't believe that the ghost of Jeremy Bentham himself could rise up and consistently condemn this statement.

I believe that speculation in grain and provisions is materially beneficial to consumers, and that the latter are better off, one year with another, and less liable to be menaced with periodical famines, than if there were no speculation in these necessities of life.

Before leaving this prolific theme of "corners" I wish to say a few words about my own experience in that line. The only "corner" in which I have ever been materially hurt during my long business experience was one manipulated by the State of Georgia.

This Sovereign State issued and granted altogether about eight millions of bonds, all bearing the great seal, properly signed and legally issued for full value. I advanced over two million dollars in good money on a part of these bonds. Shortly after this transaction, the State of Georgia ascertained through a garbled report of a committee sent to this city by the Georgia Legislature, that all these bonds were held outside of her own borders. The Legislature then passed an act of repudiation, thereby reducing the value of the bonds from par to that of waste paper. When I discovered that my little pile of two million dollars in what I considered good securities would no longer exchange for greenbacks, I had a very disagreeable sensation of having been "cornered" by the high toned and chivalrous representatives of the State of Georgia, which, through its lawmakers, claimed the sovereign right to do wrong to the citizens of a sister State.

In the Harlem "corner," which is referred to in another place, contracts to deliver at 110 were settled at 179.

About three million dollars were taken out of the pockets of the bears. Several prominent houses went down in the struggle. The result of the "corner" was that the bulls were saddled with the entire capital stock of the property.

One broker, who had sold calls at 150 and was requested to fulfil his contracts when the stock had advanced to 250, was very much in the same position as Glendower's spirits, which were called from the vasty deep but would not come. "I don't see anything here," he said, "about delivering. You can call, but I don't mind it."

There were two "corners" in Harlem. The Common Council was cornered in one and the Legislature in the other.

In the Rock Island "corner" the bulls bought 20,000 shares more than existed, and the price rose from 110 to 150.

London financiers have a fearful horror of "corners." Hence the London Stock Exchange is very chary about listing our railroads, especially those with a moderate number of shares.

"Corners" are seldom profitable, and the parties with them can hardly escape getting badly hurt unless they are prepared to own and carry the entire property. Even in that event, it is usually put out of the speculative market for a considerable time.

The Hudson "corner" was one of the most successful. paid a profit of 12 per cent. There was a profit of 4$^1/_2$ the Rock Island "corner."

The first "corner" of which there is any record in Wall Street was in Morris Canal, an old "fancy" now almost forgotten except for its "corner." It had been forced upward as fancies frequently are, until it was far above its intrinsic value, and several operators began to sell "short."

After this operation had gone on for some time a pool was formed to protect it, and the pool bought it all up and locked it up in a trunk. The operation was new to the Street and the bears were astounded, but when called upon to settle they became furious, and accused the manipulators of the "corner" of entering into a conspiracy. The "bulls" asked the "bears" why they had sold what they did not possess and could not procure.

The dispute was referred to the arbitration of the Board of Brokers, and that eminent body, then unsophisticated in the arts of speculation, took what seemed to them an equitable view of the case, and decided it in favor of the "shorts," who, on the ground of conspiracy on the part of the clique, were relieved from fulfilling their obligations.

CHAPTER 8

THE COMMODORE'S "CORNERS"

The Great Hudson "Corner."—Commodore Vanderbilt the "Boss" of the Situation.—The "Corner" Forced Upon Him.—How he Managed the Trick of getting the Bears to "Turn" the stock, and then caught them.—His able Device of Unloading while Forcing the Bears to Cover at High Figures.—The Harlem "Corner."—The Common Council betrayed the Commodore, but were Caught in their own Trap, and Lost Millions.—The Legislature Attempt the the same Game, and meet with a Similar Fate.

IN the Hudson "corner," the stock jumped from 112 to 180. Commodore Vanderbilt was the "Boss" of the situation in this "corner." He got the "bulge" completely on all the other parties connected with it, and what is more, he had the balance of the sympathy of the Street with him, for he was not the aggressor in getting up the "corner." The fighting at first was forced upon him, but he acted on the defensive in a way that made his opponents sorry for their rashness. Though he did not know much about Shakespeare, he acted in accordance with old Polonius' advice to his son by pushing the opposition to the wall.

As soon as he gained the mastery, he became severely aggressive, as he was in everything.

The beginning of this story of the Hudson "corner" is somewhat romantic. The Commodore was sunning himself on a pile of logs on the Jersey side of the Hudson while his yacht lay in the stream, and he was in the mood for enjoying a long and well-earned vacation, attempting to lay aside for a time the toil and trouble of eking out a precarious existence in speculation. While basking in the noon-day sun and gazing with delight on the luxurious foliage that arose from the New Jersey bank of the river, he was aroused from his charming reverie by a messenger from Wall Street, who conveyed to him the important intelligence that a wicked and unregenerate clique of "bears" had conspired to sell Hudson stock "short," and that it was declining with great rapidity under the repeated and unmerciful blows of their hammers.

The Commodore arose and shook off his lethargy, as a lion may be supposed to shake the dew from his mane prior to his preparation for a spring upon an unfortunate foe.

The Commodore hastened down to Wall Street and instructed his brokers to take all the sellers' options offered in Hudson. Cash stock was then taken as quickly as possible until the market was bare. A brief calculation showed that the buyers had secured either as cash or contract stock all the Hudson stock in existence with the exception of a small number of shares which were not expected to come upon the market.

The prolific brain of the Commodore then invented a new move in the game. A number of leading "bear" houses were requested to "turn" Hudson, which means to buy it for cash from the cornering party and sell it back to them on buyers' options for periods varying from ten to thirty days. This able ruse was intended to impress the bears with the idea that the cornering party was weak. It seemed as if they were short of cash. So the leading bears grasped at the good chance, as they imagined, of turning several thousand shares, and instantly threw the cash stock on the market. It was privately picked up by the brokers of the great "cornerer."

Everything having thus far progressed in favor of the ruse the trap was sprung upon the unsuspecting party. The sellers' options began to mature, and there was no Hudson to be obtained.

The "corner" was complete, and the stock rose to 180. It had been 112 a few mornings before, when the Commodore was basking in the sun, and found that the bears were taking advantage of his absence. The loss on a hundred shares was $6,800.

There were about 50,000 shares contracted for to be delivered at this rate of profit by the "cornerers." It will thus be seen that they were well fixed.

The bears were in terrible anguish.

But the worst part of the deal for these poor animals had yet to come. The bears who had turned the stock were notified that they must stand and deliver. They complained bitterly of the ingratitude of the bulls, whom they had only sought to oblige, by turning the stock. The bulls were implacable, however, and demanded their property. They proposed a compromise which was most exacting. They were willing to lend stock at five per cent. per day. Some of the bears paid this, thinking the "corner" would be of short duration, but it continued for over two weeks, and, after paying five per cent. a day for several days, these poor victims bought the stock at the high rate and settled.

This double move in turning the stock was the ablest trick that had ever been accomplished in cornering. It made Vanderbilt king of strategists in that line.

But the best part of the stratagem was that wherein the bulls saved themselves from being saddled with the whole stock, and made immense profits out of the deal.

While some of the bears were purchasing to cover at 170, Vanderbilt's private brokers were selling at 140, the clique thus craftily unloading at good paying figures. This was one of the best inside moves in the whole history of "corners."

The bulls thus saved themselves from the risk of being loaded with probably the whole, or at any rate the greater part of the capital stock, and through the Commodore's able management the load was comparatively light at the end of the deal, the property remaining as good a speculative as before, which is a rare exception in "corners."

The "corner" in Harlem was not less skilfully managed than the one in Hudson, but it had fewer complications. It was all plain sailing, so to speak, compared with the former, yet it clearly illustrated that the Commodore had a genius for "corners." When he managed the Harlem "corner" he had had no experience in railroad matters, and he had reached the ripe age of sixty-nine.

I place the Hudson "corner" first in order because it was, in several respects, the greatest, though it happened at a later date than the Harlem.

It is a curious fact that in nearly all "corners" with which the Commodore was connected, he was on the defensive, and seldom the aggressor at the beginning of the fight. He was always placed in such a position that he had to fight hard to defend his property, or let it go to the dogs.

Buying stock in Harlem was his first venture in railroad transactions. He bought it as an investment. This was in 1863. Thirty years prior to this he bad been requested to go into Harlem, but he declined, ironically remarking "I'm a steamboat man, a competitor of these steam contrivances that you tell us will run on dry land. Go ahead. I wish you well, but I never shall have anything to do with 'em."

When the Commodore went into Harlem it was selling at eight or nine dollars a share. It had been down as low as three dollars about the time I arrived in Wall Street. He put some money in the road, began improvements and the stock soon rose to 30. Many people predicted that the Commodore would lose all the money in railroads that he had made in steamboats.

The stock, however, gradually rose to 50, and speculators began to perceive that there was some inside movement going on. This was made apparent when one day in April, 1863, the Common Council of this city passed an ordinance authorizing the Commodore to build a street railroad down Broadway to the Battery. So Jake Sharp's enterprise was not original, as the Commodore was over twenty years ahead of him.

The Common Council were not immaculate in those days either, though the Jaehnes and Waites escaped punishment. They basely deceived the Commodore after taking his money; but he punished them severely. As soon as the franchise was granted, Harlem advanced to 75, and the Aldermen began to sell it "short." They thought they had the Commodore fast in their clutches, and took their friends into the secret. They expected to sell enough of stock to make several millions. Their plan was to sell "short" all that the market would take, and then repeal the ordinance, which would cause the stock to drop probably below 50. Drew was one of the great bears in this deal with the Aldermen.

The Commodore got wind of the scheme, went on buying, and got others to help him, taking all the "shorts" that were offered. The operators had soon sold a great deal more Harlem stock than there was actually in existence. There were 110,000 shares of Harlem. When the Aldermen and their friends thought they had made millions, they repealed the ordinance, and Judge Brady, in the Court of Common Pleas, at the same time issued an injunction prohibiting the laying of rails on the Broadway road.

Everybody thought that the Commodore was hopelessly ruined. Harlem stock, however, dropped three points only, to 72. This created surprise among the Aldermen and the bears. They thought it should have dropped to 50. The "shorts" went into the market for the purpose of covering. Harlem ascended with amazing rapidity to 100, to 150, to 170 and finally to 179. The Common Council were obliged to make their final settlements at the last figure. The Commodore had all the stock. The Common Council lost a million, and their friends, whom they had advised to sell "short," lost several millions. The Commodore "raked in" five or six millions, and went on his way rejoicing and improving Harlem, having now taken "Bill" in with him as vice president.

One would naturally imagine that the severe lesson which the Common Council had received in "corners" would have taught others to beware of the Commodore in this line of speculation, although it was new to him, but it did not. People as a rule will not learn either by precept or example. They must go through the rough experience themselves.

The Legislature soon fell into the same trap in which the Common Council had been caught and which they had actually set for themselves. The following year the Commodore secured control of the Hudson River Railroad through the purchase of its stock, and afterwards secured a sufficient number of the members of the Legislature to pass a bill consolidating the road with Harlem. He also won the promise of the Governor to sign the bill.

Harlem again began to rise, and went from 75 to 150. This was early in 1864.

The members of the Legislature employed to pass the bill pocketed the money of the Commodore and then hatched a conspiracy, after the manner of the Common Council, to ruin him and make millions by his fall. He had a shrewd lobbyist in the Legislature, however, who attentively watched his interests while he came down to New York to purchase stock for the rise that must have necessarily followed the passage of the bill. He had not been long in Wall Street when he was informed that the Legislature were imitating the game in which the Common Council had been so signally defeated the previous year. The Commodore sent him word to keep close watch at Albany, and he went on buying stock in Wall Street.

The bill was defeated. Harlem stock had a slump from 150 to 90. The Commodore was in a dilemma, and would have been dreadfully embarrassed only for the intense avarice of the Legislature. If they had bought and delivered at 90, they would have made millions, which the Commodore would have lost; but, like the horse leech's daughter, they cried out for more. Nothing would satisfy them until the stock should be depressed to 50. Then they could "scoop" in several millions and the Commodore would be wound up. This was probably the darkest hour in the Commodore's life. He hardly knew which way to turn. He was on the ragged edge. He has often pathetically described his feelings at this crisis to his intimate friends. He was almost on the brink of despair. He sent for old John Tobin, who had been a gate keeper at the ferry-house at Staten Island. Tobin had made quite a haul in the former deal in Harlem, and was worth over a million. He told Tobin what the perfidious members of the Legislature had done. John had been buying Harlem also in prospect of a rise.

"They stuck you too, John," said the Commodore. "How do you feel about it?" John sighed, and replied that his feelings were not the most enviable. "Shall we let 'em bleed us?" queried the Commodore.

John sighed again, but did not know what reply to make.

"John, don't them fellows need dressing down?" emphatically queried the Commodore. John answered in the affirmative, but did not see how it was to be accomplished, as "them fellows" at that moment seemed to hold the fort.

After a pause of deep reflection, the Commodore, again addressing John with intensified emphasis in his tone, said: "John, let us teach 'em never to go back on their word again as long as they draw breath. Let us try the Harlem 'corner' once more."

It was agreed to try and repeat the Harlem "corner."

John put up a million. Leonard Jerome also went into the deal. It took five millions to face the Legislature in this game, in which they had every opportunity of packing all the cards. It was virtually, at first, a silent game of whist, at which the Commodore was a noted player. He never played with greater skill than this time, except in the Hudson "corner," and in both instances he almost manifested the skill of inspiration.

The members of the Legislature completely lost their heads. The old classic maxim, "whom the gods devote to destruction, they first make mad," appeared to apply peculiarly to them, in the manipulation of the Harlem "corner." Some of them mortgaged their houses and lands to get money to sell Harlem "short." They advised all their friends that it was such a sure thing that failure was impossible, and brought all of their acquaintances whom they could influence into the speculative maelstrom of Harlem.

In the course of a few weeks, the members of the Legislature and their friends had sold millions of Harlem to be delivered at various periods during the summer, when they expected it would go 'way down, probably to 8 or 9, where the Commodore had originally bought it.

They expected, moreover, that the Commodore would have appeared at Albany either in person or by his lobby representatives to sue for terms or settlement. They were greatly disappointed. He never left the company of his brokers in Wall Street, and persisted in purchasing. The members thought he must be mad, or at least in his dotage. He was then threescore and ten, the Scriptural limit of human days.

The Commodore continued to purchase Harlem until he had bought—paradoxical as it may seem to the general reader—27,000 shares more than were in existence of Harlem stock.

When the members of the Legislature who set the trap to catch Vanderbilt, but in which they themselves were now hopelessly ensnared, went into the market to buy for the purpose of covering, there was no Harlem to be had. Vanderbilt and his brokers had every share of it safely secured in their strong boxes.

The members of the Legislature were paralyzed. They could expect no mercy from the Commodore. He owed them none, and though a good Christian prior to his death, he was then practically a stranger to the doctrine of the great Nazarene. "Return good for evil," or, "whosoever shall smite thee on thy right cheek, turn to him the other also." He was rather inclined to follow the maxim of that practical Quaker, who, when smitten on the cheek and asked to turn the other, replied, "Friend, thou didst not read far enough. It is written, 'pay what thou owest,'" and he knocked the fellow down.

This was the rule of action to which the Commodore rigidly adhered in dealing with the Legislature in the Harlem "corner."

When a compromise was mooted to him, the Commodore replied, "Put it up to a thousand. This panel game is being tried too often."

No doubt he would have put it up to a thousand and totally ruined the members of the Legislature, with the Governor and their friends included, only for the overpowering appeals of his two trustworthy friends, Leonard Jerome and John Tobin.

Mr. Jerome had no sympathy for the Legislature, any more than Vanderbilt had, but he had a patriotic desire to take care of the "Street," thus showing the large and comprehensive view of which this able financier is capable where a broad speculative question and a variety of diverse interests are involved.

"If you should carry out your threat," said Mr. Jerome to the Commodore, "it would break every house on the Street."

The Commodore yielded to that touch of nature that makes all the world akin, and under the magnetism of Jerome's prudent entreaty, like Pharaoh with the Israelites, agreed to let the legislature go—at 285 for Harlem.

In one day 15,000 shares matured at this figure. Speculators who read these lines, just pause and think of it for a moment! The stock that sold at $3 when I made my debut in Wall Street in 1857, reached 285 in 1864, and could have been put to 1,000. Don't you feel astounded at the possibilities of speculation?

Then, again, think of the one-man power that could accomplish this wonderful feat and prevail against a whole Legislature and its Governor, with the choicest assortment of "crooked" lawyers in the State, versed in all the arts of duplicity and cunning to aid and abet said Legislature and its Governor.

Think of this, and then you will have some conception of the astute mind that the Commodore possessed, without education to assist it, in the contest against this remarkable combination of well-trained mental forces. There can hardly be a doubt that the Commodore was a genius, probably without equal in the financial world. There was hardly any achievement of his life which he gloated over with such ineffable delight as the cornering of the Legislature. He would say, when referring to the matter afterwards: "We busted the whole Legislature, and scores of the honorable members had to go home without paying their board bills." Thus ended the second "corner" in Harlem.

Many large houses were ruined by the "corner," and a host of private speculators lost all they had. Daniel Drew came very near being swamped in it, but finally escaped with paying a million, chiefly through his influence at court.

It is unnecessary to speak of the celebrated Erie "corners" here, as I have treated them pretty fully in the life and speculations of Drew.

CHAPTER 9

DREW AND THE ERIE "CORNERS"

A HARMONIOUS UNDERSTANDING WITH THE COM-
MODORE.—HOW THE COMPROMISE WAS EFFECTED.—AN
INTERESTING INTERVIEW WITH FISK AND GOULD IN THE
COMMODORE'S BED-ROOM.—HOW RICHARD SCHELL RAISED
THE WIND FOR THE COMMODORE.—DREW'S SHARE OF THE
SPOILS.—HE TRIES TO RETIRE FROM WALL STREET, BUT
CAN'T.—THE SETTLEMENT COST ERIE NINE MILLIONS.—
GOULD AND FISK "WATER" ERIE AGAIN, TO THE EXTENT
OF TWENTY-THREE MILLIONS, BUT LEAVE DREW OUT.—
"UNCLE DANIEL" RETURNS TO THE STREET.—HE IS
INVEIGLED INTO A BLIND POOL BY GOULD AND FISK, LOSES
A MILLION AND RETREATS FROM THE POOL.—HE THEN
OPERATES ALONE ON THE "SHORT" SIDE AND THROWS
AWAY MILLIONS.—HE TRIES PRAYER, BUT IT "AVAILETH
NOT."—"IT'S NO USE, BROTHER, THE MARKET STILL
GOES UP."—PRAYING AND WATCHING THE TICKER.—
HOPELESSLY "CORNERED" AND RUINED BY HIS FORMER
PUPILS AND PARTNERS.

ABOUT the middle of April Drew emerged from his retreat in Jersey City, and appeared openly in Wall Street, apparently without any fear of arrest. Other members of the Erie clique had gone through the formality of purging their contempt of court, but had not made their peace with the Commodore, and things went forward without any special

interruption or excitement until July, when a settlement was made with Vanderbilt.

It was agreed that the Commodore should be relieved of 50,000 shares of Erie stock at 70, for which he was to receive $2,500,000 in cash, and $1,250,000 in bonds of the Boston, Hartford & Erie at 80. It was further stipulated that he was to receive $1,000,000 for the privilege of calling on him at any time within four months for the remaining 50,000 shares of Erie at 70. He was allotted two seats in the Erie Board of Directors. All suits between the two high contending parties were to be dismissed and all offenses whatsoever relating to the case, in the language of the law, were to be condoned.

The manner in which the compromise was effected is not the least interesting part of the famous deal in Erie. Some time after Drew had got through his famous Sunday evening interview with the Commodore, paving the way for his partners, by weeping and showing other manifestations of deep contrition on account of his inglorious flight to Jersey City, Gould and Fisk came over early one morning to see the Commodore at his residence in Washington Place. Fisk told the story of meeting the Commodore with great unction, in his bold, brazen and lively manner. "Gould wanted to wait," said Fisk, "until the Commodore should have time to get out of bed, but I rang the bell, and when the door was opened I rushed up to his room. The Commodore was sitting on the side of the bed with one shoe off and one shoe on. He got up, and I saw him putting on the other shoe. I remember that shoe from its peculiarity. It had four buckles on it. I had never seen shoes with buckles in that manner before, and I thought, if these sort of men always wear that sort of shoe, I might want a pair. He said I must take my position as I found it; that there I was, and he would keep his bloodhounds (the lawyers) on our track; that he would be damned if he didn't keep them after us if we didn't take the stock off his hands. I told him that if I had my way, I'd be damned if I would take a share of it; that he brought the punishment on himself and he deserved it. This mellowed him down. I told him that he was a robber. He said the suits would never be withdrawn till he was settled with. I said (after settling with him) that it was an almighty robbery; that we had sold ourselves to the Devil, and that Gould felt just the same as I did."

Among the friends who adhered to the Commodore in the trying hour of the "corner," besides those mentioned, were William Heath, Richard Schell and his brother Augustus, and Rufus Hatch. Richard Schell was highly practical and remarkably shrewd in the aid which he offered the Commodore to obtain money for the speculative fight. He managed, through his tact and shrewdness, to get loans on Erie after the banks had absolutely refused to lend, on account of the over-issue of the stock. After this refusal, he made inquiry at the banks, and found that most of them had New York Central stock. He then went to a bank and said: "If you don't lend the Commodore half a million on Erie at 50, he will put Central down to 50 tomorrow, and break half the houses on the Street. You know whether or not you will be among them."

The threat was repeated at other banks, and, in almost every instance, had the desired effect, and the Commodore was supplied with the sinews of war, but he was only throwing away his ammunition.

The Erie stock from the inexhaustible fountain of overissue was supplied to him without stint, and his attempts to "corner" the clique were absolutely futile.

While these gamesters were feeding the Commodore with this extemporized stuff to order, Fisk said: "If this printing press don't break down, I'll be d____d if I don't give the old hog all he wants of Erie."

The printing press did not break down, but did its work well until the Commodore was nearly "burst," and had it not been for his indomitable courage and the hold he had acquired on the courts, he would have been bankrupt. His escape seemed almost a miracle to the people of Wall Street, and Gould and Fisk were not less surprised that they had met a foeman worthy of their steel. In spite of the fact that he spilled over seven millions like water, the Commodore managed to sustain the market through it all, and prevented a crash that, in its local effects, at least, would have been as disastrous as that of Black Friday.

Certain innocent holders who had been badly crushed in the collision between the great leaders received a financial emollient for their lacerated feelings, amounting in the aggregate to $429,250. The Boston party, represented by Mr. Eldridge, was to be relieved of five millions of its precious Boston, Hartford & Erie bonds, receiving therefor four millions of Erie acceptances.

Thus, the settlement in full cost Erie about nine million dollars. The Erie stock and bondholders were saddled with this liability in defiance of law and justice.

Gould and Fisk pretended to be opposed to the settlement, leaving the public to infer that it was all the work of Drew with Vanderbilt. However this may have been, it was probably the best thing the others could have done to relieve themselves of their various complications at the time. No doubt the Vanderbilt note to Drew, for which the waiter was discharged from Taylor's Hotel, was at the bottom of the whole settlement.

Drew was left to enjoy his share of the fruits of the "corner," which netted seven millions, except that he had to pay into the Erie treasury the trifling item of $540,000 in discharge of interest and all claims or causes of action which might be presented against him by the Erie Company. The Erie Railway fell to the lot of Gould and Fisk as their share of the spoils growing out of the *entente cordiale.*

Drew then retired from Wall Street in the same way that Gould has so often retired since that time, except that Drew had probably an honest intention so far as it was possible for him to have such a conception of leaving the Street forever, but it would seem that he had not the power to do so. Once in Wall Street, always in Wall Street. It is like the doctrine of the final perseverance of the saints, as laid down in the Westminster Confession of Faith. It is impossible to get out of it when the speculator gets fairly into its fascinating grasp.

Drew might have enjoyed life and the consolations of religion on the few millions he had left if he had retired in company with his Bible and Hymn Book, to some lovely, secluded spot in the peaceful vales of Putnam county; but he was under the infatuation of some latent and mysterious force or attraction, the victim of some potent spell, like the cue in whose weird grasp Nancy Sykes was firmly held when she essayed to get away from the murderous "Bill," as described by Dickens in Oliver Twist.

Drew came back to Wall Street, and saw and was vanquished, quite unlike Caesar.

When he returned to the "Street" after a few months absence, the scene was greatly changed. His two pupils had shown themselves to be such apt scholars, that in the interim they had exceeded the wildest dreams of avarice that ever their able preceptor had conjured up or inculcated. In four months Gould and Fisk had inflated the capital stock of Erie from 34 millions to 57 millions. No doubt, Uncle Daniel was astounded at their progress, and his feelings can be better imagined than described when, in the presence of this marvellous increase of wealth, he reflected that he was no longer treasurer of Erie, and had neither lot nor part in its unprecedented prosperity.

His natural propensity to operate, however, was still strong, but when he again tried his hand at speculation, it seemed to have lost its cunning, and he felt almost as much disappointed as Rip Van Winkle did when he awoke in Sleepy Hollow, after his twenty years' nap, and began to examine the changed aspect of the country in the vicinity of Irvington, now Gould's country seat.

The speculative tactics in operation had been changed, and he soon found that it was a losing game to go on the bear side of the market. He was invited into the pool by his old partners, to have a little practice at the popular game of spider and fly. Drew had been the spider for a long time who had inveigled the unwary flies from every direction into his insidious net. He was now asked to assume the role of a fly, while his former pupils played spiders. In plain terms, he was coolly requested to go into a "blind pool" in Erie, deposit four millions, shut his eyes and open his mouth, leaving the Erie sharpers to put taffy or candy into it, just as they pleased.

He was no longer to have the privilege of pulling the wires, nor the wool over other people's eyes. On the contrary, he was to be one of the puppets that should dance to the music of Gould and Fisk, and let them pull the wool over his eyes. He was not to ask any questions, but pay his money and take his choice, that is to say, whatever Gould and Fisk chose to give him. The terms were rather humiliating, and on reflection, Uncle Daniel revolted. He did not see the point of paying the piper without having the privilege of choosing the tune. He, therefore, withdrew his funds after losing a million, and undertook the task of bearding these two young lions in their den—the den which he had constructed for them, and the two young lions which he had so carefully nurtured to destroy him. They were very wroth with him on account of what they regarded as his treachery, which virtually consisted in his refusal to be totally devoured by them. The fact is, however, Daniel could not have been true to any one, any more than they. "Can the Ethiopian change his skin, or the leopard his spots?"

After considering the matter prayerfully, as he always did in such emergencies, he resolved to operate alone, and the oracle told him to go on the short side. It was evident that the Gods had doomed him to destruction, so he rushed in madly to sell the market, which moved persistently upward.

In this emergency he took counsel of a Christian brother, who advised him to pray. He tried hard to pray, but his irresistible desire to keep constant watch on the tape of the ticker, to see the quotations, evidently distracted his devotions. This was probably the first time that he lost faith in the power that moves the arm that moves the world. He went to his Christian brother with tears in his eyes, saying: "It is no use, brother; the market still goes up." And Uncle Daniel ceased to pray, and despairingly fixed his attention on the ticker.

During November, Drew contracted for the delivery of 70,000 shares of Erie at current prices. It was then in the vicinity of 38. He proceeded on this line of operation until he was hopelessly "cornered." He then applied to the court. Application was made for an injunction in the name of August

Belmont, but Gould and Fisk offset it by applying for another injunction to their faithful Barnard. That upright Judge not only granted an injunction restraining all suits brought against his two eminent proteges, but appointed Gould Receiver of Erie. He also gave authority to the directors of Erie to use the funds of the corporation to purchase and cancel 200,000 shares of stock, the legality of whose issue had been questioned, at any price less than the par value, without regard to the rate at which it had been issued.

Gould and Fisk had issued these shares in the bear interest at 40, ran the stock down to 35, and now obtained the power to purchase it back at par in the bull interest. This they did by the authority and permission of a Judge of the Supreme Court, in spite of the law prohibiting members of corporations to deal in their own stock. So these two great manipulators "cornered" their old friend and teacher, Drew, by legally over-riding the law.

Erie became scarce after this skilful movement was performed, and was selling at 47. Drew made desperate attempts to cover at this price, but the stock ran up to 57 between Monday and Wednesday. Wall Street was in a terrible ferment, and, as the newspapers say, the greatest excitement prevailed. Erie made still another leap and reached 62. It was evident that it was bound to keep on the upward grade, and there was no apparent relief for Drew, at least for two or three days, when an incoming steamer was expected to have a considerable amount of Erie on board. It was manifest, however, that by that time Drew would have reached the end of his millions, and probably most of his credit would have vanished with his own filthy lucre. His oppressors were bearing down upon him with all their might, and were evidently determined to make short work of him.

The struggle waxed hotter as the hour of three in the afternoon approached, and these two young lions of speculation were determined to crush the old bear unmercifully and effectually.

When Drew was apparently on the very brink of utter financial destruction, and almost at the close of the market, two events happened that preserved him from total annihilation. There had been 300,000 shares of Erie issued in ten share lots, which the operators thought were safely secreted in London and Amsterdam. When the stock reached 60 these ten-share lots began to come out. It turned out that most of them had never left home, but were securely held by tradesmen, mechanics, grocers and small bankers and brokers. They were thrown on the market with great rapidity to realize handsome profits, and the efforts of the clique to absorb them before they got into the hands of Drew, made serious inroads on the reserve funds of the champion operators. As troubles never come singly, at this new juncture the banks refused to certify their checks. Drew was, therefore, enabled to make good his contracts at 47, but speculatively speaking, he was ruined. He came pretty near bringing down his desperate assailants, however, in his sad and frightful fall. The stock then fell to 42, and Erie became a drug in the market. The victors had got the spoils, but they paid dearly for them, and had come pretty near being destroyed in the moment of their triumph. They had purchased their Erie at "corner" prices, and they were obliged to carry it, for nobody wanted it. Added to this Erie was struck from the Board for a time, and had it not been for the gullibility of our English cousins, this stock would have ceased to be a disturbing element in the market for a great while longer.

Although old Drew was badly treated, yet there was little sympathy for him, since he had merely become the victim of his own avarice, vacillation, treachery and scheming to catch others in the same net.

He could not justly complain of his former partners, and Fisk told him so, for their methods of operation, and the immense inflation of the Erie stock by which he was ruined had been accomplished by the machinery which he, himself, had set in motion, only his *ci-devant* colleagues had improved upon it, and had received various new patents on inventions and improvements, which they had joined to the old one invented by "Uncle Daniel," making one of the best combinations for the purpose of creating and working "corners" that had ever been devised in Wall Street.

But the unkindest cut of all was the way in which Fisk taunted him, on the eve of his crushing defeat, with the absurdity of his complaints about the management of Erie matters.

"You should be the last man," said this worthy pupil, sneeringly, to his dear old preceptor, "that should whine over any position in which you may be placed in Erie."

It was a sad truth, heartlessly uttered by the generous "Jim." Drew had no mercy on others, and could not expect to be shown any of that "twice blessed quality" towards himself.

The private scene in the Erie office between old Drew and Fisk and Gould, just prior to their final and victorious charge upon him, was deeply pathetic, yet none of the three showed more conspicuously that they were destitute of that proverbial honor among "boodlers" than Drew himself. He had secured Vanderbilt to assist him in the courts, and also in the market, against the machinations of the Erie clique, and then, turning around, he went straight to Gould and to him betrayed his ally and the plans he had arranged with him, expecting mercy from his old colleague by this dastardly act of humiliation and deception.

He must have lost his head at this crisis, for he ought to have known Gould better. He begged and pleaded with Gould and Fisk, and was ready to throw himself at their feet. He implored them to join him, with the remnant of his fortune, in giving the old paper mill another turn to grind out more Erie stock, that he might be permitted to emerge from that cruel "corner" in which he was placed like a scorpion girt by fire, brooding over his guilty woes.

But his pupils proved that they had profited only too well by his instructions. Just as he would have acted under similar circumstances, they were perfectly relentless. They seemed to be a double incarnation of Shylock personified, or two Dromios bereft of conscience and human sympathy. Drew had no Daniel but himself, to come to judgment. There was no fair Portia to plead his cause, and if there had been such an angelic creature in the case, though she might have "broke up" Fisk, it is almost certain that Gould would have successfully resisted her charms.

When Drew saw they were implacable he bade them good night, and with the courage of despair returned to the charge in Wall Street the next morning, with the results which have been briefly related. He lost nearly two millions in that fatal struggle.

CHAPTER 10

PANICS—THEIR CAUSES—
HOW FAR PREVENTABLE

NOT ACCIDENTAL FREAKS OF THE MARKET. — WE ARE STILL
A NATION OF PIONEERS. — THE QUESTION OF PANICS
PECULIARLY AMERICAN. — VIOLENT OSCILLATIONS IN
TRADE OWING TO THE GREAT MASS OF NEW AND
IMMATURE UNDERTAKINGS. — UNCERTAINTY ABOUT THE
INTRINSIC VALUE OF PROPERTIES. — SUDDEN SHRINKAGE OF
RAILROAD PROPERTIES A FRUITFUL CAUSE OF PANICS. —
RISKS AND PANICS INSEPARABLE FROM PIONEERING
ENTERPRISE. — WE ARE BECOMING LESS DEPENDENT ON THE
MONEY MARKETS OF EUROPE. — IN PANICS MUCH DEPENDS
UPON THE PRUDENCE AND SELF-CONTROL OF THE MONEY
LENDERS. — THE LAW WHICH COMPELS A RESERVE FUND IN
THE NATIONAL BANKS IS AT CERTAIN CRISES A
PROVOCATIVE OF PANICS. — GEORGE I. SENEY. — JOHN C.
ENO. — FERDINAND WARD. — THE CLEARING HOUSE AS A
PREVENTIVE OF PANICS.

THERE are few subjects on which there is more loose the-
orizing than that of the origin and remedy of panics.
These crises are commonly spoken of as accidental freaks of
the markets, due to antecedent reckless speculations, controlled in their progress by the acts of men and banks who
have lost their senses, but quite easily prevented, and as easily cured when they happen.

These are the notions of mere surface observers. They may be in a measure true, when applied to the markets of some of the older countries, whose business moves in long-established grooves and embraces but little of the risk attendant on new enterprises. In France and Germany, for instance, the hazards of business are almost entirely confined to the accidents of political events; and such nations are comparatively exempt from panics due to purely commercial causes. In the United States, panics arise, principally, from causes from which European countries are exempt.

Notwithstanding our immense population and the large measure of well-ordered consolidation that has been effected in our various interests, we are still a nation of pioneers. In every ten years, we now add nearly fifteen millions to our population, which means that each successive decade we are piling up the equivalent of a first-class European state upon our past marvellous accumulation of empire. Inseparable from this unparalleled national growth are great ventures and great commercial and financial risks. Our new population has to subdue new territory. New lands have to be cleared; new mines have to be opened; new industries have to be established; new railroads have to be built; new banks created and new corporations founded. These new ventures are necessarily in a measure experimental. Some of them fail utterly; others succeed magnificently. They require large outlays of capital in advance of obtainable results. These outlays are, in many cases, met by borrowing; the loans being secured by liens upon the uncertain undertakings, and therefore lacking the stability of value that attaches to well developed investments.

We have thus a ceaseless stream of new issues of stocks, mortgages and commercial paper, and have, therefore, at all times outstanding a large amount of obligations which, from the uncertainty of their basis, are liable to wide fluctuations in value. Besides these absolutely new investments, we have also at all times an equal or larger amount of obligations issued against enterprises which, although not properly new, are still in an unconsolidated and experimental stage, and the value of which is, therefore, subject to wide fluctuations. Issues of this character naturally appeal to the adventurous instincts of our people and elicit a vast extent of speculative activity.

It is this peculiarity in the development and trade of the United States that renders our markets more exposed to panic than those of any other nation, and which makes the question of panics a peculiarly American one. In any and every commercial nation, trade is subject to regular successions of prosperity and depression. This oscillation results from, or constitutes a natural law.

The action of commerce, like the motion of the sea or the atmosphere, follows an undulatory line. First comes an ascending wave of activity and rising prices; next, when prices have risen to a point that checks demand, comes a period of hesitation and caution; then, care among lenders and discounters; then comes the descending movement, in which holders simultaneously endeavor to realize, thereby accelerating a general fall in prices. Credit then becomes more sensitive and is contracted; transactions are diminished; losses are incurred through the depreciation of property, and finally the ordeal becomes so severe to the debtor class that forcible liquidation has to be adopted, and insolvent firms and institutions must be wound up. This process is a periodical experience in every country; and the extent of the destructiveness of the crisis that attends it depends chiefly on the steadiness and conservatism of the business methods in each particular community affected. In addition to this ordinary and, I would even say, *natural* liability to commercial crises with a greater or lesser degree of panic, we, in the United States, have to stand the far more violent oscillations so inseparable from our great mass of new and immature undertakings.

In times of crisis, the obligations issued against such enterprises suffer instantly from the uncertainty about their intrinsic value. Holders are anxious to get rid of them; banks which have advanced money on them, call in their advances; and they become virtually unavailable assets. Every panic that has happened since the beginning of the era of railroads in this country, has been intensified many-fold by the sudden shrinkage in the value of this class of assets; and it is precisely here that the aggravation and the chief danger of an American panic centres.

In view of these facts, what is the use of discussing the possibility of averting our periodic panics? Risks and panics are inseparable from our vast pioneering enterprise; and all we can hope is, that they may diminish in severity in proportion as our older and more consolidated interests afford an increasing power of resistance to their operation. I am disposed to think that, in the future, the counteraction from this source will be much more effective than it has been in the past. The accumulations of financial resource available for market purposes at our monetary centres are increasing at a very rapid rate. Evidence of this is seen in the fact that, while the magnitude of our corporate undertakings is augmenting every year, we are also every year becoming less dependent on the money markets of Europe, and our large corporate loans are now made principally at borne. These accumulations afford elasticity to our financial system and serve as a buffer against the violence of great financial disturbances.

I do not see how we can in any other way satisfactorily explain how it is that, while we have had two distinct waves of commercial depression since the great crisis of 1873, such as have ordinarily been attended with more or less panic, we have had no disturbance that can be regarded as a fully developed panic. The only approach to it was the disturbance brought about by the Grant & Ward failure in May, 1884, which was merely a restricted and comparatively temporary affair.

But, whilst maintaining that panics cannot be avoided in a country situated as ours is in its present incomplete development, I cannot avoid expressing the opinion that conditions are permitted to exist which needlessly aggravate the perils of these upheavals when they do occur. In every panic very much depends upon the prudence and self-control of the money lenders. If they lose their heads and indiscriminately refuse to lend, or lend only to the few unquestionably strong borrowers, the worst forms of panic ensue; if they accommodate to their fullest ability the larger and reasonably safe class of borrowers, then the latter may be relied upon to protect those whom the banks reject, and thus the mischief may be kept within legitimate bounds. Everything depends upon rashness being held in check by an assurance that deserving debtors will be protected. This is tantamount to saying that all depends on the calmness and wisdom of the banks. They may easily mitigate or aggravate the severity of the crisis, according as they are prudently liberal or blindly selfish. It is, perhaps, safe to say, that the banks never do all they may; but the banks of this city must be credited with having shown great sagacity under repeated derangements of this kind within the last twenty-five years. They have largely succeeded in combining self-protection with the protection of their customers; and the antecedents they have established will go far toward breaking the force of any future panic.

But, unfortunately, the law imposes restraints upon the national banks which seriously interfere with the wise discretion of those institution. As the law now stands, the banks are liable to be wound up at the order of the Government if they permit their lawful money reserves to fall below 25 per cent. of their legal deposits. This establishes a "dead line" which is so dreaded when approached that it becomes almost a panic line. When that limit is reached, the banks are compelled to contract their loans; and, in certain conditions, the contraction of loans means forcible liquidation, without regard to consequences. Thus the very contrivance designed to protect the banks becomes a source of most serious danger to their customers and therefore to the banks themselves; and, in times of monetary pressure, it is the most direct provocative of panic. Were the banks allowed to use their reserves under such circumstances, a fund would be provided for mitigating the force of the crisis, and the danger might be gradually tided over; but, as it is, the banks can legally do little or nothing to avert panic; on the contrary, the law compels them to take a course which precipitates it; and when the crash has come, they have to unite in common cause to disregard the law and do what they can to repair the catastrophe that a preposterous enactment has helped to bring about. This is one of not a few unwise restrictions upon our national banks which needs to be stricken from the statute book. These periods of the breaking-down of unsound enterprises and of the weeding out of insolvent debtors and of liquidation of bad debts can never be wholly averted; nor is it desirable that they should, for they are essential to the maintenance of a sound and wholesome condition of business; but it is a grave reproach to our legislators if, when the day of purgation comes, the law treats the deserving and the undeserving with equal severity.

GEORGE I. SENEY.

The most prominent characters in the short lived panic of 1884, as every observing person knows, were Ferdinand Ward, James D. Fish and a few others who acted minor parts in connection with the methods of financiering which precipitated the crisis in Wall Street.

There are many people who think that Ward—the Young Napoleon of finance, as he was popularly called—was able to dupe everybody, his accomplices included, and that he was chiefly responsible for all the trouble. But this is an exaggerated and unscientific view of the case.

Among the financiers who came to grief in the general embarrassment caused by the peculiar methods of the two financiers referred to, was George I. Seney. Seney gave his money away, and it was placed in the wrong quarters for any tangible return. He was a great patron of the churches and religious institutions. If he had studied the life of Daniel Drew, he might have discovered that investments in such enterprises as these were not particularly profitable. In his financial difficulties, Seney was left high and dry without friends who would come to his rescue. The result was, that the two financial institutions the Metropolitan Bank and the Brooklyn bank with which he was thoroughly identified, had to go under as the result of Mr. Seney's misfortunes. And an insurance company in Brooklyn, which had loaned about all of its surplus to Mr. Seney, taking Metropolitan Bank stock as collateral, was swamped as well.

There are few of the speculative magnates who succumbed to the crash of 1884, whose financial histories are more interesting than that of Mr. Seney. He is the son of a Methodist minister, and was born at Astoria, Long Island, about sixty years ago. He has always manifested the deepest devotion to his paternal church, and in the very height of his prosperity the church was the first object of his financial care. He was educated at the University of the City of New York, and shortly after he graduated, and when about 22 years of age, entered the Metropolitan Bank as a clerk. He was afterwards teller and then cashier. This was when Mr. Williams was President and when Mr. Jacques was Vice-President. Mr. Jacques resigned that position several years ago and made a prolonged journey to Europe. Mr. Williams died a few years ago, and Mr. Seney became his successor as President of the bank.

Mr. Seney's wonderful financial abilities were a comparatively recent outgrowth of his mental evolution, at an age when very few men exhibit signs of new developments.

Up to a date shortly prior to the panic, he was generally regarded as slow and phlegmatic, without manifesting any special parts that indicated superior brilliancy as a financier. He first distinguished himself in Wall Street during the speculative furore of 1879, and came to the front then with sudden and surprising activity. He carved out an original course for himself in speculation—so original, in fact, as to stamp the enterprises with which he became identified with his name. The Seney properties became almost as familiar to the financial world as the Goulds, the Vanderbilts and the Villards.

Mr. Seney's chief securities (so-called through the courtesy of speculative parlance) were Ohio Central, Rochester and Pittsburgh, East Tennessee, Virginia & Georgia, and the celebrated "Nickel Plate" Road. These were known as the Seney Syndicate properties, and the system of handling them was entirely novel in the history of Wall Street, causing the financial veterans of Wall Street to stand and stare at the boldness and rapidity of the Seney movements.

Instead of starting with moderate issues in amount, as has usually been the custom of most men handling railroad and telegraph properties, and doing the watering process by degrees, Mr. Seney boldly began the watering at the very inception of the enterprise, pouring it in lavishly and without stint. There was nothing mean or niggardly about his method of free dilution, the sight of which threw some of the old operators into a fit of consternation. The stocks were strongly puffed, and as they were so thoroughly diluted their owners could afford to let them get a start at a very low figure. The future prospects of the properties were set forth in the most glowing colors, the public took the bait, and the stocks became at once conspicuous among the leading active fancies of the market.

The cause of the vigorous life and amazing activity so suddenly imparted to the stocks of the Seney Syndicate can only be revealed by a careful perusal of Mr. Seney's checkbook, which, if still in existence, will show commissions paid for the execution of the orders to buy and the orders executed to sell, both by the same pen and in the same handwriting.

These transactions, in the language of the "Street," are called washed sales. In this way Mr. Seney was understood to have made a very large amount of money, and from being almost one of the poorest men in Brooklyn, he soon became marked as the richest. While he continued to thrive it was a singular fact that the majority of his financial friends seemed to fall into a decline.

When the affairs of the Seney enterprise were wound up, it was discovered that these people had little left except the certificates which bore the high-sounding term of the Seney Syndicate Property.

One peculiarity about Mr. Seney in his social relations was, that while he appeared almost bereft of sympathy for used-up friends whom his schemes had ruined, he drew largely on his immense gains for philanthropic purposes, and in the aggregate must have distributed over $2,000,000 in a very magnanimous manner.

It would seem that Mr. Seney at one time aspired to be a great philanthropist, and had it not been for the unfortunate exposè which was the result of the panic, he might one day have stood in as high and lordly a position as the renowned Peabody, with even a greater reputation as a financier. It is sad to picture the contrast presented by the *denouement* with what might have been, in a career which began with so much promise, dating from the time that Mr. Seney was installed as President of the Metropolitan Bank, whose standing and credit were the highest in the State.

Mr. Seney's speculative career affords an example of the way in which this kind of speculation reflects on the stability of our best banking institutions. The lesson is one that should be carefully taken to heart by the financiers of this country.

It is due, however, to Mr. Seney to state that he alone was not responsible for the misfortunes of the Metropolitan Bank, although he was the ruling spirit; for it could hardly be possible that the directors of that institution could have been ignorant of its affairs in connection with the Seney speculations. The Metropolitan Bank cannot be compared with the Marine Bank, which met a similar misfortune, for it was no family affair, and Mr. Seney had none of his relatives connected with it, as Mr. Fish had with the Marine Bank.

It appears that it was chiefly owing to the fact that Mr. Seney had so little personal interest in the Metropolitan Bank that be was so anxious to gut the concern, knowing that the loss would fall upon others.

The most important point for speculators and investors, however, connected with the enterprises of these men is, that the terrible shrinkage of Stock Exchange values at the time, amounting to over $1,000,000,000, was in a large measure brought about by a foregone conclusion on the part of the sagacious bear cliques that disaster would sooner or later overtake the institutions over which Mr. Seney and Mr. Fish presided.

This should afford a wholesome lesson, through the medium of practical experience, to speculators and investors for all future time. For this very reason the facts are worthy of being put on permanent record as a reminder and a guide, particularly to Wall Street men, who are too often prone to forget the past and thus leave themselves liable to be caught in a similar net again.

The transactions of the four prominent speculators who played the most conspicuous part in the events which resulted in the panic of May, 1884, should be preserved for reference, as a guide when similar cases arise, for in spite of the deep disgrace, shame and misery that have followed in the wake of their enterprises, these men will have hosts of imitators for many years to come. Ward, Fish, Seney and Eno, with probably the one exception, Fish, are, by many, considered smart men, who simply had the misfortune to become involved, but who had a fair chance of coming out of all their troubles, great millionaires and publicly honored for their ability and success.

It must be admitted that there are some examples in the financial world whose careers will fully support this theory and belief but they are the exceptions which only prove the rule in speculation, as in other lines of business, that "honesty is the best policy." These men, who have been apparently so successful through dishonest methods, are never free from dread of being tripped up at any period of their inflated prosperity. They are always subject to be called upon by the application of the stern methods of honest financiering to give an account of their stewardship, and to have the transactions of a lifetime eventually gauged by the standard of public honesty. It is the winding up that tells the tale, and exposes the duplicity of the ablest financiers, who vainly imagine that dishonest methods will always prevail.

JOHN C. ENO.

Of the four famous "financiers" mentioned who were most prominent in the Summer panic of 1884, the speculative history of John C. Eno was in some respects the most remarkable and most interesting.

Eno was a young man, not more than twenty-six years of age, and a representative of that class of ardent and youthful speculators who plunge into the market with all the recklessness incident to young and sanguine imaginations, with many roseate schemes of wealth and greatness, for which inexperienced youth is proverbial. Eno was a victim of that rashness, impulsiveness and desire for extravagance, by which the possessors of these attributes frequently get themselves and many of their associates embroiled in numerous difficulties and embarrassments.

Another point of interest in the curious career of Eno was his position as President of the Second National Bank of New York, up to the time of the panic. Seldom does it fall to the lot of a youth of his tender years to have conferred upon him a position of such responsibility and dignity. The manner in which he made use of this position of trust, for appropriating money which did not belong to him, was notable for its peculiar ingenuity.

Most of the money lent by the bank was upon collateral securities, which, for convenience, as well as for safety, were kept, not at the bank, which was situated under the Fifth Avenue Hotel, but in a vault down town.

The capital stock of the bank was $100,000, and it had $4,000,000 of deposits, all of which was appropriated to speculative use by this smart young man, who decamped to Canada in company with a Roman Catholic priest.

Eno happened to have a rich father, who had made his money by thrift and economy during a long and prosperous life. To his credit, it must be said, that he came promptly to the rescue of this wayward and erring son, and paid the bank, of which he was director, three and one-half millions of dollars, on condition that the other half million should be contributed by the other directors, all of whom were very rich men. The directors willingly accepted the proposition, and thus the entire deficiency was made good by this generous arrangement, so that none of the depositors suffered the loss of a dollar.

The methods which Mr. John C. Eno, the President, resorted to for the purpose of capturing the institution root and branch, were ingenious and unique in their character, inasmuch as they had a tendency to inspire the fullest confidence in his vigilance and honesty regarding the affairs of the bank, instead of exciting any suspicion.

He discouraged the custom of keeping the securities of the bank in its own vaults, on the pretense that they were not sufficiently secure, and suggested that a safe should be rented in one of the down-town safe deposit companies. This was done at his request. He argued, further, that the funds on hand being mostly family deposits, the depositors were not of a class that often required to be accommodated with discounts, and that the money was not taken by the bank to be locked up and kept on hand so as to have the name of having it, but to be used to the best possible advantage consistent with safety, to make profitable returns through interest. Consequently, he was allowed to use the money of the bank freely to make loans to Wall Street brokers on interest, with approved collaterals, and he represented to the directors that he was carrying out this course.

As the bank was located so far up town, (at Twenty-third street,) the distance from Wall Street made it extra hazardous to send securities back and forth, as adventurous thieves might seize the messenger on the way. This has frequently happened in this city. It was, therefore, desirable to have the safe deposit vault in close proximity to Wall Street. Of the combination to the safe in this vault Mr. John C. Eno was the sole possessor. Having things fixed in this manner it was indispensable that the President himself should go down town every day, so as to accommodate the brokers in the loaning of money. The directors were by this plan convinced that the risks, through the careful methods adopted by the President, were no greater than if the bank was located in Wall Street. These conservative methods, so skilfully planned and plausibly explained, increased the confidence of the directors in the able and careful management of Mr. Eno, and nobody was so much surprised as they, when the wool was raised from their eyes and they discovered that these various and ostensible "safeguards" were ingeniously devised for the sole purpose of screening their skilful inventor in the accomplishment of his huge defalcations.

Instead of loaning the money to Wall Street brokers, as he represented to the directors, he placed it as margin with his own brokers in various speculative ventures, and in that manner he made away with the entire $4,000,000 of the bank's deposits without exciting the least suspicion in the confiding breasts of the directors.

Such another instance of a clean sweep of the deposits of a bank by any of its officials, is probably not on record in the whole history of this kind of manipulation.

When the President represented to the Cashier, every evening, that he had lent specified sums on certain securities, his word was taken, and his checks for the amounts duly honored, without exciting a feeling of suspicion. Thus, by degrees the books of the bank showed $4,000,000 of call loans upon unexceptionable collaterals, when in fact the money had all gone to the President's private account.

Eno speculated with the greater portion of the money in stocks that were continually declining in price, and at length the time arrived when he was obliged to make a clean breast of the terrible condition of his affairs to his father. As I have stated, the old gentleman, Mr. Amos B. Eno, nobly came to the relief of his prodigal son, and saved the bulk from suspension.

As Eno senior is still worth about $25,000,000, he will never suffer the pangs of poverty through this great loss; but it will take a long time to enable him to survive the disgrace which the flagrant acts of his son have brought upon an honest and highly respected name.

THE CLEARING-HOUSE AS A PREVENTER OF PANICS.

In this panic the boldest and most remarkable instance of self-sacrifice on record was manifested by the Clearing-House banks. The panic of 1884, in its incipient stage, was different

to any that had preceded it—at least any of the financial con-
vulsions within my recollection—owing to the influence exercised upon it by the prompt and liberal policy of the banks.
In every respect their action was notable, showing that those
at the head of their management had largely profited by the
lessons of former panics.

It was chiefly due to the masterly management of the
banks, together with the magnanimous conduct of Mr. Amos
B. Eno and his associate directors of the Second National
Bank, that the panic was short-lived and so narrowly circum-
scribed. Had it not been for the determinate and instantaneous joint action of these parties there would have been
a very serious crash, which would have been far-reaching in
its results.

The results of the timely action taken on the part of the
managers of these institutions in this crisis, proves that
panics can be arrested by proper methods, and that quick
and determined action is indispensable in the incipient stage
of the emergency. If bank presidents could only be relied
upon by the business community to act promptly and in
unison with the business men, as they did in this instance,
threatened panics need have but little terror for the people,
who now live constantly in dread that these outbursts of
business disaster may be sprung upon them at any time in
any decade.

In the past history of panics bank managers, as a rule, have
acted without system, without judgment and almost entirely
without any well defined plan of action. There has been an
astonishing lack of vigor in their methods and purposes,
which were weak and vacillating in their character—frequently
more like the acts of children than those of business men.

If the panic of 1873 had received the same vigorous treatment in its origin as that of 1884, it could just as easily have
been checked as the latter, and the entire country would
have been saved a large portion of the depressing effects of
that serious collapse and its attendant disasters, which caused
a state of general prostration for five or six years succeeding
the event. These years, from a business standpoint, appear as

a blank in the history of the country's progress. Indeed, they constitute a black mark.

In 1884 the bears indulged in much adverse criticism in regard to the action of the Clearing-House in taking Mr. Seney's pictures as collateral. At the time, this method of financiering was without precedent; but the result has fully justified the policy of the Clearing-House Association and its management. Such an exceptionally fine collection of paintings in a country like this, now filled with connoisseurs who have sufficient wealth to gratify their tastes, stimulates the demand for these luxurious articles of value and transforms them into the best collateral to be found in the market. When the Seney pictures were offered for sale at auction they attracted greater competition in the purchase, at good prices, than could have been obtained for almost any class of railroad securities connected with Wall Street for months afterwards. While Mr. Seney seems to have been as much of a virtuoso as the late Mrs. Morgan, he did not permit his love of the beautiful to rise to such a pitch of exaltation as would cause him to pay the extravagant prices which almost ruined that eccentric woman. He never forgot that the picture had a "market" value, and never permitted his enthusiasm for the fine arts to make him a victim of sharp and unconscionable dealers. In fact he appeared to have been more wide-awake in picture buying than banking, and demonstrated that the former, rather than the latter, was his forte. If the bank presidents had not acted in the praiseworthy manner referred to, the financial revulsion of that panic would have been very serious. Several millions of deposits in the Metropolitan and Second National were promptly drawn out, and forthwith entered into circulation. This saved the community from the evil influence of a large number of panic makers in the persons of the depositors of these banks. Instead, therefore, of helping to stir up the excitement—as they would have done by pursuing the selfish policy formerly resorted to in similar circumstances—every person with funds in these two institutions, assisted very effectively to allay suspicion and create confidence, instead of distrust.

It was the disturbing element of panic makers, who generally constitute one of the most potent factors of disruption to be dealt with in seasons of business trouble, that caused the greater part of the trouble at the time of Jay Cooke's failure. The holders of the Northern Pacific bonds then, finding that the security was no longer equal to that of Government bonds (as they had been taught to believe), but was apparently worthless, became panic-stricken at their losses, and were all transformed into panic-makers, infusing the spirit of distrust into every person with whom they came into contact, until, like a fatal virus, it inoculated the whole country, spreading business disaster far and wide.

CHAPTER 11

OLD TIME PANICS

THE PANIC OF 1837.—HOW IT WAS BROUGHT ABOUT.—
THE STATE BANKS.—HOW THEY EXPANDED THEIR LOANS
UNDER GOVERNMENT PATRONAGE.—SPECULATION WAS
STIMULATED AND VALUES BECAME INFLATED.—PRESIDENT
JACKSON'S "SPECIE CIRCULAR" PRECIPITATES THE PANIC.
—BANK CONTRACTIONS AND CONSEQUENT FAILURES.—
MIXING UP BUSINESS AND POLITICS.—A GENERAL
COLLAPSE, WITH INTENSE SUFFERING.

THE first panic of any great importance was that of 1837.
This panic had its origin in a misunderstanding between
the United States Bank, with headquarters located at
Philadelphia, and President Jackson, whose election the officials of the bank had opposed.

The bank had been chartered in 1816, and went into operation in 1817. Its charter had twenty years to run. The bank
had been kept in operation with varying success until 1830,
when it was considered to be on a very stable footing, so that
the Finance Committee of the United States Senate were
enabled to testify to its efficiency as follows: "We are satisfied
that the country is in the enjoyment of a uniform national.
currency, not only sound and uniform in itself, but perfectly
adapted to the purposes of the Government and the community, and more sound and uniform than that possessed by any
other nation."

This was the second United States Bank; the first had been
chartered in 1791.

The bank applied to Congress, in 1832, for a renewal of its charter, which would expire in 1836. A bill was passed by Congress to re-charter the bank. The bill was vetoed by the President for the reason above stated. In the following year the Treasurer announced, by order of the President, that the public funds, amounting to $10,000,000, would be drawn from the custody of the bank because it was an unsafe depository.

The transfer of the Government funds to the State banks created great agitation in political and financial circles. The State banks, under this favorable turn of Government patronage, quickly assumed a thriving condition and began to expand their loans and circulation. This stimulated speculation in all parts of the country, but especially land speculation. Large purchases of land were made from the Government, and payment was made in notes of State banks.

With the rapid sales of its lands the Government was soon able to pay off the public debt, and had still a surplus of $50,000,000 in the Treasury. This apparent prosperity continued for the next year or two, money was plenty and speculation was greatly stimulated and values became inflated.

The crisis came in 1837, and was hastened by the "Specie Circular," which was the last official act of President Jackson, and which pricked the bubble of inflation. This circular, which was issued from the Treasury in July, 1836, required all collectors of the public revenue to receive nothing but gold and silver in payment. The purpose of the circular was to check the speculation in public lands, but it caused too sudden a contraction in values, and created widespread disturbance in business circles generally.

The public protest against the "Specie Circular" was so strong and universal, that a bill went through both houses of Congress partially repealing it. "Old Hickory" did not yield to Congress, however, and though he did not veto the bill, he delayed signing it until after Congress adjourned, thus preventing it from becoming a law.

The State banks sought to tide over the troubles arising from the Jacksonian method of financiering by loans of public money to certain financial concerns and individuals, but this plan only made matters worse. There was a sudden expansion of paper money, which encouraged a wild spirit of speculation and excessive importations, and imparted an unnatural stimulus to business and commercial affairs. This state of overtrading and reckless speculation was suddenly checked by bank contractions, and in the spring of 1837 there were failures amounting to $100,000,000 in New York city alone.

The shock was communicated to the entire country, and a state of general paralysis in business circles ensued.

In the meantime the Bank of the United States continued in operation, and did not even suspend in 1836, when its charter expired, but obtaIned another charter from the State of Pennsylvania, which was entitled "An Act to repeal the State taxes on real and personal property, and to continue and extend the improvement of the State by railroads and canals, and to charter a State bank to be called a United States bank."

This United States bank did not expire until 1839, though it suspended specie payment with the State banks in 1837, when by this method they escaped a general collapse, and dragged through an agonizing existence for two years longer. The circulating notes and deposits of the Bank of the United States were paid in full, but the $28,000,000 of capital were a total loss to the stockholders, who never obtained a dividend. Such were the good old times of financiering when General Jackson and his successor, Martin Van Buren, sat in the Executive chair.

The entire capital stock of the bank was $35,000,000, of which $7,000,000 were to be subscribed by the Government.

The real cause at the bottom of the failure of this bank was its error of mixing up its legitimate business of banking with politics and speculation, showing that keeping those matters as distinct as possible is one of the great secrets of success in each of them.

The panic of 1837 was further aggravated by the action of the Bank of England which, in one day, threw out all the paper connected with the United States. The banks on this side refused to discount paper, and as a retaliatory measure in self-defense the business men and speculators withdrew their deposits from the banks. This had a tendency to cripple business still more, and cause utter prostration. In their selfish frenzy bankers and merchants completed the ruin of each other, hastening the catastrophe from their inability to take a broad, cool and generous view of the situation.

There was a general suspension of the New York banks on May 10, 1837, and the banks throughout the country followed in their wake within a week afterwards, producing a financial convulsion unparalleled in the history of the Republic. The country was brought to the verge of bankruptcy from the effects of which a long time was required for recovery.

After two years' struggle to regain the credit and stability lost through false methods of financiering, the banks suffered a relapse, and underwent a severe process of weeding out the weakest, nearly one-third of which happened to be of this description. Out of 850 banks, 343 closed their doors permanently.

The Sub-Treasury at New York was established the following year, 1840, by an act of Congress which provided that the officers of the Government should keep the public funds in their own custody, that coin alone should be received in payment to the United States, and bank notes were to be no longer received and paid out at the Treasury.

While this short chapter deals with matters which go back beyond my personal recollections of twenty-eight years in Wall Street, still as the panic of 1837 was the first of the great upheavals of its kind, that had a marked effect on Wall Street affairs, it properly falls within the scope of this book to chronicle the chief incidents of that great business convulsion.

For this reason, therefore, I find room for it, in some measure commensurate with its importance, and the space which can be afforded to it, as a matter of financial history, the facts of which were still fresh in the recollection of several speculators, bankers and business men, with whom I had the honor of being acquainted shortly after my advent in Wall Street immediately succeeding the panic of 1857.

Of those who gave me lively descriptions of their vivid recollections of that panic, but few now survive.

I think, therefore, it is well for me to do my part in helping to preserve the leading features of this important episode in the early history of Wall Street, as there will soon be none of those, who took an active part in the exciting events of that period, left to tell the tale.

CHAPTER 12

THE TRUE STORY OF BLACK FRIDAY TOLD FOR THE FIRST TIME

THE GREAT BLACK FRIDAY SCHEME ORIGINATES IN PATRIOTIC MOTIVES.—ADVISING BOUTWELL AND GRANT TO SELL GOLD—THE PART JIM FISK PLAYED IN THE SPECULATIVE DRAMA.—"GONE WHERE THE WOODBINE TWINETH."—A GENERAL STATE OF CHAOS IN WALL STREET.—HOW THE ISRAELITE FAINTED.—"WHAT ISH THE PRISH NOW?"—GOULD THE HEAD CENTRE OF THE PLOT TO "CORNER" GOLD.—HOW HE MANAGED TO DRAW AMPLE MEANS FROM ERIE.—GOULD AND FISK ATTEMPT TO MANIPULATE PRESIDENT GRANT AND COMPROMISE HIM AND HIS FAMILY IN THE PLOT.—SCENES AND INCIDENTS OF THE GREAT SPECULATIVE DRAMA.

IN the year 1869 this country was blessed with abundant crops, far in excess of our needs, and it was apparent that great good would result from any method that could be devised to stimulate exports of a part, at least, of the surplus.

Letters poured into Washington by the thousand from leading bankers, merchants and business men, urging that the Treasury Department abstain from selling gold, as had been the practice for some time, so that the premium might, as it otherwise would not, advance to a figure that would send our products out of the country, as the cheapest exportable material in place of coin, which, at its then artificially depressed price, was the cheapest of our products, and at the same time the only one undesirable to part with. So the Government decided to suspend gold sales indefinitely.

Jay Gould and others, being satisfied that this was to be the policy of the Administration, commenced at once buying large amounts of gold, actuated, doubtless, by the purest of patriotic motives, namely, to stimulate cotton and cereal exports. They succeeded in accumulating a considerable amount of gold at prices ranging from 135 to 140, covering a period of three months' steady buying.

This was the honest foundation on which the great Black Friday speculative deal was erected.

The eruption on Black Friday was really caused by the erratic conduct of James Fisk, Jr., who actively joined the movement on Thursday, the day before, and became wild with enthusiasm on the subject of high gold. He began on Friday, early in the morning, to buy large blocks through his own brokers, William Belden and Albert Speyer, running the price up very rapidly.

The original syndicate consisted of Jay Gould, Arthur Kimber, representing Stern Brothers, of London, and W. S. Woodward, of Rock Island corner notoriety. The two latter, however, sold out their interest to Gould, who directed the deal to the end, with the assistance of several able and wicked partners. Their office was located in Broad street, on the present site of the Drexel Building.

When the excitement arising from the above causes was at its height, I sent a telegram to Secretary Boutwell, and one to President Grant, representing the exact condition of affairs in Wall street, and urging the sale of gold without delay. I also prevailed upon General Butterfield, the New York Sub Treasurer, and Moses H. Grinnell, the Collector of the Port, to send similar telegrams, which they did, and timely action was taken at once by an order coming to sell $5,000,000. The moral effect of this Government action was to strike terror to the holders of gold, and a general rush was made to sell out, thereby driving down the premium from 160, in less than two hours, to 132. The down grade produced an excitement quite equal to the early furore in the up movement. Albert Speyer had from Fisk a verbal *carte blanche* order to buy, in million lots, all the gold he could get at 160; while he was thus buying millions upon millions at this figure, on the opposite side, and in other sections of the room, sales were freely made in moderate amounts at 140, 145, 147 and 150, almost simultaneously; and even when 135 was reached, which was soon thereafter, Speyer still kept on bidding 160 for a million at a time, making one of the wildest and most ludicrous spectacles ever witnessed among men not idiots. Fisk afterwards repudiated the contracts made on his account by Speyer & Belden, simply denying having given the orders, and as they were not in writing, they could not well be proven, hence both brokers failed, throwing immense losses upon an innumerable number of others. Quite a noted firm sold Speyer some of his million lots, which they bought back at 140, being satisfied with the profit of 20 per cent.; when they had finished buying, the price instantly broke to 132, and the announcement of Speyer's failure, which was made before the close of the day, caused them also to fail, as well as half the members of the Gold Room. Owing to the serious complications prevailing, and the disaster being so widespread, it was found impossible to continue the clearances through the Gold Bank, and the Governing Committee of the Gold Room were at once convened, and passed a resolution to suspend all dealings in gold for one week, in order to enable the members to adjust their difficulties and differences between themselves privately. The Gold Bank also suspended business in the meantime. While Albert Speyer was vigorously buying and continuing to bid 160 for one million after another, the clique were as actively engaged in selling all the market would take at ten points less, and also busy making private settlements with the shorts.

As the transactions were purely phantom in their nature, the great parties in the speculative contest did not really lose much. Contrary to popular opinion about such transactions, they did, virtually, incur heavy losses, but in one way or another they managed to evade them. Gould's losses were estimated at over four millions. Fisk's were equally large, but he repudiated all of them. Others were heavily saddled, however, with the burden which he should have borne.

Importing merchants were among the greatest sufferers, and a large number of them were forced to cover at high figures.

The suspension of the Gold Board caused many important failures. Private settlements were made during a period of sixty days following, in many instances on the basis of a compromise.

When Fisk heard that Secretary Boutwell had ordered gold sold, he exclaimed that it would knock spots out of phantom gold, and send him and others with their long stuff "where the woodbine twineth." The full effect of the disaster became more fully realized when the Gold Board and Gold Bank suspended and the numerous large failures were announced; then it almost seemed that a general state of chaos reigned, and how to unravel the complications was the problem to be solved. No one that had any connection with gold dealings during the eventful day could positively tell how they actually stood, or how to estimate their losses or gains; such was the uncertainty as to future results, and the doubt as to who was, and who was not, going to pay the differences due. The Board Room was crowded almost to suffocation, and the scene just prior to its close partook of the appearance of Bedlam let loose; in fact, it had not been much different during the entire day. Late in the afternoon, a formidable body of enraged sufferers assembled at the doors of Smith, Gould & Martin's office, and many and boisterous were the threats that were indulged in against the members of the firm, in consequence of which a police guard was detailed for their protection.

The gold furore brought many Israelites to Wall Street, who since, by their numbers and natural shrewdness, have become quite formidable in our midst.

One of them, being very long of the precious metal, on its break from 160 to 140, fainted; water was soon obtained to bathe his feverish brow and rubbing was also adopted. When, finally, he had sufficiently recovered to raise his head and open his eyes, looking all around he said: "What ish the prish now?" Upon finding it still lower, he closed his eyes again, and fell into another swoon. He was finally carried from the Gold Room a sick and ruined, but a wiser Hebrew, and is now in the "ole cloe" business on the East side.

This is the history in brief, but the scenes and incidents of that day would furnish material for an interesting volume.

Although I am not much given to the sensational, I have collected a few of the leading events in detail, which I think are worth putting in permanent form, if I may presume that this book itself may happily partake of that character.

The inside history of the conspiracy to put up the price of gold is also full of interesting material, and shows how deeply laid the scheme was to take advantage of the circumstances and of the feeling which existed in favor of stimulating our exports at the time. I shall, therefore, give an epitome of the salient points behind the scenes of the great speculative plot, and the bold attempt made to involve President Grant and his family in the conspiracy.

As I have intimated, Jim Fisk, Jr., or Jim Jubilee Junior, as he was then popularly called, was eventually put forth as the active member of the manipulating coterie. The clique made very good use of him, also, at intervals during the period they were concerting their plans.

Fisk had originally been a peddler in New England, as his father had been. He appeared in Wall Street a few years previous to the great gold conspiracy as one of the confidential men of Daniel Drew. Having shown that he was too sharp for some of the people in the broker's office where Mr. Drew made his headquarters, he received a polite hint that his presence there was undesirable. Mr. Fisk then opened an office of his own, and united his speculative fortunes with those of Mr. William Belden. The name of the firm was Fisk

& Belden. It was of but short duration. It seems that they had difficulty in finding bankers to accommodate them to the extent required, and they closed up the business. But though Fisk failed of success in this instance as a broker, his resources were not by any means exhausted. He made himself generally useful to Mr. Drew, who still adhered to him.

As the result of this friendship and his own smartness, in a short time afterwards Mr. Fisk was elected to the directory of the Erie Railroad Company, and Mr. Drew, who had forwarded his interest in that direction, was left out. This is an instance of the way Fisk made the best use of his friends.

As the result of Fisk's election to the Erie Board, forty thousand shares of new stock were issued. Bold attempts were made to gobble up other railroads through the same instrumentality. Fuller information on these matters is given in my chapters on Drew, Gould, and the struggle with Vanderbilt.

Fisk began to be considered a universal genius at that time, and had acquired the soubriquet of Prince of Erie. Though he had no money to operate with when he made his debut in Wall Street, soon after this large issue of Erie stock, he began to show signs of wealth very rapidly. He had the reputation of being the fortunate owner of several railroads and steamboats, an opera house, at least one bench of judges, an unlimited number of lawyers and a bevy of ballet girls.

The Head Centre of this gold conspiracy needs no introduction here, as I have attempted to do him ample justice in another chapter. He was also the power behind the throne in Erie as well as in the Gold clique. He pulled the wires while Fisk was the imposing factotum who was exhibited to an admiring public. He managed the courts, the judges and the lawyers, while Fisk got the reputation of doing this fine work, but was simply the mechanical executive. He had made himself solid with the Legislature also, and had acquired a hold on Erie that enabled him to use that property just as he pleased for his own personal benefit, ambition and purposes.

Erie was a mighty power at that time, with a wonderful leverage for raising money. When cash was needed to purchase another railroad, a legislature or a court, all that was necessary was to sell a few hundred thousand of Convertible Bonds and turn them into Erie shares. Mr. Gould was thus fortified with ample means of raising money on call at the time he played the heavy role in the events which culminated in the disaster of Black Friday.

Though the circumstances at that time were all in favor of success in such a plot, it required a mind with great grasp and wonderful powers of generalization to take advantage of all the bearings of the situation, and to utilize everything toward the great end in view. Gould did his work as chief of the conspiracy with rare tact and marvellous sagacity.

A resume of the conspicuous points in the situation and the plot will make this clear.

The supply of gold in the New York market then did not exceed 25 millions. The Government held less than 100 millions, and about one-fourth of this was in the form of special deposits represented by gold certificates, part of which were deposited in the banks and the remainder circulating throughout the country. Gold was then being sold by the Treasury at the rate of a million a month, in accordance with a plan that had been adopted as the best financial policy, both for the administration and the prosperity of the country. This had always a tendency to keep the price down, but on account of the circumstances briefly related in the beginning of this chapter, this policy of selling gold, owing to our commercial relations, was no longer considered for the best interests of the country, and Mr. Boutwell, with his coadjutors in the Treasury, were bound to give ear to the opinions of the bankers and business men in the interest of our export trade.

Although the policy of stopping the sale of gold had been agreed upon in deference to the views of the best financiers of the country, yet Mr. Gould and his fellow strategists thought it was best to make assurance doubly sure on this point, in order that nothing might stand in the way of the great speculative intrigue, to get a "corner" in gold. President

Grant was conservative on the subject. The conspirators, therefore, conceived the design of arranging things so that Secretary Boutwell could not depart from this policy, no matter what emergency might arise.

This bold and wicked strategy could only be successful by first getting President Grant convinced that the theory of stopping the gold sales was the only commercial salvation for the country in the then condition of business stagnation and the possible panic threatened. The theory was then to impress him with the necessity of giving Secretary Boutwell an absolute order not to sell gold, and afterwards to fix things so that it would be impossible for the President to revoke that order until the brilliant speculative purposes of the clique in cornering gold should be accomplished.

The scheme was but little short of treason, regarded from a patriotic point of view, and it is very questionable if the perpetrators would have stopped short of this dastardly act, had they not been convinced that their purpose was fully compassed by a method less villainous and shocking. It was considered indispensable by the conspirators, for the consummation of their plans, that Grant should be got out of the way by some means or other. Fortunately for him, and for the honor of the nation, the plan succeeded without the necessity of offering him any violence.

Before explaining how this was done it is necessary to describe briefly a few of the preliminary events which formed a portion of the plot.

It was arranged that General Grant should accompany a party, one beautiful evening in the middle of June, who were going to attend the great Peace Jubilee of Patrick Sarsfield Gilmore in Boston: Jim Fisk did the executive work in the arrangement. There was a fine champagne supper on board the Boston boat, and several gentlemen were present who were thoroughly conversant with financial questions, and could talk glibly on the state of the country. The subject of exports and the policy of stopping the sale of gold were thoroughly discussed. It was a feast of reason, and those who have imagined that it was all flow of soul, on that festive occasion, do very scant justice to the intelligence that was at the bottom of the deep design of the nocturnal excursion, planned by Gould, Fisk & Co. General Grant was an eager listener to all that was said on the most interesting subject of that day, but his mind, it would seem, was not then thoroughly made up that the best policy for the prosperity of the country was to stop the sale of gold. He was undecided on that point, and it required well directed reasons to convince him. Mr. Gould observed this and foresaw what was necessary to be done. The drift of the conversation, when this point was brought clearly out, was very succinctly described by Mr. Gould in his testimony before the Garfield Investigating Committee. He said: "The President was a listener. The other gentlemen were discussing. Some were in favor of Boutwell's selling gold, and some were opposed to it. After they all interchanged their views, some one asked the President what his views were. He remarked that he thought there was a certain amount of fictitiousness about the prosperity of the country and the bubble might as well be tapped in one way as the other. That was the substance of his remark. He asked me what I thought about it. I remarked that I thought if that policy was carried out it would produce great distress and almost lead to civil war; it would produce strikes among the workmen, and the workshops, to a great extent, would have to be closed; the manufactories would have to stop. I took the ground that the Government ought to let gold alone, and let it find its commercial level; that, in fact, it ought to facilitate an upward movement of gold in the fall. The fall and winter is the only time that we have any interest in. That was all that occurred at that time."

It may be necessary to observe that I am merely quoting Gould from the report, and am not by any means responsible for his confusion of ideas and grammar.

This is sufficient to show how ably Mr. Gould played his part in attempting to get the President into the proper frame of mind to enable him to endorse a policy so vital to the interests of the country and to the success of the gold clique.

"I took the ground," says Gould, "that the Government ought to let gold alone and let it find its commercial level."

This reference to "its commercial level" is rich, coming from the head–centre of the plotters who wanted to put the article up to 200. Then, in another afterthought, he says: "It (the Government) ought to facilitate an upward movement of gold in the fall."

How artfully insinuating was this suggestion in the interest of our foreign commerce! It showed clearly the power the man possesses of rising to the patriotic height of the occasion. This is a characteristic of Mr. Gould that few people know how to appreciate at its true worth. It has stood out conspicuously in his character in many other exigencies. It reminds one of the unkind but vigorous remark of the famous old English critic, Dr. Samuel Johnson: "Patriotism, Sir," said the old cynic, "is the last refuge of a scoundrel."

About the time the above events were transpiring, the Assistant Secretary of the Treasury, Mr. H. H. Van Dyck, resigned his office in this city. Mr. Gould's chief ambition at that time was to name his successor, in order that he might be able to control the Treasury when the time to get a "corner" in gold should be ripe. Mr. Abel B. Corbin came in quite handy at this juncture to help to further the designs of Mr. Gould. He was a man of fair education and considerable experience both in business and politics. He had been a lobbyist in Washington for some years. He was well informed on financial matters, a pretty good writer, and could "talk like a book." His wife was a sister of Mrs. Grant, and he had good opportunities for reaching the Presidential ear, which he employed to the best advantage.

A gentleman named Robert B. Catherwood, who was married to a step-daughter of Mr. Corbin, was approached by Gould and Corbin on the subject of the assistant–treasury-ship. They were anxious that Mr. Catherwood should take the office, and told him he could make a great deal of money in a perfectly legitimate manner if he were once installed.

So Mr. Catherwood stated in his testimony before the Investigating Committee, but he adds, "My ideas differed from theirs in what constituted a legitimate manner, and I declined the office."

The office then sought another man in the person of General Daniel Butterfield. He received the intimation of his appointment in a very different spirit from Mr. Catherwood, showing that he was fully equal to the occasion. He wrote a letter to Mr. Corbin thanking him kindly for the offer, saying that he was under numerous obligations to him, and expressing a hope that he would be eminently successful in his undertaking. General Butterfield received his commission in due course.

This made perfect another link in the chain of Mr. Gould's speculative design, as he supposed. It made Corbin "solid" with Gould also, a position which they both highly appreciated. Mr. Gould paid the following tribute of admiration to the true value of Corbin in the enterprise: "He was a very shrewd old gentleman. He saw at a glance the whole case, and said he thought it was the true platform to stand on; that whatever the Government could do legitimately and fairly to facilitate the exportation of breadstuffs and produce good prices for the West, they ought to do so. He was anxious that I should see the President, and communicate to him my views on the subject." Corbin talked with Grant until he received a positive assurance that Boutwell was not to sell any more gold. At a meeting in Grant's house, where Gould and Corbin were present, the President said: "Boutwell gave an order to sell gold, and I heard of it, and countermanded the order."

It was not until Gould had received positive assurance from the President's own lips, that he considered his scheme perfect. But the links of this strategic chain were now nearly all forged. The bankers and merchants were largely in his favor through commercial necessity, the Sub-Treasury was "fixed," as he thought, and the Executive fiat had placed the Treasury of the United States itself where it could not spoil the deal if Grant did not change his mind. There were reasons, of course, to apprehend that he would do so in case of an emergency; for he never was privy to the scheme, no matter what his traducers and political enemies may have said.

To ensure perfect safety, then, Grant must be put out of the way temporarily. This was the crowning effort of the conspirators. After the Boston Peace Jubilee, this Cabal spent the remaining part of the summer in maturing its designs. Large enterprises of this nature always require time and patience. I am told that "Billy" Porter, "Sheeny" Mike and other eminent burglars will work assiduously from six to twelve months studying all the ins and outs of a bank or other financial concern before coming to the point of using the "jimmy," blowing the safe or chloroforming the janitor.

It seemed necessary that all the members of the Cabal should be fully acquainted with the combination to Grant's purposes as regarded his orders to Boutwell, and that his ideas should remain fixed on the theory of increasing exportation for the country's safety. Accordingly it was arranged that Jim Fisk should visit the President at Newport, where he was on a visit, some time about the middle of August, a month or so prior to Black Friday. It would seem that Grant at this date was still wavering, and adhering to his policy of selling gold in spite of the order which he had given Boutwell. He may have been suspecting that the anxiety of Gould, Corbin & Co. for the prosperity of the country was not altogether genuine. The necessity of bringing further pressure to bear upon him was therefore clearly manifest.

Referring to the interview at Newport, Fisk said: "I think it was some time in August that General Grant started to go to Newport. I then went down to see him. I had seen him before, but not feeling as thoroughly acquainted as I desired for this purpose, I took a letter of introduction from Mr. Gould, in which it was stated that there were three hundred sail of vessels then on the Mediterranean, from the Black

Sea, with grain to supply the Liverpool market. Gold was then about thirty-four. If it continued at that price, we had very little chance of carrying forward the crop during the fall. I know that we felt nervous about it. I talked with General Grant on the subject and endeavored, as far as I could, to convince him that his policy was one that would only bring destruction on us all. He then asked me when we should have an interview, and we agreed upon the time. He said: 'During that time I will see Mr. Boutwell, or have him there.'"

The President was carefully shadowed after this by the detectives of the clique, and great care was taken to throw men across his path who were fluent talkers on the great financial problem of the day, the absolute necessity of stimulating the export trade and raising the premium upon gold for that patriotic purpose. In this way, President Grant began to think that the opinion of almost everybody he talked with on this subject was on the same side, and must, therefore, be correct.

About the 1st of September it was considered that the opinions of the President had been worked up fairly to the sticking point, and Gould bought $1,500,000 in gold at 132 1/2 for Corbin. Gould, however, was timid in his purchasing at first, as he had heard that a number of operators who were short of gold were making arrangements to give Secretary Boutwell a dinner. On further assurances from Corbin that the President had written Boutwell to sell no gold without consulting him, Gould prepared to go ahead with the execution of his great scheme. Nothing remained to be done in the completion of the plot except to stow away the President in a place of safety until the financial storm should blow over.

Things were so managed that the President was placed in a position that his honor was seriously in danger of being compromised, yet so ably was the matter engineered that he was perfectly unconscious of the designs of the plotters.

He was prevailed upon to go to a then obscure town in Pennsylvania, named Little Washington. The thing was so arranged that his feelings were worked upon to visit that place for the purpose of seeing an old friend who resided there. The town was cut off from telegraphic communication, and the other means of access were not very convenient. There the President was ensconced, to remain for a week or so about the time the Cabal was fully prepared for action.

Sometime about the period of the President's departure for Little Washington, Fisk bought seven or eight millions of gold. Gould then said to Fisk: "This matter is all fixed up. Butterfield is all right. Corbin has got Butterfield all right, and Corbin has got Grant fixed all right, and in my opinion they are all interested together."

This was patriotism with a vengeance. Just think of the audacity of it! Gould enters into a scheme to place the President in a position where he could not interfere with the plan of getting a "corner" in gold, and then be turns around and accuses the first Magistrate of the Republic with being privy to a plot that was calculated to create a panic, and cause widespread disaster in business circles, and render him an object of universal contempt.

Gould and Fisk, through Corbin, also attempted to compromise Grant's family, as well as his private Secretary, General Horace Porter. This intention was fully disclosed through the interview of Fisk with Corbin. Fisk testified: "When I met Corbin he talked very shy about the matter at first, but finally came right out and told me that Mrs. Grant had an interest; that $500,000 in gold had been taken at 31 and 32, which had been sold at 37; that Mr. Corbin held for himself about two millions of gold, $500,000 of which was for Mrs. Grant and $500,000 for Porter. I did not ask whether he was General or not. I remember the name Porter. This was given out very slowly. He let out just as fast as I did when he found that Gould had told me about the same thing. I said: 'Now, I have had nothing to do with your transactions in one way or the other. We have embarked in a scheme that looks like one of large magnitude. Mr. Gould has lost as the thing stands now. It looks as if it might be a pretty serious business before getting out straight again. The whole success depends on whether the Government will unload on to us or not.' He said: 'You need not have the least fear.' I said: 'I want to know whether what Mr. Gould told me is true. I want to know whether you have sent this $25,000 to Washington, as he states?' He then told me that he had sent it, that Mr. Gould had sold $500,000 in gold belonging to Mrs. Grant, which cost 32, for 37 or something in that neighborhood, leaving a balance in her favor of about $27,000, and that a check for $25,000 had been sent. Said I: 'Mr.Corbin, what can you show me that goes still further than your talk?' 'Oh, well,' the old man said, 'I can't show you anything, but,' said he, 'this is all right.' He talked freely and repeated: 'I tell you it is all right.' When I went away from there, I had made up my mind that Corbin had told me the truth."

An attempt was made to prove, before the Garfield Committee, that a package containing $25,000 was sent to Mrs. Grant through the Adams Express Company, but expert testimony failed to decide whether the amount was that or $250, as the two noughts at the extreme right were crowded into the cents column, and it was difficult to determine whether or not a very light "period" was placed between them and the "$250."

The design of the clique was manifest, however, to implicate the family of the President in some way or other, in order that they might make use of the Executive influence to help accomplish their great speculative purpose. But as the Garfield Committee truly said in its report: "The wicked and cunningly devised attempt of the conspirators to compromise the President of the United States or his family utterly failed."

The scheme might have succeeded if Fisk had been possessed of the coolness and penetration of his partner, but his impetuosity, anxiety and enthusiasm aroused suspicion and partially spoiled the plot.

Fisk was so eager to be satisfied that Grant was all right that he overdid the thing by urging Corbin to write Grant a letter to stand firm and not to permit the Treasury to sell gold under any consideration. The outcome of this afforded clear proof, if any were wanting, that Grant had no guilty knowledge of the base purposes for which he was being used. Fisk had this letter from Corbin sent by a special messenger from Pittsburgh, who rode twenty-eight miles on horseback, and delivered it in person to the President. He read the letter, and had his suspicions at once aroused. He said laconically to the messenger, "It is satisfactory; there is no answer." He began to see through the game, and at once desired Mrs. Grant to write to Mrs. Corbin requesting her husband to have nothing more to do with the Gould-Fisk gang.

Mrs. Grant wrote to Mrs. Corbin to say that the President was greatly troubled to learn that her husband had been speculating in Wall Street, and that she should desire him to disconnect himself immediately with the party who were attempting to entrap the President.

Corbin hastened to obey the mandate from Little Washington. He was greatly agitated, but the ruling passion of avarice was strong; in bidding Gould farewell, and before taking his final adieu of the clique, he requested the arch plotter to hand him over his share of the profits. Referring to this incident, Gould said: "I told him I would give $100,000 on account, and that when I sold, if he liked, I would give him the average of my sales. I did not feel like buying any gold of him then."

This was the denouement of the plot against the President, who immediately hastened to big Washington.

Now, let me again ask the reader to turn his attention for a moment to the concluding scenes in the speculative drama in Wall Street on Black Friday. How the clique tried to manipulate Assistant-Secretary Butterfield was kept as profoundly secret as possible, and as it turned out, he did not have as much power over the events of that great day as was expected. When somebody charged Fisk with tapping the telegraph wires, however, to obtain information from the Government, he replied: "It was only necessary to tap Butterfield to find out all we wanted."

This was very likely a vain boast of Fisk.

On Wednesday, the 22d September, two days preceding Black Friday, the clique, it is believed, owned several millions more gold than there was in the city outside the vaults of the Sub-Treasury. Belden bought about eight millions of gold on that day, while Smith, Gould, Martin & Co. were also heavy purchasers. The clique held a caucus in the office of William Heath & Co., in Broad street, and concluded that it had gold enough to put the price to 200, if it could carry the gold without lending and compel the "shorts" to purchase. But the idea of finding a market for over thirty millions of gold was also a gigantic problem, and they felt the risk of being ground between the upper and the nether millstones of their scheme.

On the morning of Thursday another council of war was held in the office of Belden & Co., on Broadway. At this meeting, Gould, Fisk, Henry N. Smith and William Belden were present. The proceedings of this meeting were kept a profound secret, but one result of it was that Belden gave his clerk the famous order to put gold to 144 and keep it there. On that day Belden purchased about twenty millions of gold, the price opening at 141$\frac{1}{2}$ and closing at 143$\frac{1}{2}$.

The chiefs of the Cabal had another private meeting up town that evening. The great question of closing up the transactions on the following day was the chief topic of discussion. These operators held contracts for over $100,000,000 in gold. Gould said that the "short" interest was $250,000,000. The total amount of gold in the city did not exceed $25,000,000, and the difference between this and the aggregate amount of the contracts of the clique was the enormous amount that would have to be settled in the event of a "corner."

Fisk proposed that the clique show its hand, publish the state of affairs, and offer to settle with the shorts at 150. His plan was rejected by his brother conspirators.

On the morning of the fatal day, Belden and William Heath had an early breakfast together at the Fifth Avenue Hotel, and repaired immediately to their offices. Belden announced that gold was going to 200. "This will be the last day of the Gold Room," he added. Moved by Belden's threat, a large number rushed to cover. In the language of Henry N. Smith, "They came on with a rush to settle." He was settling in the office of Smith, Gould & Martin, at 150 to 145, while Albert Speyer, acting as broker for Fisk and Gould, was bidding up to 160 for a million at a time. It was only when the price came down to 133 that Speyer realized the humorous absurdity of his position. He had then bought 26 millions since morning at 160.

A voracious demand for margins about midday brought the work to a crisis. The scene at the office of Heath was indescribable when Belden went there to see Gould and his confederates, to find out what was to be done next with the frenzied purchasers. An eye-witness thus describes the scene at Heath's office: "I went outside while Belden went in. I walked up and down the alley-way waiting for him to come out. Deputy sheriffs, or men appearing to be such, began to arrive and to mount guard at Heath's office to keep out visitors. After waiting a prodigious long time, as it seemed to me, Jay Gould came creeping out of the back door, and looking round sharply to see if he was watched, slunk off through a private rear passage behind the buildings. Presently came Fisk, steaming hot and shouting. He took the wrong direction at first, nearly ran into Broad street, but soon discovered his error, and followed Gould through the rear passage. Then came Belden, with hair disordered and red eyes, as if he had been crying. He called: 'Which way have they gone?' and, upon my pointing the direction, he ran after them. The rear passage led into Wall street. At its exit the conspirators jumped into a carriage and fled the Street."

They did not fly the Street, however, but went to the Broad street office of Smith, Gould & Martin, where the crowd assembled, evidently with riotous intent, apparently bent upon an application to Judge Lynch for justice; and had any of the gentlemen appeared outside the confines of the front wall, the chances were that the lamp-post near by would have very soon been decorated with a breathless body. To ensure their safety inside, however, a small police force kept guard outside, which made the barricade complete. These gentlemen remained under this shelter until the small hours of the morning, busily endeavoring to find out where they stood in the result of the gold deal, and the more they pondered over it, the greater grew the doubt in their minds whether they were standing on their heads or their heels.

Although the Black Friday "corner" was a temporary calamity, perhaps it was worth all it cost, in teaching us a useful lesson in financial and speculative affairs. In my chapter on "Panics, and How to Prevent Them," I think I have made several points clear that can be utilized by financiers, speculators and investors to advantage, in case of an impending panic or "corner."

CHAPTER 13

OUR GREAT
AMERICAN PANICS
FROM FIRST TO LAST

THE panic of 1907 naturally revived public interest in all our previous panics, and therefore a brief historical our review of these is timely. The small one that followed the throwing overboard of the historic tea in Boston harbor in George the Third's time, and which was the prelude to the War of Independence—the victorious struggle of the old Thirteen Colonies to throw off the British yoke—was of no importance, owing to the country's scanty trade and banking development, and the corresponding scarcity of credits. It was a tempest in a teapot, this sequel to the Boston tea party.

The panic of 1812 was the first of much magnitude in the history of the United States, and it resulted from overtrading and undue expansion in all directions, but was precipitated by our war with England in that year. The banking capital of the country was then only seventy millions of dollars, yet more than ninety banks failed in the run upon their deposits that ensued, and the Government found great difficulty in raising a war loan. Meanwhile, trade and manufactures, which had been very active and prosperous before the declaration of war, suddenly became almost paralyzed.

The change from undue inflation to the undue contraction born of fear was disastrous in its wholesale destruction of market values and credits. But the Government war expenditures, after it had succeeded in disposing of its securities, gradually stimulated recovery from the worst effects of the panic, and industries that had been suspended were resumed, thus re-employing labor that had been left idle.

Not much has been recorded of the panic of 1823, which caused trade depression till 1825, so it was evidently much milder and less disastrous than that of 1812. It was another instance of the reaction that follows over-trading and an over-extension of credits, without any war or other great event to precipitate it.

The panic of 1837 was, however, much more serious and disastrous, because it involved far greater results owing to the growth of the United States in extent, population, and wealth in the interval. Like its predecessor, and indeed all other panics, it was due to the over-extension of trade, speculation and credits, but it was precipitated by the troubles of the United States Bank, and President Jackson's hostility to that institution.

Speculation had been running wild, particularly in land and new railway projects, which were then in their infancy in England. The achievements of George Stephenson, the builder of the first locomotive engine there, had quickly kindled the fire of railway enterprise in this country, and promoters busied themselves in raising capital for building and equipping railways here; and incidentally it gave a strong impulse to the widely prevailing speculation in land.

The panic of 1857 was, of course, infinitely greater .in its extent and consequences than that of 1837, owing to the same causes that made the latter greater than that of 1812, namely, the growth of the territory, population, and wealth of the United States. Its main cause can be traced to the enormous increase of speculative enterprise in this country, especially in railway building, following the great gold discoveries of 1849 in California. But its immediate cause was the general alarm produced by the failure of the Ohio Life and Trust Company, which had its principal agency in Wall Street.

There, at the corner of Nassau Street, it had long been regarded as a pillar of financial strength, and no institution in the United States stood in higher credit or commanded greater confidence, although without any good reason. When it suspended payment, the news came upon the public with the suddenness of a thunderbolt from a clear sky. The unexpected shock filled the financial and mercantile community with dismay, and from one end of the country to the other credit was destroyed.

This, indeed, was panic. Bank-notes were everywhere distrusted, and presented for redemption; whereupon the banks everywhere suspended specie payment, except that the Chemical Bank of New York redeemed its own notes. Business depression and thousands of failures from Maine to California followed, and nearly three fourths of the railways, and other large corporations, defaulted in their interest and other payments, and went into the hands of receivers. The depression grew deeper from month to month for more than a year after the panic, and some of the best railway stocks declined to $3 to $5 a share, including Michigan Southern and Harlem. Meanwhile corporate foreclosure sales and reorganizations told the story of the financial wreckage of the time.

The country had not long recovered from the effects of this great panic when, on the 4th of March, 1861, Lincoln was inaugurated President, and the Civil War broke out. There was severe depression—a war crisis—then, but it was so slow, insidious, and prolonged that it was never called a panic. It may be said to have commenced—in anticipation of the threatened war of the South against the North—with Lincoln's election in November, 1860, and to have continued till the Government began to issue the paper money of the war era in 1861, after the suspension of specie payments.

One feature of the panic of 1857, and the prolonged depression that followed it, duplicated the experience of 1837, and that was the almost universal prevalence of what were called "shinplasters." These were practically I O Us given as change by anyone who had received a bank-note or check for more than the amount due him in payment for anything. In New York the notes of solvent New York banks were never refused in payment, while those of banks elsewhere were tabooed; but in making change, no specie was given, the banks having suspended specie payment. So, unless the exact amount was tendered, shinplasters were given for the balance.

The city was flooded with these personal evidences of debt for small amounts, issued by storekeepers, hotels, restaurants, saloons, barbers, and the rest of mankind, and many of these were passed from hand to hand till they became too dirty and dilapidated to be handled. They were the worst kind of filthy lucre, and understood to be only redeemable on a return to cash payments by the banks. But of course many of them never were redeemed. They ranged in amount from one cent to several dollars, and this sort of scrip was more or less extensively issued from Maine to Texas.

The Black Friday Gold Panic was a Wall Street convulsion, and not far reaching, like the others. It occurred on Friday, September 24, 1869, and was the result of a conspiracy, headed by Jay Gould, to corner gold, and force the "shorts" and importers to buy at a high premium. The Tenth National Bank, in Nassau Street, which he, and those associated with him, managed to control, became conspicuously involved in the corner through over-certifying their checks to the amount of about $7,500,000 on that day, and, as a result, it was closed by the Government bank examiner. Several scandals cropped out in connection with this conspiracy to corner gold, one of which involved the resignation of the New York Assistant Treasurer, and another two brokerage firms employed by the gold cornerers to buy and receive their gold. Gold, after being bid up by the conspirators day by day from 119 1/4 to 162 1/4, broke thirty per cent on the announcement that the Government would sell five millions of gold. This was followed by the suspension of the Gold Clearing House Bank, and the Stock Exchange was also closed to check the panic in stocks that ensued. While not a commercial panic, Black Friday was very disastrous to many in Wall Street.

Next came the tremendous panic of 1873, which, commencing in Wall Street, on September 13, with the failure of several prominent banking and brokerage firms, including

Howes & Macy, Kenyon Cox & Co. (in which Daniel Drew was a special partner), Fisk & Hatch, and then Jay Cooke & Co., rapidly spread, and soon covered the entire country. Many other failures followed these from day to day, and crowds of sightseers besieged Wall Street from morning till night, while the Stock Exchange was closed, and remained closed for ten days to prevent the sacrifice of stocks.

The severity of the distress that prevailed may be inferred from the fact that on the 19th of September twenty-two Stock Exchange firms suspended payment. Rumors of bank and trust company troubles flew thick and fast, and there was a heavy run on their deposits, while the Union Trust Company was temporarily forced to close in order to raise money on its assets to meet the run upon it. Several banks were known to be unable to stand the general run any longer, when, on the evening of September 20th, the New York Clearing house resolved to issue $10,000,000 of Clearing House loan certificates, in accordance with the resolution adopted to meet the crisis of 1860–61. It was on the same date that the Stock Exchange was closed by its governing committee.

On the 24th of September an additional issue of $10,000,000 of certificates was authorized, and on the 27th, so great and widespread had the panic become that all restrictions upon their issue were removed. The banks, instead of paying checks in cash, except for small sums, to depositors, certified them, payable through the Clearing House, and the weekly bank statement of the Association was suspended on September 27th, and not resumed till December 28th. The amount of Clearing house loan certificates attained its maximum—$22,400,000—on October 20th. In the interval business was resumed on the New York Stock Exchange on September 30th, after its ten days of suspension. While it remained closed there was a curb market on Broad Street for stocks and bonds, but sales for cash there could only be made at panic prices. The crisis of 1873 was far more severe than that of 1907, and recovery from it was very slow. The panic of 1884 extended far beyond Wall Street, but was most severely felt there.

There was a stock market panic in 1890, due to the failure of Baring Bros. & Co., in London, and heavy gold exports from this side to allay the panic there, but it did not spread much beyond Wall Street, and was soon over. The panic of 1893 was, however, severe and extensive, and 15,000 failures were attributed to it throughout the country. As usual, it resulted from undue speculation and expansion in trade, stocks, and new enterprises. But it was more immediately caused by the agitation of the 16-to-1 silver heresy, which led to a run on the gold in the United States Treasury till the amount of free gold held by it, at all points, was less than twenty millions, while the amount in the Sub-Treasury in New York was reduced to only about $8,700,000. It was then, in February, 1893, that President Cleveland made his famous gold purchase for United States bonds from the Morgan-Belmont syndicate, namely 3,500,000 ounces of gold for $62,312,500 of four per cent bonds. This, aided by the syndicate's efforts, stopped gold exports and replenished the supply of gold in the Treasury, and so restored confidence. Therefore the run ceased; and after that the largely increased customs duties gradually swelled the gold belonging to the Government to a far larger amount than it had ever held before.

Coming down to the panic of 1907, we are confronted by its causes. These were cumulative, but, as in every preceding crisis, the main cause was far too large a mass of credits— that is, of debts—for the amount of cash in which they were redeemable. Trade and speculation had been long so active, and too often recklessly expanded, that this disproportion had become dangerous, and a menace to our safety, as I pointed out several times months before the crisis actually came. I said that a serious reaction, a serious revulsion, was inevitable unless we moderated our pace and mended our ways in the matters that I have elsewhere referred to and criticised.

From my knowledge of banking, and my personal experience of our previous panics, dating from that of 1857, I could foresee that this vast and growing disproportion between the volume of credits and cash would finally lead to collapse. This disproportion is always large, and always becomes larger in periods of activity in trade and speculation. But in this country, and particularly among our speculative Wall Street millionaires and promoters, it had become unwieldy, while, very largely, liquid capital had been converted into fixed forms that were unavailable in raising cash.

Yet the people generally did not see the danger and take alarm till, on October 21, the New York Clearing House was notified by the Bank of Commerce that it would not clear for the Knickerbocker Trust Company after the following day; and simultaneously the Clearing House made an examination of the Mercantile National Bank, and ordered all its officers and directors to resign at once, preparatory to assisting it.

Then the public suddenly took fright, and the run upon the deposits of the Knickerbocker Trust Company caused it to close its doors about two hours after it had opened them the next day. This added fuel to the fire of distrust, and the run on the Trust Company of America and its Colonial Branch, and also on the Lincoln Trust Company, began; and six banks and a trust company suspended in Brooklyn, and the Hamilton Bank in Harlem, on the day following.

At the same time there was a heavy withdrawal of deposits from all the banks and trust companies, and the money thus withdrawn was not deposited in other institutions, but hoarded. Hence the severe monetary stringency that ensued, which caused call loans on the Stock Exchange to command as much as forty to fifty per cent per annum at one time, and from fifteen to twenty-five till the end of the year.

The New York Clearing House saw the urgent need of promptly fortifying the banks in the Association against the drain on their deposits, and, on October 26, resolved to issue Clearing House certificates against such satisfactory assets as they might deposit, these certificates to be used by them instead of cash, in paying their daily balances at the Clearing House. This gave immediate relief to the banks, and was the signal for every other bank clearing house in the large cities to do likewise, besides which many of the country banks issued checks of their own, from one dollar up, in payment of checks against deposits.

The other principal features and details of the crisis I have given elsewhere. But it must not be overlooked that, severe as it was in its actual effects, it was very largely sentimental in the sense that it was precipitated by fear—fear born of distrust. That is the immediate cause of all panics, but without the superinducing causes this fear would not exist. In our case it was the very seriously impaired credit situation, arising from a multiplicity of contributory causes, which inspired the fear that caused the runs on the banks and trust companies, and the hoarding of the money withdrawn, as well as the withholding of other money which, in the absence of distrust, would have been deposited. To fill the vacuum caused by hoarding, we outdid all our previous efforts by importing about a hundred millions of gold.

This hoarding, and consequent stringency, apart from the issue, in all, of $81,000,000 of Clearing House loan certificates, was responsible for the premium on currency, which at one time was quoted at four to five per cent, for it practically forced the banks to a partial suspension of payments involved in requiring checks to be made payable through the Clearing House, except in cases where they were willing to accommodate depositors with small amounts of currency. But fortunately the premium, which had dwindled to $1/4$ @ $3/8$ on the 31st of December, disappeared at the beginning of 1908. Meanwhile, all through the crisis, large employers of labor had found great difficulty, and incurred much expense, in obtaining currency enough to pay wages; and in Pittsburgh and other labor-employing centers, wages were paid largely in scrip issued by the banks or employing corporations. This scrip was so generally issued that in Pittsburgh all the street car lines accepted it for fares.

No wonder that these conditions seriously checked buying of all kinds, and caused demoralization and semi-paralysis in industrial corporations, and that hundreds of thousands of operatives were thrown out of employment by the stoppage or curtailment of work in mills and other manufacturing establishments. But the storm being over, and the money market again easy, there is every prospect of gradual, if not rapid, recovery to a normal standard of prosperity in our trade and manufacturing industries. It was not till January 11, 1908, that the Clearing House reported the deficit in the bank reserves wiped out, and a surplus of $6,084,050 accumulated against a deficit of $11,509,550 on January 3d, and at one time of $81,000,000.

It should not be thought, because we imported a hundred millions of gold from Europe to relieve the monetary stress produced by the crisis, that we thereby placed this country under obligations to any other country. The gold we imported we bought and paid for from our own resources, equivalent to cash, in the shape of exports of cotton, grain, petroleum, copper, and other American produce.

These commodities were even more necessary to Europe than the gold we purchased there was to us. So the transactions on both sides were mere matters of bargain and sale, no favor being shown on either side. Indeed, both England and France did all they could to restrict our importations of gold. The extraordinary advance of the Bank of England rate to seven per cent, and its retention there till we discontinued our purchases of gold, furnished practical proof of this. This was justifiable, of course, as a defensive and protective measure for the bank, but none the less it was an obstacle placed in our path.

Its proclaimed purpose was to prevent our taking gold from Europe as much as possible, yet in the face of this heavy handicap we bought and paid for and imported all the gold we wanted, and it was not till after we had stopped buying that the Bank of England lowered its rate to six per cent. This showed that we controlled the Bank of England more than the Bank of England controlled us. We were not assisted; we assisted ourselves, and neither asked nor received favors.

This important fact testified to the strength and wide sweep of our resources, both financial and commercial, and also to the solidity and soundness of our business position, and the foundation on which it rested. The firmness, too, with which we bore the enormous strain of the crisis, and the good order and condition in which we emerged from it, were equally eloquent in testifying to the same effect, and showing that ours is indeed a great country—the greatest of all nations in its material resources and acquired wealth.

The advantage of this is largely shared by us with the rest of the world, both in our enormous foreign trade and the vast amount of money spent every year by American tourists in Europe. If the hundred and fifty millions of dollars spent by them there in 1907 had been kept at home, it might have obviated the necessity of our importing gold to relieve the crisis. Europe has good reason to return thanks for all it gets from us; and what would the trade and commerce of Europe be, in this progressive age, without the United States of America?

The strength, the resolution, and the courage with which the country, as a whole, bore the brunt of the crisis of 1907 augurs well for a rapid recovery from its effects, and paves the way to renewed prosperity and progress; and there is every probability that it will recuperate more swiftly from the great and trying ordeal than it did from the memorable panics of 1812, 1837, 1857, 1873, 1884, and 1893, for its wealth, population, and general resources are now so vastly greater than they were at any of those periods that comparisons are out of the question.

The growth of our banking system alone since 1873 is indicated by the fact that in the very severe panic of that year the New York Clearing House issued only $16,000,000 of Clearing House certificates to the banks belonging to it, whereas in the panic of 1884 it issued $21,000,000, in the panic of 1893 $41,000,000, and in this last panic of 1907 no less than $81,000,000. The crisis was severe but it was purifying, and eliminated a vast amount of unwholesome and dangerous, if not dishonest, speculative elements from the management of many of our banks and large railway and industrial corporations, and left in its place the legacy of a higher standard of business morality than we had before. Hence, perhaps we may say, with Shakespeare, all's well that ends well, and, with the Bible, out of evil cometh good. At least we have plucked the flower Safety from the nettle Danger.

This view of our country, and the situation, is shared by the banking community of the Old World, who also absolve President Roosevelt from blame or responsibility for the crisis. In this connection a leading London banker, Mr. H. H. Raphael, a member of Parliament and one of the most influential and popular financial men in Great Britain, said, in December:

"We regard President Roosevelt as not only one of the most courageous, but one of the ablest of all your long line of distinguished Presidents. We admire him for his courage and independence. No wonder the heart of the American people is with him; he is giving you a good housecleaning, and you well need it; and although you are passing through financial storm and stress now, we know something of the wonderful recuperative power of the United States, and it will not be long before America will be forging ahead on the highway of economical progress, cleaner and stronger than ever."

This opinion is well worth quoting because of its evident sincerity. There is no suspicion of politics or office-seeking about the allusion to President Roosevelt, and if one man more than any other in this great country of ours deserves the resounding applause of a national "Hip! Hip! Hurrah!" for his public services, it is President Roosevelt.

CHAPTER 14

BOOMS IN WALL STREET

WALL Street has lately been enjoying quite a boom in some respects differing from any in its previous history. Probably the most interesting feature about this boom is that it is not in any sense spectacular. In that respect it is unique. Prices of many stocks are higher and intrinsic values greater than they have ever been before. The market has all the qualities that normally would cause intensest excitement and focus the attention of the entire country on the Stock Exchange. Yet in spite of these conditions, the Street is in a normal state of mind, and it is doubtful if the general mass of the people, who get their information from the newspapers are fully aware that there is even an ordinary boom in Wall Street. This unusual condition is due, I believe, to the fact that the boom we are enjoying is built on a foundation that reaches clear to the bowels of the earth. There is nothing unnatural or artificial about it. Wall Street is simply one of the centres that reflects the general prosperity throughout the country. Farmers, merchants, mechanics, mill workers, and miners are all so intent in keeping pace with the progress in their own pursuits that they have no time to cast eyes our way. The same conditions that are booming stocks, are booming everything else in the country at an equal rate, so that we are in nowise singular or deserving of special attention.

Another factor too, has developed in the Street that prevents the usual excitement and hurly burly incident to a rising market. This is the absence of a pronounced central figure, or controlling force. Usually a boom centres about some one man who stands boldly out in the open, or whose hand it is known is manipulating values. At present the manipulation is being carried on in a method that is as quiet as it is novel and unusual. That the market is being manipulated, is apparent enough even to the most casual observer. But the source of this manipulation is probably known only to a few; all others are but students in the Street. They know that a new order has come, and that this order is due to the most powerful and resistless influence that has ever manifested itself in Wall Street. This influence is very largely composed of the Standard Oil Combination, who have introduced in their Wall Street operations the same quiet, unostentatious, but resistless measures that they have always employed heretofore in the conduct of their corporate affairs. Beside this group, every other man or combination of men that has ever operated in the Street are materially belittled by comparison. The heretofore conspicuously big operators that have flashed up and across the horizon, appear comparatively small beside the men who are running things for us now.

At his best, Jay Gould was always compelled to face the chance of failure. Commodore Vanderbilt, though he often had the Street in the palm of his hand, was often driven into a corner where he had to do battle for his life, and so it has been with every great speculator, or combination of speculators, until the men who control the Standard Oil took hold. With them, manipulation has ceased to be speculation. Their resources are so vast that they need only concentrate on any given property in order to do with it what they please. And that they have so concentrated on a considerable number of properties outside of the stocks in which they are popularly credited with being exclusively interested io a fact well known to every one who has opportunities of getting beneath the surface. They are the greatest operators the world has ever seen, and the beauty of their method is the quiet and lack of ostentation with which they carry it on. There are no gallery plays, there are no scareheads in the newspapers, there is no wild scramble and excitement. With them the process is gradual, thorough and steady, with never a waver or break. How much money this group of men have made, it is impossible even to estimate. That it is a sum beside which the gains of the most daring speculator of the past were a mere flea bite, is putting the case mildly, and there is an utter absence of chance that is terrible to contemplate. This combination controls Wall Street almost absolutely. Many of the strongest financial institutions are at their service in supplying accommodations when needed. With such power and facilities it is scarcely conceivable what these men must be making, what they can do on either side of the market. So far, fortunately, their manipulations have all been one way, upwards, and in conjunction with the general prosperity it has resulted in making large sums of money for nearly everybody in the Street.

Here and there we have heard of losses, some of them fairly large, but in comparison with the general money making these are hardly to be taken into consideration.

The last preceding boom that Wall Street enjoyed was as different from the present as it is possible to imagine. It had all the elements which this one has not. It centred about one man who stood out in the lime-light clear and distinct. It kept the Stock Exchange in a constant state of ferment. It filled the newspapers with column upon column of sensational stories. It made millions for an army of retainers, on paper, and it kept the market jerking up and down for months. Roswell P. Flower, ex-governor of the State of New York, was the leader of the boom, and a more picturesque figure has never been seen in Wall Street, which is saying a great deal. Mr. Flower was an individual of very plain exterior. He often used language that was noticeable more for its force and directness and emphasis, than it was for polish. He had an ambling gait and looked like a well-fed farmer. He was rarely seen without a huge quid of tobacco that almost filled the left side of his mouth. Spittoons were an essential part of the furnishings of his office. His clothing hung on his person not unlike meal sacks. His hat was rarely brushed, and for days at a time, apparently, he forgot to shave. Altogether he was the last person, in appearance, who might be expected to lead in a district that is famous for its well groomed men. His education was certainly not collegiate; doubtless all his peculiar traits the ordinary man would have judged a handicap, still they were Mr. Flower's strongest aids. The lack of artificial polish gave people confidence in his statements. His limited education enabled him to think clearly along certain lines without being hampered with mental digressions, which would probably have come with a higher original mental culture.

As the administrator and manager of the estate of his brother-in-law, Henry Keep, he came into the Street twenty or twenty-five years ago. He in that way controlled a large amount of funds, which by conservative direction he increased very substantially. He scarcely ever figured in the speculative field to any great extent, until after he had completed his term as Governor of New York State. When he returned to the Street from Albany, he naturally came with a considerable prestige. Ex-governors of the Empire State are not very plentiful in and about the Stock Exchange. He also brought with him a large political following. In both of the great parties in New York State there are many men of standing and influence who like to take a flyer in Wall Street. Almost to a man they associated themselves with Mr. Flower, who, during his term at the capital had made hosts of friends with Republicans and Democrats alike, and this, though his party loyalty had never been questioned. He also had close associations with most of the big capitalists. After he had settled down to business, on leaving politics behind, Mr. Flower picked out several stocks as his specialties, Chicago Gas, Federal Steel and Rock Island being some of these. Under his manipulation all these properties went up and soon began to show a big advance, unusual strength and great activity. The bears made frequent assaults on his position and now and then pushed him towards the wall, but he always fought his way to the front again, and came out master in every encounter. When he had himself pretty well entrenched in the specialties he was handling, he suddenly plunged into Brooklyn Rapid Transit, and for months he kept things stirred up in a way that even Wall Street has not seen very often. He picked up the stock commencing at six dollars a share, and in an incredibly short time ran it up to over 138. Almost every politician in the State made a fortune on paper. Mr. Flower was immensely popular with the Wall Street news reporters, who helped his boom along through the glowing accounts they wrote from day to day.

Under the impetus of the swirl in Rapid Transit, practically every property in the Street went flying upward, until the end did not seem to be in sight. The bears were beaten to a standstill every time they showed their heads, the only result of their attacks being that Flower stocks would jump up a notch higher. The ex-governor preached Americanism and confidence, until everybody believed that if a stock was only grounded, and the property located in America, you could buy it at any price and still be on the safe side.

That a terrible panic did not grow out of this boom was due only to one fact: Mr. Flower's sudden death. Had he lived thirty days longer, the bubble must have been pricked, and the result would have been disastrous. Mr. Flower went to the country for a day's rest, ate freely of ham and radishes and washed his frugal meal down with a copious supply of ice water; he naturally, in consequence, died in a few hours afterwards of an attack of acute indigestion; his death alone saved the Street.

The Rockefellers, the Vanderbilts and his other wealthy friends rushed into the market with millions and sustained values. They were in a position to attribute the threatened reaction to his death and pointed out the absurdity of letting such an incident affect the value of stocks. They discounted the break that must have come in the natural course of events under the forcing process that was going on. Reasoning such as this spread broadcast through the papers stopped the break. Where the bottom would have fallen out entirely there was only virtually a moderate break all along the line; why it was not worse was due to the market being bolstered up by the Standard Oil Combination and others with them coming to the rescue just in time to prevent a big smash. The small speculators operating on moderate margins were of course all wiped out almost to a man, but many of the big fellows were saved. It is probably the only instance on record where the death of a big operator saved a general smash. Those hurt were numerous politicians and small fry operators who instead of getting away with snug fortunes in the shape of profits, lost their all.

An interesting circumstance of the Flower boom was developed involuntarily by young Joe Leiter. Leiter himself, although he had gone to the wall some time previously, indirectly had brought about certain conditions that served Mr. Flower's purpose admirably. These conditions were the general release of hundreds of millions of dollars on mortgages on farm lands. When Leiter began to corner wheat, it was ruling down in the neighborhood of sixty cents a bushel. He lifted it to considerably over a dollar before he went broke. This enabled thousands of farmers to realize on their crops at the dollar figure and above, which brought prosperity almost over night to the wheat growing belt. With the money realized from their wheat the farmers paid off their mortgages to the extent of two or three hundred million dollars. These mortgages were generally held in the East. This released that much Eastern capital, causing that vast volume of money to seek investment. The men controlling this money were overjoyed when Mr. Flower made an opening for them through the Wall Street boom, and hence it was a comparatively easy matter for a time to push up values.

J. Pierpont Morgan, now a noted character, was trained as a clerk in the one-time famous banking house of Duncan, Sherman & Co. Later he made a connection with Anthony J. Drexel, probably the wealthiest banker in his time in America. Out of this grew the house of Drexel, Morgan & Co., with Mr. Morgan as the managing partner in New York. When Mr. Drexel died, Mr. Morgan absorbed the entire business, and a few years later when his father died, Mr. Morgan became the head of the London house of J. S. Morgan & Co. as well. This put him in a very prominent position. He soon thereafter demonstrated his influence by reorganizing the bankrupt Richmond & West Point Terminal Railway & Warehouse Co., changing its name to the Southern Railway Co. A number of small roads were added to it, many of which were in financial straits, and practically all of them had been badly managed. He combined them into one system under the one head. This railroad combination is now one of the great properties of this country. Mr. Morgan next turned his attention to the reorganization of the Reading and the Erie roads, which were in a bad way. He soon produced order out of chaos there, and that resulted in a boom in railroad stocks all along the line. He had several sharp tussles, however, with some of the big stock holders, who tried to stand out against him on account, as they thought, of his plans being too drastic; and during these tussles he not infrequently resorted to the usual methods to break values, buying at the reduced prices so as to strengthen his control.

The people who followed Mr. Morgan's lead in these transactions generally made money.

A different sort of deal was engineered a few years before by S. V. White, popularly known as Deacon White, because of his position as deacon in Plymouth Church. Mr. White is one of the oldest operators in the Street, and one of the most striking figures. He has made half a dozen great fortunes in speculation and lost them, but he is as undaunted as ever, and in spite of the fact that he is now over seventy years old, he is still active daily in the market.

Probably one of the most unique stock deals ever carried out in the Street resulted from the transaction of Joseph Bannigan when President of the Rubber Trust. The history of this deal which for a time resulted in a great boom in industrials, has never been told, and is known to but very few persons, most of whom, by the way, were its victims.

Bannigan was an uneducated Irishman who could hardly read and write. He commenced life in a New England rubber factory and worked for $1.50 per day and died worth five million dollars. He was shrewd and bright and knew the value of money. He saved to such good purpose that when the Rubber Trust was formed he was at the head of one of the biggest factories in the country, located in Providence. His knowledge of the trade was so thorough that despite the fact that he almost invariably used small i's in writing a letter, he was made President of the Trust, his holdings amounting to about forty thousand shares. When matters had been moving along for some time, Bannigan made up his mind that the other men in the trust, the big fellows, were not treating him right, and that the best thing he could do was to get out. So he packed his stock certificates in a grip sack, left Providence on the night boat, landed in New York bright and early, had his breakfast and then made a bee line for a stock brokers' office. He had assured himself in advance that this stock broker was to be relied on and told him frankly what he intended to do.

"I want to sell out bag and baggage," he said. "I want to get rid of every one of my forty thousand shares. Here they are, put them on the market and sell them." The stock broker told him that that would never do. If he wanted to realize full value for his holdings he would have to go about it in a different way, for if he threw his forty thousand shares into the market it would knock the bottom out and he would get little or nothing for his stock. Mr. Bannigan saw the point, and asked what he was to do.

"Buy," said the broker.

"But I don't want to buy; I have got more now than I want."

"That is all right; buy anyway, that will make a market for the stock, and then you can unload when the time comes."

"How much must I buy?"

"Oh, about $250,000 worth."

"But I have not got $250,000 in cash to go and buy Rubber stock."

"Well, you can borrow it; a man in your position, Mr. Bannigan, would have no difficulty in borrowing $250,000."

Much against his will the old man was finally persuaded to do as he was told. About two weeks later the broker wrote to him that he must buy some more, this time, $200,000 worth. Mr. Bannigan used rather strong language, but finally yielded as he had before. He borrowed $200,000, and turned it over. With this additional capital to work on, the brokers continued to manipulate the market. The insiders soon discovered that some strong party was buying; but they did not know who, Bannigan having carefully kept himself in the background. His brokers operated skilfully in the stock, one day buying, the next, selling to keep the stock active. The brokers after awhile commenced to borrow large amounts of the stock. This convinced the insiders that there was a big short interest somewhere, and they got together in order to squeeze the shorts. The inside holders who held most of the stock, who had combined to squeeze the shorts out, as they thought, put the price up to 61, and at about that figure Bannigan's was all unloaded. Bannigan now found himself full of money and the other fellows had his stock. They never awakened to the fact that the President had sold out on them until his shares were delivered against their purchases, as they thought, of short stock. Rubber soon thereafter did not stop tumbling until it had gone from 61 to 16. This deal had all the elements of a comedy-drama and the playwright who can do it justice will find material there which will make him an everlasting fortune and reputation. I have touched but lightly on a few of the important incidents. It is not often, however, that newcomers in the Street fare as well as this in the end. For a time they will go on merrily enough, and send things booming; but in the end many get the worst of it. A. B. Stockwell is a good illustration of the truth of this. He is still around the Street somewhere, but is one of the "has beens," like numerous other former conspicuously large and supposed to be brilliant operators. At one time he was worth many millions of dollars. To-day, he is upside down. His start in life was as purser on a Lake Erie steamboat; his father, it is said, kept a livery stable in Cleveland. On one of his trips, Stockwell was in a position to show considerable attention to Elias Howe, the inventor of the eye at the upper end of the sewing machine needle. Mr. Howe was accompanied by his daughter. Stockwell made himself agreeable to Miss Howe also, and with such good effect that he managed to win her affections and soon thereafter married the young lady. When Mr. Howe died, Mrs. Stockwell came into possession of her father's millions. With this nest egg Stockwell started in Wall Street, and before anyone realized what had happened he was the most talked of man in the district. He put all his wife's millions into Pacific Mail stock, and secured entire control of the Company. He came into the Street as plain Stockwell, then as the news of his liberality and good fellowship spread, he became Mr. Stockwell; after he got hold of Pacific Mail he was Commodore Stockwell, by common consent. Everybody bowed and scraped to him and no man was so high and mighty that he was not proud to shake his hand. Stockwell took hold of Pacific Mail at about 40 and sent it up to 107. It was at this period that he was worth over fifteen million dollars; but he found, unfortunately, when it was too late to retreat, that while Pacific Mail was up to 107, it was not worth that figure when the unloading commenced. He was landed high and dry with it all and the Street told him he was welcome to it. He tried to sell, and found that there was no market. Then came violent demands on him to pay up his numerous call loans, and in order to respond thereto he had to sell regardless of price and thus created a whirlpool, which finally sent the stock down to the price at which he commenced his original purchase at 40. In this one upset, he lost all his paper profits and his wife's millions besides. This catastrophe not only stripped him of all his worldly possessions, but reduced him to the position of being plain Stockwell again, and there are many also who even go so far as to call him "that little red–headed cuss." That was the most famous boom in the history of Pacific Mail, notwithstanding Leonard Jerome's previous brilliant ups and downs in that former erratic property.

Leonard and Addison Jerome had a good time with Pacific Mail for a while. They ran it up to high figures several times;

but finally meeting with the same experience that Stockwell did. The two Jeromes from being among the wealthiest and most dazzling operators in the Street, were in the end practically wiped out. Leonard Jerome, who was the father of Lady Randolph Churchill, had nothing left to bequeath his daughter except an equity in the house now occupied by The Manhattan Club on Madison Avenue, which yields an income of about $15,000 a year, of which Lady Churchill gets $10,000.

These are a few of the booms that have stirred up things in Wall Street at one time or another, as did the Keene booms, of which there were several, the Gould booms, and the Vanderbilt booms, all of which have been referred to in previous chapters in this book.

The question of trusts or trade combinations has, in recent years, excited a good deal of interest. One of the most interesting figures in this connection is John D. Rockefeller, who will undoubtedly be regarded by the future historian as a striking character in the business history of the nineteenth century. And be it remembered that history now concerns itself, not so much with the doings of governments; not so much with the personalities of emperors, kings, presidents or even with political parties, as with the life of the people themselves. This is clearly shown by such historians as Lord Macaulay and John Bach McMaster. And looking at history in this way, surely John D. Rockefeller must be regarded as one of the most interesting types of the great commercial powers of the day. He was a pioneer, a commercial Daniel Boone, striking out into a new and untrodden field of enterprise, taking great risks, undergoing grave financial perils of a novel kind and at length winning a complete and lasting success—a success which has filled business history with his achievements and the world with his fame. It was a great stride from the little farmhouse in Tioga County, New York, to the place which he fills today. Born in 1838 he is now in the prime of life. Reared by strict, church-going people, his word is as good as his bond; he is the soul of business integrity, and a striking example of what thrift, enterprise and persistency will

do for a young man who starts out in life with apparently little or no chance of success. His old schoolmaster, it seems,
was the first to get the young man to look into the refining
of petroleum. Not so many years ago, they used sperm oil,
and it cost $1.50 a gallon. How to refine the thick, ill-smelling
oil found in the water courses of Pennsylvania was a problem.
It was black slime, and John D. Rockefeller, by hitting upon a
method of refining it and introducing it in the home throughout the world has made a fortune that recalls the fable of
Midas. Before he was twenty-one. he formed a partnership
with a man named Hewitt and at first engaged in the warehouse and produce business. Then came the great oil craze
in Pennsylvania. Poor farmers suddenly became rich; thousands flocked to the oil fields. Young Rockefeller kept his
head. Asked to make investments in oil wells for Cleveland
friends he dissuaded them from the project on the ground
that the thing was being overdone, and with Samuel Andrews,
who was familiar with the general processes of distilling,
engaged in the refining branch of the petroleum trade. The
firm subsequently became Rockefeller, Flagler & Andrews,
which rapidly expanded its field of operations, and in 1870
organized the Standard Oil Company with a capital of
$1,000,000. It started pipe lines to ship the oil to the sea-
ports. It made millions in by-products once considered worthless. It established markets all over the known world,
cheapened its methods of production and outstripped all competitors. Little wonder then, that its "extra" dividend in the
year 1899 amounted to $23,000,000 over and above the regu-
lar dividends on the whole capital stock. Mr. Rockefeller
attributes his success to early training and perseverance. That
is, like other men who have stamped their individuality upon
the affairs of mankind, he is what is termed a causationist; in
other words, he believes that nothing is got for nothing; that
effects proceed from causes, and the cause of success he
believes to be largely perseverance. He believes that perseverance overcomes almost everything, even nature itself, and
in that opinion this practical business man is at one with the
philosophers of antiquity.

He and his associates in the Standard Oil Company are naturally a power in the stock market. They are, of course, very large holders of railroad stocks and bonds and at times their influence is as irresistible as the laws of gravitation. John D. Rockefeller's influence alone could be so, as he is supposed to be the richest man in America and indeed the richest man ever known in human history. His is believed to be the greatest fortune ever accumulated by any man within his own lifetime. That he feels the responsibilities of his great wealth is obvious from his munificent gifts to educational and charitable institutions, to churches to a hundred other praise-worthy objects. His princely donations to schools, colleges and universities rival those of that other public-spirited citizen, Andrew Carnegie. They are equally strong in their belief that the greatest charity lies in helping others to help themselves.

CHAPTER 15

WALL STREET'S WILD SPECULATION, 1900–1904

MCKINLEY'S REËLECTION AND THE DEFEAT OF BRYANISM
SET THE BIG BALL OF SPECULATION ROLLING ON THE
STOCK EXCHANGE. — THE TREMENDOUS VOLUME OF
SPECULATION BY BOTH LARGE AND SMALL CAPITALISTS. —
THE RUSH TO INCORPORATE NEW COMPANIES AND CREATE
INDUSTRIAL TRUSTS AND RAILWAY COMBINATIONS. — THE
ENORMOUS CAPITALIZATION OF THE UNITED STATES
STEEL CORPORATION AND OTHER COMPANIES IN EXCESS OF
REAL VALUES. — THE RAPID GROWTH AND POPULARITY
OF NEW AND OLD TRUST COMPANIES AND THE EFFECT OF
THEIR COMPETITION IN FORCING BANK CONSOLIDATIONS.
— THE BOLD AND RECKLESS SPECULATIONS IN RAILWAY
STOCKS OF THE NEWLY ENRICHED WESTERN CAPITALISTS. —
THE GREAT NORTHERN PACIFIC PANIC OF MAY 9, 1901. —
THE CAPTURE OF CONTROL OF THE LOUISVILLE &
NASHVILLE RAILWAY BY JOHN W. GATES, AND ITS
REDEMPTION BY J. P. MORGAN & CO., ACTING IN THE
INTEREST OF THE LOUISVILLE & NASHVILLE AND SOUTHERN
RAILWAY. — THE SLOWING DOWN OF WILD AND RECKLESS
SPECULATION IN STOCKS AFTER SEPTEMBER, 1902,
THROUGH THE INFLUENCE OF THE BANKS AND
CONSERVATIVE BANKERS, THUS AVERTING FURTHER
INFLATION AND A GREAT CONVULSION. — THE LIQUIDATION
AND DEPRESSION OF 1903 A NATURAL REACTION FROM THE
INTOXICATION OF THE PRECEDING PROLONGED BOOM. —

The Great Rise in Cotton and the Collapse of the
Tremendous Bull Speculation Led by Daniel J. Sully
when He Failed.—The Sudden Fall in the Iron
Barometer in 1903, and the General Situation
in 1904.

WALL Street changed with almost magical suddenness
from depression and apprehension to confidence and
buoyancy with the defeat of Bryan and his silver heresy, and
the reëlection of McKinley in November, 1900. Large capitalists all over the country began to buy stocks and bonds on so
heavy a scale that prices shot up rapidly, like the celebrated
Gilderoy's kite, and very soon orders poured into the Stock
Exchange from people of smaller means everywhere, and a
tremendous bull market for stocks resulted, with too many
men staking, or ready to stake, their bottom dollar on the rise.

The speculative capitalists and large operators of Wall
Street, not of course excepting many of the active Standard
Oil magnates and James R. Keene, naturally availed themselves of this state of affairs to manipulate stocks on a grand
scale. Having loaded up with them early at low prices, they
boomed them with vigor; and we witnessed the beginning of
a carnival of speculation, and an unexampled rush to form
combinations of industrial and railroad interests, or trusts,
and generally to capitalize the concerns taken in for many
times the amount of their previous capital or real value. The
stock thus created, after being admitted to dealings in Wall
Street, was made active and bid up by the promoters to high
figures to catch buyers, while the public, which had become
crazy to buy, took it in enormous amounts. It bought in haste
to repent at leisure, for, I regret to say, most of the buyers
have it still; and the aggregate loss its shrinkage in price rep-
resents is to be counted by very many hundreds of millions
of dollars.

But it was fortunate for both Wall Street and the nation
that the inflation which ran riot till September, 1902, was then

checked by the conservative action and warnings of the banks and men like myself, for if it had been allowed to continue for another half year it would have ended in a disastrous convulsion, a bursting of the bubble, which would have been felt all over the United States, and in every department of business, as in and after the panics of 1857 and 1873. I was one of the first to sound the alarm and call a halt in this dangerously wild speculation in my weekly letter dated September 13, 1902, in the following words:

A man becomes an inebriate by getting himself into a condition where he ceases to recognize effect as following cause. Under the influence, at times, of the intoxicating beverage he will defy both law and order. This is due to the callous condition he has allowed himself to get into. The stock market of late has been productive of a similar condition of mind with a majority of people. They have been engaged now for such a prolonged period in buying, buying, buying, making profits on all their ventures, as to make them like the inebriate, callous to all adverse factors whenever they come up. High prices don't frighten them; scarcity and high rates for money don't frighten them; cautionary signals don't frighten them; strikes don't frighten them. Buying and holding on have simply become chronic with them. This may not unlikely continue to be the condition of the stock market until compulsory liquidation sets in, which the strain in the money situation will sooner or later produce. I recommend great caution on the buying side, and, better still, not buying at all at the prevailing high prices. I see no possibility of relief to the money market excepting through the importation of gold. The activity of business all over the country, together with the moving of the crops, is going to keep money thoroughly employed at high rates from now onward and all the way through the new year; therefore, those who buy stocks to carry hereafter, excepting on big concessions from present prices, may meanwhile be overtaken with discomfort from depreciation in values as well as from the difficulty of obtaining money at reasonable rates.

HENRY CLEWS.

The intoxication of the time having gradually given place to sobriety, and a slow but heavy downward reaction in prices, we escaped the violent and widespread panic that threatened us, and that would have been inevitable had we not "slowed down" in time. As it was, the decline was long-continued and severe, and impoverished or ruined hundreds of thousands of people, including a vast number of formerly very rich men. Both big and little speculators became the victims of the downward plunge of prices: but the country as a whole was saved from serious disturbance and depression—that is, from the effects of such a tremendous collapse and crash as menaced Wall Street during nearly the entire year 1903. This was very fortunate for all our material interests; and the conservative element in Wall Street is to be congratulated on having so successfully put on the brakes in time to prevent a collapse that would have involved and disturbed the nation from the Atlantic to the Pacific.

The year 1901 was the most remarkable in the financial history of the United States, and Wall Street was a theater of action whose performances astonished not only the entire country, but the world. Their like had never been seen before, not even during the great war between North and South. It would take volumes to fully describe and give retrospective clearness to the leading events of that extraordinary period which made the Stock Exchange continually the scene of wild excitement, daring manipulation, and unexampled inflation.

To say that Wall Street astonished the natives and made conservative business men stand aghast is no exaggeration. There were six influential factors actively at work in that year, namely, the consolidation of railroad and industrial companies at enormously inflated prices, including the disastrous Northern Pacific skyrocket "corner," the restless sea of reckless stock speculation that swept the American people into its vortex, with all its razzle-dazzle extravagance, the transformation of this country from a heavy lender in Europe to a heavy and urgent borrower, the partial failure of the corn crop, the decline in prices for nearly all the staples except grain and iron, and the collapse in earnings and dividends of many new industrial combinations. These included The Amalgamated Copper Company, and the panicky decline in its stock, which impoverished or ruined many thousands of investors, it being first run up to 130 and then rapidly down to 60 by the manipulators, who sold out and then sold "short," and who are said to have made more than fifty millions by the up and down movement. Subsequently even this low price was cut nearly in two, as the decline did not stop until 32$^1/_2$ was reached.

A mere recital of events as they occurred would be an eloquent serial story to those familiar with the alphabet of Wall Street; and there is no more interesting or exciting serial story than the stock ticker tells, from day to day, to those interested in the stock market, or one that often excites more joy or sorrow, or carries with it more weal or woe, prosperity or ruin. But the ticker, like Tennyson's brook, will go on forever during business hours, for we shall never be without a stock market and speculation.

The transactions of the New York Stock Exchange in 1901 were so tremendous in volume as to excite wonder. But they only represented the speculative spirit, the intoxication of the time. The sales in the first half of the year aggregated 175,800,600 shares of stocks and $637,100,800 of bonds at par value, an increase of 109,906,300 shares and $346,900,700 in bonds over the same six months in 1900.

As prices soared the volume of speculation increased, and on January 7th the day's total sales amounted to 2,116,500 shares, and then went on increasing till they reached 3,271,000 on April 30th. Then came the Northern Pacific bombshell, the panic of May 9th, when stocks came down even faster than Captain Scott's coon, and the actual sales were still larger, but owing to the intense excitement, demoralization, and confusion that prevailed, it was impossible to keep track of them all, and the ticker registered only 3,073,300 shares.

This sudden catastrophe convulsed the stock market in a way that alarmed money lenders, destroyed confidence, and caused a general rush to sell stocks which brought them down with a crash, involving many thousands in ruinous losses. The revulsion of feeling, the change in the sentiment of the Street was as startling as a violent earthquake, and the consequences were fraught with grave disaster. Up to the very eve of this great convulsion in the stock market the dance of speculation had been fast and furious, among both "the big men" and the little, and its unlooked-for occurrence reminded one of Byron's lines on the Brussels ball, given on the eve of the battle of Waterloo, when the sound of cannon unexpectedly boomed above the music:

> "On with the dance! Let joy be unconfined;
> No sleep till morn when Youth and Pleasure meet
> To chase the glowing hours with flying feet.
> The lamps shone o'er fair women and brave men;
> A thousand hearts beat happily; and when
> Music arose with its voluptuous swell,
> Soft eyes looked love to eyes that spake again,
> And all went merry as a marriage bell;
> But hush! hark! a deep sound strikes like a rising knell,
> Arm! arm! it is—it is—the cannon's opening roar!"

Fortunately, in the midst of the Northern Pacific panic, the financial belligerents combined to stop it. Their competitive buying for control of the stock had caused the "corner." But the extraordinarily high prices to which it was bid up by those short of it were reached after the competitive buying had ceased for the want of sellers. The contestants saw the wisdom of coming to terms to restore confidence and check the havoc that was being wrought on the Stock Exchange, where prices had fallen from fifteen to fifty per cent. that day, while Northern Pacific common stock had sold up to $1,000 a share. So J. P. Morgan & Co., the bankers of the Hill-Burlington-Great Northern party, and Kuhn, Loeb & Co., the bankers of the Harriman-Union Pacific party, met in haste, and came to an agreement as to the Northern Pacific stock they had bought, the formal announcement of which caused a violent recovery of prices the next day, but not before the sweep of the besom of destruction had caused several Stock Exchange failures to be announced. The recovery was followed by a relapse of equal violence under a fresh rush to sell, which carried stocks nearly as low as in the panic, and then by a fresh recovery, a usual feature in a crisis where credit has been severely shaken and many have been crippled.

The outcome of this agreement between the two sides was the formation of the Northern Securities Company, practically as arranged for by J. P. Morgan & Co. and Kuhn, Loeb & Co., Mr. Morgan naming the directors by mutual consent. Into this repository, or holding company, the Hill and Harriman companies—that is, both sides to the controversy—put their Northern Pacific stock, as well as Great Northern stock, and the Northern Securities Company later issued its own stock to them in exchange for it.

But when, in 1901, the Northern Securities Company was held by the United States Supreme Court to be a violation of the anti-trust law, and it became necessary to distribute its assets, a new controversy arose. Its directors proposed to make an equal, or pro rata, distribution of the Northern Pacific and Great Northern stocks deposited with it, whereas President E. H. Harriman, for the Union Pacific, which deposited the lion's share of the Northern Pacific, namely, $78,000,000, wanted all its stock back again; in other words, to eat his cake and have it, too. As this, if assented to, would have given the Union Pacific control of the Northern Pacific, President Hill, for the Great Northern Burlington system, naturally objected, and we all know of the litigation that followed, and in view of the glorious uncertainty of the law, it would have been rash to have predicted its final outcome.

On the Stock Exchange, April was the most active month of 1901, the sales aggregating 41,689,200, a daily average of 1,812,600. On April 24th no less than 652,900 shares of Union Pacific were sold. These specimen bricks furnish a practical commentary on the rampant speculation then in progress.

The new incorporations of the year represented an amazing amount of capital, the total being far in excess of any previous year, even that of 1899, when many of the large trust combinations were formed. The largest and probably the most heavily watered combination launched was the United States Steel Corporation, with its $508,478,000 of common stock, $510,277,300 of preferred stock, and $304,000,000 of bonds. The mania for organizing new companies and making combinations of old ones on largely inflated capital spread to every State in the Union, and the promoters of industrial enterprises, in particular, seemed to be trying to surpass each other in piling Pelion on Ossa in excessive capitalization. Their obvious purpose in most instances was to sell the stock to the public, and the poor public took the bait and suffered accordingly, for much of the stock in a great many of the new schemes became almost entirely worthless, both as collateral and in the stock market, and the rest experienced very heavy depreciation, and, figuratively speaking, like the shaky corporations it represented, went limping along with an uncertain gait and a ragged and down-at-the-heel appearance suggestive of reduced circumstances and hard times.

In every State there was a flood, if not a deluge, of new companies. In New Jersey, 2,346 were formed in 1901, with a capitalization of $4,773,702,000, against 2,181 in 1900, with a capitalization of $1,350,208,400; and in New York, Ohio, and Texas the incorporation mills were proportionately active in grinding out new companies with fictitiously large capital stocks.

Commercial and manufacturing corporations were practically unknown, that is, in any substantial form, in the United States till about 1850, and then they followed the development of the railways. In 1848 the first general corporation act, known as the Manufacturing Act, had been passed in this State, and companies began to be organized under it; but the law limited their capital and imposed other restrictions, whereas companies may now be incorporated for a thousand years with an unlimited amount of capital. The contrast between 1850 and this era of trusts marks the great and rapid progress of the country in the interval in population, commerce, manufacturing industry, banking, railway building, and general material prosperity.

The growth of trust companies has been the natural outcome of our industrial and economic development, and the
freedom allowed by our laws in monetary affairs. In England,
France, and other European countries the laws restrict corporation rights and privileges so rigidly that such companies
would find it impossible to do business there as they do here.
Hence trust companies have practically no existence except
in this country. How immensely they have prospered of
recent years the banks know to their cost. In 1882 the gross
deposits of all such companies in the United States were
$144,841,000. In 1892 they were $411,659,000; but after the
new industrial combination era began, in 1897, they shot up
with amazing celerity, and new companies sprang up like
mushrooms in all our large cities, and here and there in
small towns.

Being competitors of the banks they shared their business,
and so prevented or limited their natural growth, and forced
many of the bank consolidations that have since taken place.
At the end of June, 1902, their deposits had mounted up to
$1,525,887,000. Here was an increase of $1,114,228 in ten
years to about half of the total individual national bank
deposits of the country, for these on July 16, 1902, were
$3,098,875,772. Moreover, in the city of New York the trust
company deposits exceed, or did exceed, the individual
deposits of the national banks, those of the latter on
September 15, 1902, aggregating $603,565,374, while on June
30, 1902, the deposits of the trust companies, as shown by
their semiannual reports to the State Superintendent of
Banking, were $760,776,124. This comparison is a very sug-
gestive revelation of where the money goes and how the
trust companies prosper at the expense of the banks.

In 1902, again, a few leading factors, or influences, controlled American finance, and shaped the real financial history
of the year. These were the good corn crop, following the
bad one, and other satisfactory harvests; the overstraining of
American bank resources to supply the vast requirements
of the new trust and flotation enterprises when the capital
and currency of the country were required for its regular

trade and ordinary business; the enormous increase in our foreign importations contemporaneously with a very heavy decrease in our exports; the great rise in the price of the raw materials used in our manufactures, as well as in the cost of labor; the strenuous efforts of large speculative capitalists to extend and hold permanent control of their respective railway and industrial enterprises and undertakings; the reckless and unprecedented Vesuvius-like eruption of speculation in railroad and other stocks by wealthy and newly enriched Western stock operators known as "the Chicago Crowd" and "the Pittsburgh Crowd," respectively, aided by heavy bank loans at high rates; and finally the refusal of the public to follow them any longer as buyers. This accords with what I have said about the influence of the conservative banks and bankers in calling a halt on the wild speculation for a rise which raged up to the latter part of September in that year.

The exploit, in 1902, of John W. Gates, backed by his speculative associates, in buying a majority of the Louisville & Nashville Railway stock, was his last successful venture to make a big haul of millions on the Stock Exchange. After that he and they met with very heavy losses in their continued efforts to boom stocks. But Mr. Gates was paid a profit of ten millions of dollars on his Louisville & Nashville purchases by J. P. Morgan & Co., a partner in that firm having made the bargain with him at the Waldorf-Astoria Hotel, at three o'clock in the morning, after it had been discovered that Mr. Gates had really bought control of the stock.

It transpired, in evidence, that Mr. Perkins had gone there at that hour for this purpose, and found Mr. Gates in bed. The object in giving him so large an amount above what he had paid for the stock he had just bought was to get him out of the way as a mischief-maker, for with him in control of the Louisville & Nashville, there was no telling what he would do to demoralize the Southern Railway system. He was looked upon as a bull in a china shop, to be coaxed and tempted out, regardless of expense, before he began to toss the crockery with his horns.

So when he said to Mr. Perkins, "As you want the stock so badly, to keep the Belmont board in control and protect the Southern Railway, I will let you have it if you will pay me ten millions more than it cost," the proposition was promptly accepted; and the deal was closed on this basis. The Louisville & Nashville and the Southern Railway companies were supposed to have been jointly interested in the purchase, but the Gates stock was finally turned over to the Atlantic Seaboard Air Line.

Buying control of the Louisville & Nashville by Mr. Gates was a far bolder operation than President Hill's purchase of the stock of the Burlington & Quincy for the Great Northern, or than the Moore Brothers' purchase of control of the Rock Island and their subsequent great inflation of its stock and bonded debt, because Gates bought it merely as a speculation, without any desire to manage the road. He was fortunate in being able to sell it so easily to those he had frightened by his daring coup.

It is interesting to compare the leading influences, or principal factors, in Wall Street in 1903 with those of 1901 and 1902. Stock Exchange transactions in that year were very much smaller than in 1902, but not nearly as much so as the total in 1902 had fallen below those of 1901, the year of the greatest activity and excitement in this memorable speculative period. The sales in 1903 aggregated 161,099,800 shares, against 188,497,600 in 1902 and 265,945,700 in 1901. The largest total on any one day in 1903 was 1,539,000, against 1,996,000 in 1902 and 3,202,200 in 1901. The largest in any month in 1903 was that of January, 16,002,300, against 26,568,000 in April, 1902, and the smallest in 1903 was 10,731,000 in November, against 7,884,900 in June, 1902.

The barometer of the iron trade was still rising at the opening of 1903. Good crops had been gathered and were being sold at good prices; railway earnings were large, and railway companies were making heavy expenditures for new equipment and improvements, and every department of business and manufacturing industry seemed prosperous, with the iron trade enjoying its full share of that prosperity. So heavy, indeed, was the demand for iron and steel that the capacity of our works was unequal to it, and we were importing iron and steel largely, as we had been in 1902.

But in June the iron industry experienced one of its time-honored lightning changes. That barometer suddenly fell. The demand subsided with surprising celerity in all lines, and by November prices in some of these were fifty per cent. lower than in January. The boom in the iron trade which commenced in 1899 was at an end after lasting for four years. At the end of the year, however, the trade began to revive, and 1904 witnessed a slow but steady improvement in it, as the reports of the United States Steel Corporation's earnings have shown. Consequently that highly inflated company, after being forced in 1903 to suspend dividends on its common stock, was encouraged to continue them at seven per cent. on its preferred stock. But this carried cold comfort to the hundreds of thousands who had been impoverished by buying these stocks at the high prices at which they were floated here and in Europe.

Before the end of 1903 liquidation on a large scale in stocks had run its course and exhausted itself, and the market quieted into comparative steadiness; and in 1904 we had, on the whole, nothing more than a dull trading market, with the outside public very largely absent. But there has been a general tendency toward slow improvement, although the net earnings of both railways and industrial companies have, on the average, shown a heavy shrinkage, a reflection of the reduced volume of trade and more or less industrial depression following the overstimulated boom of previous years. Just as 1901 was the year of the most unbridled and unrestrained inflation, 1902 witnessed a constant battle against the tendency to a downward reaction, and 1903 saw and felt the reaction, which was all the more severe because it bad been so long delayed.

In the cotton market, however, as wild and extraordinary a bull speculation raged in 1903 and the early part of 1904, under the lead of Daniel J. Sully in New York, and William P.

Brown and a Southern clique in New Orleans, as ever excited the Stock Exchange. Through their manipulation, helped by the statistical position of cotton and the prospect of reduced production, cotton rose, under an enormous and unprecedented volume of transactions, from about eight cents a pound here to seventeen cents, with frequent violent fluctuations, and Mr. Sully was avowedly planning to carry it up to twenty cents, when he found his resources insufficient to carry, on a falling market, the amount of cotton sold to him. So after going up like a rocket, he came down like the rocket stick, although his previous profits by the rapid rise had run into several millions. It was well that a halt was thus practically called to this excited speculation and excessive advance in cotton, for it had inflicted heavy losses upon spinners and caused the closing of many mills. Sully's failure was the logical result of a too daring speculative campaign, and reminds us of that vaulting ambition which overleaps itself and falls on the other side.

Glancing at other countries, I find that Canada made more material progress in 1903 than in any previous year in her history, business increasing substantially in nearly every branch of trade and finance, stimulated by bountiful crops and 150,000 immigrants. But in England the continued decline of British Consols to the lowest prices in a generation reflected a low financial barometer, the legacy of the costly South African war. France, however, made the best showing of the year in Europe in finance and general prosperity, while in Germany a vigorous industrial revival lifted that country out of its previous depression consequent on over-speculation and bank failures.

One question of great interest in relation to our new industrial combinations is whether a proper readjustment of their hugely inflated capital and excessive charges will place them permanently in a condition of efficiency, productiveness, solvency, and prosperity, or whether they will ultimately drift, one by one, into the hands of receivers through their inability to make both ends meet, or become hopeless wrecks, like the Shipbuilding Trust. The same fate is liable to overtake many other large flotations into which there was a too copious flow of water, supplemented by chicanery and misrepresentation. Many of these have been organized in disregard and defiance of legitimate finance, and have exposed the stock market and all the monetary interests depending upon them to risks and disastrous disturbances inseparable from organizations whose foundations rest largely on wind and water and on prospectuses and bookkeeping that often failed to tell the truth, the whole truth, and nothing but the truth.

It was well that a stop was practically put to the creation of such inflated industrial combinations, as well as to needless combinations and highly inflated stock issues among the railroads for power and profit and stock-jobbing purposes, by the course of the Wall Street banking interest, to which I have referred, in coming to the conclusion that the over-watering of new companies, the marketing of new stocks, and the rise of prices on the Stock Exchange had been carried beyond the point of safety, and that the outside public had bought more speculative industrial and railway stocks than they would be able to carry on a falling market.

They argued, therefore, that their buying power and their inclination to buy were nearly exhausted, and that the stock market had become largely a field of action for certain heavy and reckless speculators, each of whom had suddenly made many millions by the formation of new trusts and railway combinations. Some of these had become multimillionaires through the early sale of the heavy amounts of United States Steel stock they received in exchange for their plants when that huge corporation was launched in its sea of water. In this they were like some others who enriched themselves by their industrial combinations in the West before they branched out in Wall Street.

Very large bank loans to the brokers of these big operators were gradually called in and fresh accommodations refused them. Without loans it was impossible for them to buy and run up stocks to inordinately high prices, as they had been doing. Therefore they found that, to a large extent, their occupation was, like Othello's, gone. They were eagles with clipped wings.

The heavy liquidation by large and small operators in 1903 caused a heavy and almost continuous decline in prices on the Stock Exchange. Many rich men were compelled by this shrinkage and the calling in of their loans by the banks to sell out heavy lines of both railway and industrial stocks. Not a few of these lost practically all their capital, while nearly all the rest sold a large part of their best holdings to protect the remainder, which became unmarketable.

This period of liquidation and depression left Wall Street and the country at large in 1904 thickly sprinkled with poor rich men, capitalists with a good deal of property, real and personal, including stocks, but all unsalable in the market except at an almost ruinous loss. Their policy is naturally to hold on to what they have left till the tide turns, and if they are strong enough to be able to do this they will doubtless meet with their reward. History repeats itself in Wall Street as well as elsewhere, and with this prospect in view they can cheerfully say, as the old song says, "There's a good time coming, boys; only wait a little longer."

Meanwhile, those who were active in Wall Street during this eventful period of inflation and speculation must note, more than others, the vast change that has come over sentiment and opinion in Wall Street and everywhere else.

Both Wall Street and the outside public have lost the faith that they had in many of the stock-market leaders, the men who were once followed blindly in their schemes of inflation and regarded as omnipotent in their execution. The power and prestige of these leaders, for the present at least, have passed entirely away, and none are so poor as to do them reverence. The devotees of the Street no longer worship the old idols.

Wall Street and the public also lost faith in all new ventures and new railway and industrial bond and stock issues, as well as in the good judgment and good faith of the promoters and corporations concerned. The revelations of fraud, chicanery, and excessive capitalization that have been made in the courts and elsewhere, have undeceived even the dullest and most credulous believers in the schemes and schemers that took the country by storm in the days of Wall Street's wild and pyrotechnical speculation.

Out of evil there cometh good, and this great change from blind credulity and inordinate inflation to discriminating distrust and severe contraction has exerted a wholesome effect in paving the way to a sounder, safer, and generally better state of things both in and out of Wall Street. But meanwhile one bad sign is noteworthy. The large corporations, being unable to market new bond issues, are borrowing heavily from banking syndicates at five to six per cent. on notes running from one to three years. There is danger in this, and the way of the borrower on these terms may, like that of the transgressor, be hard. But the end may justify the means; and the nation is still growing as rapidly and as grandly as ever in our history from ocean to ocean.

There is nothing to provoke pessimism in the magnificent strides we are making in the march of progress; Wall Street is always sure to reflect this progress and our growth in material prosperity, as well as any periods of depression we may encounter, for it is the great barometer not only of the country and the times, but very largely of the world.

CHAPTER 16

THE UPS AND DOWNS
OF WALL STREET

ILLUSTRATED BY PERSONAL REMINISCENCES OF ITS LEADERS.

THE mutations and vicissitudes, the ups and downs, of Wall Street can be best illustrated by sketches, from life, of the career and experience of its leading operators, who have often, though not generally, gone up like a rocket and come down like a stick.

I will not begin with those now foremost in the Wall Street arena, but go back to Jacob Little, whose name is still a household word on the Stock Exchange.

He died in the sixties, while the war between North and South was raging, and he had gradually ceased to be a power in the Street after the panic of 1857. He remained a bear on the rising tide of currency inflation following the outbreak of the war, and was submerged and wiped out.

He was an odd fish—singular in appearance, manner, and business methods, but for more than twenty years he had a great name in Wall Street. To speak colloquially, he was the cock of the walk by self-assertion and common consent.

He was the successor of Jacob Barker, who came from Philadelphia, and was the first great leader Wall Street had known. He was trained in his office, and began as a stock operator on his own account in 1835.

The panic of 1837 made his reputation and his fortune, for, being naturally a bear, he was largely "short" of stocks. That panic swept the whole United States with the besom of destruction, and sent prices down to zero. It left him a greater bear than ever, a preacher of distrust and a prophet of failure. He thrived on calamity, and grew richer and richer during the years of depression that followed that memorable revulsion.

From 1835 to 1846 he was in his glory and his prime, and no one disputed his leadership in the world of Wall Street. But then he met with a great reverse, not, however, through continuing to "bear" stocks, but through a "bull" operation in Norwich and Worcester Railroad stock. He attempted, with a Boston clique, to control it, and personally bound himself to the clique, in the sum of $25,000, not to sell his stock below 90.

He went to work to put it up, but it "bulled hard," and refused to stay up. So he paid the forfeit, and sold out at the best prices he could get, losing a million, which was looked upon in those days as ten or twenty millions would be now. This was the only large bull operation he ever engaged in, and it confirmed him in his natural bearishness.

He more than recovered from this disaster, however, by breaking the "corner" in Erie stock not long afterwards. He was largely "short" of it, and the cornering clique had bought up all the stock on the market. They put the price higher and higher from day to day, but Jacob Little remained unterrified, and refused to "cover" his contracts. He was the only one "short" who stood out against the cornerers, and made no effort to buy in his stock. The eyes of all Wall Street were watching him, and the prevailing opinion was that he would be forced to "cover" at a ruinous loss, or fail.

But he had "a card up his sleeve" that the cornerers had never suspected, and just when they were expecting his surrender, or failure, at the maturity of his contracts to deliver, he produced a big bundle of new Erie certificates of stock and filled his contracts by delivering them. These had been issued to him in exchange for the company's convertible bonds, unknown to the clique, the issue of the bonds with the convertible clause being also unknown to them.

Such a surprise and checkmate Wall Street had never known before, and the "corner" was broken, with resulting demoralization and disaster to the cornering clique, and great profit and eclat to Jacob Little. But subsequently he failed several times on the "bear" side, yet always managed to pay in full out of later successes. He was equally generous as a creditor, and compromised on easy terms, so as to give his debtors a chance to recuperate. Hence he was liked and respected notwithstanding his aggressiveness and the havoc he often wrought among speculators on the opposite side of the market.

He was a born speculator. Speculation was his daily bread. He liked it for its own sake. His ambition was to control the stock market, and he was willing to run extra hazardous risks to achieve this end. He once said: "I care more for the game than the results, and, winning or losing, I like to be in it!"

It was this feeling that kept him in Wall Street after his money power and his prestige of success, as well as his health, had passed away. He was out of debt, but without money in any considerable amount. He was a mere shadow of what he had been, a name and nothing more. Nevertheless, he risked his small operations with zest. But his health gave way more and more, and he fainted one morning in the board room, in Lord's Court, and his end came not long afterwards.

He said, "I die poor!" But from the ashes of his estate and unsettled accounts his family succeeded in collecting about $150,000, which he had neglected to look after, for he had always been careless and easy-going in money matters, and attached little value to money except for its use in speculation. He was the very reverse of a miser, for he had never cared to hoard.

It was Anthony W. Morse who gave the finishing stroke to the career of Jacob Little, for, while Little was operating for a decline in the early sixties, Morse sprang into the speculative ring as a rampant bull, and bid prices up on the Stock Exchange, while it was still in Lord's Court, in a way that astonished him and the other fossils of the board. They considered him utterly reckless. But Morse foresaw that the great war issues of United States currency—greenbacks as they were called—then being made would inflate the prices of stocks largely, and he accordingly, metaphorically speaking, rushed in where angels feared to tread.

He became the storm center, the hub, the pivotal point, in the wildest riot of stock speculation this country has ever known, or probably ever will know again; and who was he? A slight, fair-complexioned country lad, he came to New York without a dollar, and became a clerk in a stockbroker's office. Then he married a woman with some money, and induced her to let him speculate a little for her, and was successful in making something for her, and enough for himself to buy a seat at the Stock Exchange, which then cost only $500, the initiation fee.

That was in 1862, up to which time he was both insignificant and unknown. But the bold, dashing style in which he immediately began to astonish the natives and rattle the dry bones of the fossils, by his rapidly advancing bids for railway stocks, showed that he was a man of the time, fully up to date. Had he not proved to be right on the market he would have been ruined at the start, but the market went with him, and it went with a rush that made the old fogies of the board say: "Well, well! this young fellow got the start of us—we are not in it!"

He first put up Cleveland & Pittsburgh with the ease and celerity of a man who thought it a mere trifle to handle. Then he successfully took hold of Ohio & Mississippi, Rock Island, Erie, and Fort Wayne, and put them up in the same pyrotechnical and flamboyant way. He, in one day, marked Fort Wayne up from 118 to 152. He had unlimited confidence in himself, because he saw that he was on the right track, and the Street and the public followed him. He ran Pittsburgh up from 65 to 108 amid great excitement, and bid 100 for the whole capital stock, "seller one year." He then sold all his Pittsburgh between 96 and 108. His firm, Morse & Co., were overrun with commission business at their large ground-floor office in

William Street. By the early part of 1863 he had punished the bears badly, and made, it was estimated, at least $1,250,000, and his career of riotous success ran for just two years, during which he was supposed to have made enormously. There was a rush to join every pool he formed, so great was his prestige. Men crowded the sidewalk in front of his office trying to find out what he said, or what he was doing, so that they might do likewise; and if he gave a "bull" point on any stock, nearly all who heard of it acted upon it, feeling confident that it was a dead certainty. His fellow-brokers in the board largely followed him, like the rank and file, and rag, tag, and bobtail of the Wall Street crowd, because he had been always right. Never indeed was a Wall Street leader, before or since, more blindly followed than Morse. The whole country joined in the mad speculation there, and he was on the crest of the wave.

One night at the Evening Exchange Morse bid 112 for 10,000 shares of Erie stock, and Daniel Drew sold them. Then be bid the same price for 20,000 more, and Drew sold them. A day or two later Drew "covered" at a heavy loss. When Morse took hold of Ohio & Mississippi he jumped it from 49 to 69 in a couple of days.

Money was cheap and abundant, owing to the currency inflation, and speculation so active that many stock houses kept a relay of clerks for night work. Meanwhile speculation in gold was as rampant as in stocks, and hundreds of new mining and petroleum companies were launched, and the stocks of these were actively traded in at high and rapidly rising prices, while old and worthless stocks, like Bucks County Lead, were resuscitated and boomed with the rest.

Clergymen and women were drawn into this whirlpool of speculation, and any stock with "gold" in its name went off "like hot cakes." One stock was considered about as good as another to buy, as all were going up. Morse led the crazy multitude in everything, and, among his other achievements, he put Rock Island up from 106 to 149, and, in doing so, bought the whole capital stock, which was then only 56,000 shares.

Morse's doom was sealed by Mr. Salmon P. Chase, who as Secretary of the Treasury sought to stop the wild inflation, and particularly the tremendous bull speculation in gold, by selling gold for currency, and locking the currency up in the Sub-treasury, so as to make a tight money market. This had the desired effect, for it made money so scarce and dear that it forced the large speculative holders of stocks to sell, through the banks calling in their loans, and brought on a panic, just at the time when Morse was more heavily loaded with stocks than he had ever been before.

Broken in health, and looking weary and haggard, he tried to sell, and this set every one of his followers selling like a flock of sheep, and prices tumbled from bad to worse under the general rush to realize. Fort Wayne fell at the morning session of the board on that fatal Monday of the Morse panic, on the 18th of April, 1864, from 153 to 119. Then Morse left the room for the last time, and, going to his office, said to his partner, "The game is up!" Reading had also fallen that morning nineteen per cent.; Pittsburgh, seventeen; Hudson River, twenty-three; and all other active stocks about as much.

This monetary tornado, that found Morse overloaded with stocks, there and then swept him out of the Stock Exchange, for, knowing that he was hopelessly mined, he wrote an announcement of the suspension of Morse & Co., and sent it to the board a few minutes after he had left it. The failure proved a very bad one, and the firm was unable to settle or resume. Morse was no longer the leader of Wall Street, and many of his customers, in a semifrantic condition, rushed in upon him and denounced him bitterly. The king had been dethroned, never to regain his crown, nor ever to get a fresh start.

Pandemonium reigned during the rest of the day, and at the Evening Exchange uptown at night. Speculation had been so widespread, and Morse had been so implicitly trusted as a leader, that the collapse ruined thousands, including many women, and a raving, cursing mob crowded into the Evening Exchange and overflowed into the Fifth Avenue Hotel. There was a night of horror in hundreds of homes. Morse was upbraided and cursed, and many of his customers, as is usual when they lose their money in a broker's office, blamed him for their losses.

Then for a year Morse disappeared. When he returned he looked more haggard than ever, and he died poor soon afterwards. No one ever accused Morse of being dishonest, therefore his Waterloo defeat gained him widespread sympathy. Few Wall Street magnates had more friends than Anthony W. Morse from start to finish of his career.

John M. Tobin, who had been a ferry gatekeeper for Commodore Vanderbilt on Staten Island, figured largely as a speculator in the gold room, and also as a stock operator, during the two years of the Morse campaign, and saw many ups and downs. He began to loom up still more after Morse sank below the horizon in 1864. He was known to be the agent of Commodore Vanderbilt in cornering Harlem stock, and shone in Vanderbilt's reflected light, although a large operator on his own account.

The Harlem "corner" was a memorable event. Through the winter of 1863–64 the stock had been selling at about 60, and Vanderbilt was a director and large stockholder, and, moreover, determined to make what he called "a big thing" out of it. The road was, however, generally considered of little account except for carrying milk. So, in connection with his street-railway projects for improving its value, he engineered the stock up to 117. He counted upon getting a charter from the Common Council; but its members tricked him, and after passing a favorable resolution they sold the stock "short" and then rescinded the resolution, and it fell to 72. So they made money at his expense.

He then applied to the Legislature at Albany for a Harlem franchise to lay rails in Broadway; and the legislators saw there was room for stock speculation in this. They made a favorable report on a bill granting Vanderbilt's application, and on this Harlem stock rose sharply to 150. Then they and their friends, including the New York Common Councilmen, sold it short largely, thinking they had a sure thing; and Tobin bought for Vanderbilt all that was offered. On March 25, 1864, they voted, by prearrangement, against the bill, and Harlem stock fell to 101.

The sellers of Harlem rejoiced, for they had large profits on paper; but Tobin still continued to buy the stock, and under his purchases it rapidly recovered. The commodore was determined to punish them. Within ten days Harlem was up to 150 again. A week later it touched 185, and thereafter, for ten days, fluctuated between 175 and 200. Daniel Drew sold calls on it for 30,000 shares, thinking it could not stay up long, and the professional speculators, both in and out of the Stock Exchange, took a hand in selling it "short" on the same theory. The Morse panic swept over it in April, but still it stood up, like a pyramid in the desert, and Tobin still continued buying for Vanderbilt.

In May the price of Harlem was put up to 300. It stood at 285 on the day 15,000 shares had to be delivered, and they were settled for at this price. Daniel Drew compromised by paying $1,000,000 to Tobin in settlement of his own Harlem "shorts," but the claim against him was $1,700,000. He, however, threatened a suit for conspiracy. Tobin's share of the profits of the corner was about two millions, and this made him worth three.

Commodore Vanderbilt chuckled, and disposed of the Harlem road by leasing it at eight per cent. on the stock to the New York Central & Hudson when he got control of it. So Harlem proved a bonanza to him till the end, and is still one of the splendid assets of his descendants. After the "corner," Tobin bulled gold on a tremendous scale in the face of the Union victories that terminated the war. He bulled it from 198 to 211 against the "short" interest at the beginning of 1865, and then it broke on him so heavily that he lost more than $1,500,000. After that he met with a succession of disasters in the stock market, and lost every dollar that he had, besides running in debt with his brokers. He then retired to live with his sister on a farm on Staten Island, and was never seen again in Wall Street. He saw ups and downs with a vengeance. So did his contemporary of the open board, E. A. Coray, who made and lost about as much.

Addison G. Jerome had a career in Wall Street more brief than that of Anthony W. Morse, but he is still well remembered there as a shining light. He entered Wall Street as an operator early in 1863, after being a merchant in the dry goods trade, and during the rest of that year was called "the Napoleon of the public board," so conspicuously active, bold, and successful was he in his operations. He was a friend and broker of John Tobin's, and cooperated with him in bulling Harlem, with the result that he made a very large amount of money out of it, first by the rise from 60 to 117, when Commodore Vanderbilt was dealing with the New York Common Council, and next when he was punishing the legislators at Albany for going back on him, as he phrased it, in the 1864 "corner."

He became a brilliant leader, and had a host of followers, and was successful in everything he undertook until he bulled Michigan Southern, and, with a clique that he formed, bought control of it. He put it to high figures, and was sure of his position. But Henry Keep, the treasurer of the company, and a keen operator in stocks, stepped in, and turned Jerome's success into utter and disastrous failure.

Henry Keep knew something that Jerome was unaware of, namely, that a clause in the Michigan Southern's charter permitted its directors to increase its capital stock. So he called a secret meeting of the board, and an increase of 14,000 shares was voted. Then, with this increase for future delivery, he sold the stock against it, and borrowed to make his deliveries, which made Jerome think Keep was largely "short" of Michigan Southern. He and his clique, therefore, kept on buying and advancing the price, while Keep kept on selling more and more. The final result was that Jerome called in all his loans of the stock, so as to force the "shorts" to "cover," and that Keep responded by delivering the 14,000 shares of new stock, which caused a fall of twenty per cent. in Michigan

Southern in one day. This involved the loss of nearly all the three millions of money Jerome had so quickly made, and killed him as a leader, although he was respected as an honorable man. He took the loss of his fortune and prestige so much to heart that he sickened and died in the following year of some obscure disease, a virtually ruined man. But, fortunately, during his nine months of phenomenal success he had settled enough on his wife to keep the wolf from the door. His ups and downs were remarkably swift even for Wall Street.

Leonard W. Jerome, a younger brother of Addison's, was prominent in Wall Street and society, and as the driver of a four-in-hand, long before the latter appeared, and continued in the Street long after Addison passed away. His career was also marked by memorable ups and downs. In 1863 he was a large holder of Hudson River Railroad stock, which the bears had hammered down to 107. So he formed a strong clique to bull it against the "short" interest, and bought all the stock that was offered until he had taken nearly all the capital. Then he bid up the price gradually till it reached 175, and made the stock so scarce that he loaned it to the bears to make their deliveries, at five per cent. a day. The shorts, estimated to represent about 50,000 shares, finding there was no help for them, covered at a very heavy loss, while Jerome made a great deal of money by squeezing them, presumably two or three millions.

His prestige increased with his wealth, and he became a social as well as a financial lion. He had been watching Pacific Mail since it succeeded the Nicaragua Transit Company in 1856. In 1861 its stock fell to 69, but in the next year its earnings were enormous, and 26,000 of its 40,000 shares were bought by a combination of operators, mostly its directors, who transferred it to Brown Brothers & Co., to be held in trust for their benefit for five years; and they selected Leonard Jerome to bull the stock in the open market. Under his manipulation it rose to 160 in thirteen months after he commenced operations for the ring. There was a large "short" interest in it by that time, and, to force the "shorts" to settle, he put it to 200, and kept it there, and they settled.

In 1865 Pacific Mail's capital was increased from four millions to ten, and yet its stock stood at 240, and it paid twenty per cent. a year in dividends. The year after, it was increased to twenty millions, yet it sold at 180, with Jerome still bulling it. But in 1867 he met his Waterloo in it. To use his own words, he had bitten off more than he could chew. The company's earnings fell off largely, and its report showed assets reduced from thirty-four to twenty-two millions; the Government paper-money issues were being rapidly contracted, and the flood of "water" injected into the stock was beginning to tell upon it. Moreover, Jerome had agreed to buy the old five-year combination's stock at 160. Owing to all this, accompanied by a generally weak stock market, Pacific Mail broke, under enormous sales, from 163 to 115 in a few days on his hands, and he lost practically everything he had, except some real estate. After being thus ruined by Pacific Mail, Leonard Jerome ceased to be a power in Wall Street. He had no longer any prestige there, and soon retired from it entirely, and died, at the home of his daughter, Lady Randolph Churchill, in London, a poor man. He had experienced his full share of the ups and downs of Wall Street.

Pacific Mail was nothing to Leonard W. Jerome after he lost his money, nor he to Pacific Mail. The company had seen its most palmy and prosperous days, and its water-logged stock was heavy on the market. It suffered from reduced traffic and bad management, and in 1871–72 its stock had sunk to so low an ebb that the directors felt it was necessary to do something to mend matters. So, having little of the stock, they decided, instead of trying to reëlect themselves, to give up the ship. They retired to make room for a new board in November, 1871, with Alden B. Stockwell at the helm as president. Nominally the new board selected him, but really he selected them to do his bidding.

His name was then very little known in Wall Street, but he was known to have been a steamboat clerk on Lake Erie, and more recently to have married the daughter of Elias Howe, the sewing-machine inventor and manufacturer of Bridgeport, Conn., and thus acquired wealth and become the president of the Howe Sewing Machine Company and the Willcox & Gibbs Company.

He had come to Wall Street to see what he could do, and finding Pacific Mail stock down to the 40's in 1871, he began to bull it with a vigor that excited some wonder; and the wonder grew when it was found that he had secured stock and proxies enough to elect his own board of directors. He elected them and himself by a vote of 118,000 shares, and became Commodore Stockwell at a bound. His wish was law to his codirectors, and the irreverent called it a dummy board.

With the assets of the Pacific Mail Company under his control, and acting for it, he soon managed to get control, and become president, of the Panama Railway Company. He began, on this acquisition of the Pacific Mail Company, to bull Pacific Mail stock anew by making splendid promises. In October, 1872, while the company's steamers were foundering and burning with alarming frequency, he claimed that it had increased its property by large purchases, and was earning more than eleven per cent. a year in excess of the Government subsidy. This, he said, would enable it to pay twelve per cent. on its capital stock from January 1, 1872. Then he asked for authority from the Legislature at Albany to reduce its capital stock from twenty millions to ten, which was granted; but the company never availed itself of this authority, and to this day its capital remains at twenty millions.

The stock, that had been as low as 40, responded to his "bull" statements and manipulation, for Wall Street saw that the intention was at least to put the stock up. It rose, after a good deal of see-sawing, to about 107, and Commodore Stockwell was the sensation of the time in Wall Street. He became, like Leonard W. Jerome, what was called a "big swell." He had one of the largest houses in Madison Avenue and one of the showiest turnouts in the city, and yet he had been commodore for less than a year.

He did not confine himself to Pacific Mail and the other interests mentioned, but took hold of that railway cripple, Boston, Hartford and Erie, and bought 30,000 shares of Atlantic and Pacific Railway preferred at 25, a stock of uncertain legal status, although the certificates had been printed by the company, because there was no legal authority for its issue. But this did not prevent the stock from being made active for a short time in Wall Street at prices a good deal above cost.

Before long, however, it became discredited, and so also did Boston, Hartford and Erie stock, while Pacific Mail suffered under fresh losses and reduced earnings. The stocks of the three companies were vigorously attacked by the bears and they all went down together, Stockwell being unable to support them, and all that he had made was lost. This state of things involved him in a snarl about the 27,000 shares of the Pacific Mail Company's treasury stock, and a compromise was the result, by which he is said to have given his note to the Pacific Mail Company for $1,140,000, indorsed by the Howe Sewing Machine Company.

Then, at the next election, he ceased to be its president, and a new board of directors was elected. He was also dropped from the Panama Railroad directorate and the Atlantic and Pacific board. He had lost his money and his prestige, and there were none so poor as to do him reverence. He led a precarious existence as a small speculator afterwards, and, not long before his death, failed for a small amount as a member of the Consolidated Exchange.

He was a man of popular manners, and, in describing his change of fortune, he humorously remarked: "When I first came into Wall Street, it was asked, 'Who is that man Stockwell?' But I was respectfully spoken of as 'Mr. Stockwell' after I had made a good deal of money bulling Pacific Mail; and when I was elected president of Pacific Mail, I was styled 'Commodore Stockwell' and 'a Wall Street leader,' and a great man generally. But when Pacific Mail broke, and broke me, I became 'That red-headed cuss Stockwell.'" Thus are the ups and downs of Wall Street, and Wall Street opinion, illustrated in real life.

Of all the great operators of Wall Street, however, Daniel Drew furnishes the most remarkable instance of immense and long-continued success, followed by utter failure and hopeless bankruptcy. His early success as a stock speculator was all the more surprising because he was an illiterate man, who had barely learned to read and to write enough to be able to sign his own name in a sprawling, illegible hand.

He had been a cattle drover, and after that the keeper of the Bull's Head Tavern, at the New York Cattle Yards, and was without any experience of banking or Stock Exchange affairs when he first came into Wall Street; and he never even read a newspaper. But he succeeded in making money from the start, and then joined others in putting capital into Hudson River steamboats; and his investments in these became large and proved very profitable, although he knew nothing about running steamers himself.

His shrewdness enabled him to make millions by stock speculation, and before long, without knowing anything of the stock brokerage business except as a customer, he entered into a Stock Exchange partnership, his firm being Drew & Robinson. For many years this house was prosperous and prominent, and Drew, after it was dissolved, and when at the summit of his prosperity, said to a friend who rated him at twenty millions, "I guess sixteen will cover it."

After that Drew's cunning and sagacity seemed gradually to fail him. He met with a succession of disasters through bad judgment, but was more liberal than before in endowing the Drew Theological Seminary and other Methodist institutions. Yet, instead of giving the endowments in cash, he gave his notes for them, and paid interest on these. The consequence was that when he finally lost every dollar that he had, and was declared a bankrupt, without any assets, the notes were worthless. While in this bankrupt condition and dependent for a home on his son, he died, and his death was as unnoticed as that of any other Wall Street wreck. He had gone out of sight, and out of mind, when his money was gone. Never did anyone go further up or further down in Wall Street as a stock speculator than Daniel Drew.

Charles F. Woerishoffer was a brilliant Stock Exchange operator, who made a large fortune out of nothing and then lost most of it again by overstaying his market as a bear after the panic of 1884.

James R. Keene came to New York with several millions, made out of mining stocks in California at the time of the great Bonanza gold discovery at Gold Hill, when Flood and O'Brien, Mackay, and John P. Jones made their millions. But Keene, after adding to his "pile," lost all he had through overextending his operations in bulling stocks and grain in the eighties. He, however, got a fresh start through being employed by large interests to manipulate stocks for them, and after several more ups and downs he is rich again.

Henry N. Smith, a former partner of Jay Gould, made five or six millions as an operator in stocks, only to lose them again and die poor. The brief meteoric Wall Street career of Ferdinand Ward, who lured General Grant into forming the firm of Grant & Ward, is well remembered. He went up so high that when he came down he landed in Sing Sing prison. Fish, the president of the Marine Bank, did the same, after being long in good repute.

It is unnecessary to dilate on any of the Vanderbilts, or Goulds, or Russell Sage, or Henry Keep, or Henry Villard, or William E. Travers, because they had no totally overwhelming reverses in their Wall Street career; but John F. Tracy, the president of the Rock Island Railroad in the sixties, was ruined by his stock speculations after being worth more than five millions, and he had to relinquish his presidency, and died in poverty. Cyrus W. Field, too, lost nearly all his large fortune through overloading himself with Manhattan Railway stock; and Addison Cammack, the Ursa Major of Wall Street, died worth little in comparison with what he had once possessed.

How violent the vicissitudes of Wall Street are at times we may easily infer when we recall the tremendous convulsion produced by the gold conspiracy of Black Friday, on September 24, 1869, which involved thousands in enormous losses, and caused both the Stock Exchange and the Gold Clearing House, and Gold Exchange Bank, to be closed; or when we think of the devastating Northern Pacific panic of

May 9, 1901, or of the far-reaching and long-continued havoc worked by the panic of 1873.

The memorable failure of Jay Cooke & Co., early in the last-mentioned panic, will be recalled by many as vividly as the collapse of the Ohio Life and Trust Company that started the panic of 1857.

All these reminiscences of the ups and downs of Wall Street will serve to remind my readers that, while it is often easy to make money, it is still easier to lose it. Therefore, boldness should be always tempered with caution in the pursuit of the Almighty Dollar in Wall Street.

CHAPTER 17

GRANT'S SECOND TERM

THE BEST MAN FOR THE POSITION AND MOST DESERVING OF THE HONOR.—HOW THE "BOOM" WAS WORKED UP IN FAVOR OF GRANT.—THE GREAT FINANCIERS AND SPECULATORS ALL COME TO THE FRONT IN THE INTEREST OF THE NATION'S PROSPERITY AND OF THE MAN WHO HAD SAVED THE COUNTRY.—THE GREAT MASS MEETING AT COOPER UNION.—WHY A. T. STEWART REFUSED TO PRESIDE.—THE RESULTS OF THE MASS MEETING AND HOW THEY WERE APPRECIATED BY THE FRIENDS OF THE CANDIDATE, LEADING REPRESENTATIVES OF THE BUSINESS COMMUNITY AND THE PUBLIC PRESS GENERALLY, IRRESPECTIVE OF PARTY.

I wish to relate briefly the part which I took in the reelection of General Grant, whose defeat, when he was spoken of as a candidate for the second term, was foreshadowed among a large number of politicians of every stripe. There were serious divisions in the ranks of his former friends and adherents, and an organized effort was made to destroy his prospects a long time in advance of the meeting of the Philadelphia Convention.

All the political machinery of his enemies, and of disappointed office seekers and their friends, was put in force, and all the tactics and prejudices employed that were put into operation with greater success four years later.

I felt assured that the nomination of any other man might result in the defeat of the party, and that it was absolutely necessary to its strength, maintenance and autonomy that General Grant should again be our choice. He had been tried for one term and found to be a very satisfactory executive. There was no important risk involved in trying him for a second term, while the experiment with another man in the then sensitive, unsettled and tentative condition of reconstruction, might have been injurious to the best political and industrial interests of the country; and the experiment would have been especially risky if the nominee should have been a Democrat.

The people of the South were not then in a proper frame of mind to be trusted with any power implying the mere possibility of obtaining a controlling influence in the affairs of the Government. I perceived it was important that the Republicans should make a nomination that had a fair prospect of being successful, and I felt satisfied that the result would be extremely doubtful if we should nominate any other man.

Besides, no other man was more deserving of the national compliment, considering that he had done so much to terminate the struggle for national existence, and had been the chief force in suppressing the Rebellion. His genius and courage had been chiefly instrumental in preserving to the country the blessing of a Republican form of Government. For this boon no people could ever be too profuse in the manifestations of their gratitude.

This was the patriotic feeling deep in the hearts of the people at large, but there was a secret movement engineered by "sore-head" politicians, behind whom were even more dangerous enemies, to thwart patriotic purposes. Some of these conspirators had been brooding over latent schemes of anarchy for a long period, and had been attempting to put them in organic shape before half the first term of General Grant had expired. They were hard at work training public opinion, by every means in their power, to prevent Grant's renomination.

This hostile element was sedulously hatching scandals and ventilating them in subsidized newspapers, and through various other disreputable channels.

This opposition increased in violence and intensity, and as the time approached when the country was to choose its next President, the renomination of General Grant became a matter of serious doubt, even to some of his most enthusiastic supporters. It had become a foregone conclusion that the Democrats would draw largely from the Republican ranks, and the anxiety on this point was intensified by the hostility of the *Tribune,* and the prospect of Horace Greeley's candidacy. It was absolutely necessary, therefore, that an energetic effort should be made, and the requisite steps taken to ensure General Grant's success at the Convention.

I entered into this feeling with a great deal of personal enthusiasm. What was my motive? some one reading this may ask.

Because I believed the sacredness of contracts, the stability of wealth, the success of business enterprise, and the prosperity of the whole country depended on the election of Grant for President.

If the reader wants to get at the selfish motive, as all readers do, I shall be perfectly candid with him in that respect also. Of course I knew that Wall Street business would boom in the wake of this general prosperity. That was the selfish motive, from which no man is free. Of course, I expected to share in Wall Street's consequent prosperity.

I did not want office, as several of the highest were offered me which I respectfully declined; and no office in the gift of the people would have compensated me financially; and moreover, my highest ambition has been satisfied in my own line of business.

I went to work then in the interest of Grant for the second term. I employed numerous canvassers at my own expense, to find out the minds of the representative business men on the subject, and to talk the matter up with those interested in Republican success. These men reported to me daily, and in a short time I had sounded the minds of that part of the business community who had the greatest stake in the country, and whose influence is always most felt when any important achievement is to be compassed. I sent out a petition, and obtained the names of a splendid array of merchants and business men of all shades of opinion and politics in favor of Grant. Following is the heading of the petition:

"A PUBLIC MEETING.

"To the merchants, bankers, manufacturers and other business men in favor of the re-election of General Grant:

"The undersigned, desiring publicly to express their earnest confidence in the sagacity, fidelity, energy and unfaltering patriotism, so signally displayed by Ulysses S. Grant in securing the restoration of peace at home, upholding national rights abroad, and in maintaining throughout the world the honor of the American name, do hereby invite their fellow citizens to assemble in mass meeting at the Cooper Institute, on Wednesday evening, the 17th of April, 1872."

This call was chiefly the result of the personal canvass which I had instituted a few weeks previously. I selected the names of the persons to be called on from day to day, and kept these men working the matter up, until I had secured almost all the reputable business firms in the city of New York. The following, whose original signatures I have still in my possession, were prominent in the list:

WILLIAM E. DODGE,	R. H. McCURDY,
JOHN C. GREEN,	JOSEPH SELIGMAN,
HENRY P. VAIL,	THEODORE ROOSEVELT,
GEORGE T. ADEE,	WILLIAM ORTON,
REV. SAMUEL OSGOOD,	CHARLES R. KIRKLAND,
WILLIAM H. FOGG,	PETER COOPER,
BENJAMIN B. SHERMAN,	HUGH J. HASTINGS,
ROBERT L. STEWART,	SAMUEL B. RUGGLES,
WILLIAM HENRY ANTHON,	CORTLANDT PALMER,
E. D. MORGAN,	JONATHAN EDWARDS,
JAMES BUELL,	CHARLES KNEELAND,
H. B. CLAFLIN,	S. R. COMSTOCK,
W. R. VERMILYE,	PITT COOK,
WM. M. VEHMILYE,	THOMAS J. OWEN,
CHARLES L. FROST,	OTIS D. SWAN,

NATHANIEL HAYDEN,
JESSE HOYT,
WILLIAM BARTON PEAKE,
EMIL SAUER,
JACOB OTTO,
JOSEPH STUART,
J. STUART,
THOS. GARNER ANTHONY,
FREDERICK S. WINSTON,
MORRIS FRANKLIN,
WM. C. BRYANT,

GEORGE OPDYKE,
HARPER & BROS.,
JOHN C. HAMILTON,
GEO. W. T. LORD,
SAMUEL T. SKIDMORE,
JONATHAN STURGES,
WM. H. VANDERBILT,
SHEPARD KNAPP,
WM. H. ASPINWALL,
J. S. ROCKWELL.

It is sad to reflect that these are all now numbered with the mighty dead.

These names will serve to show the great number of prominent people gradually departing from us every few years.

The name of the number of those yet alive who signed that petition is legion. In fact those who did not sign it were those whose names were not worth having. To put it mildly, I secured through their own signatures, by this method, all whose names were desirable. Our forces having been mustered in this way, the next thing was to disconcert the enemy, and inspire our own party by showing our available strength, and the power and enthusiasm behind the movement. This we proceeded to do by calling a mass meeting at the Cooper Institute for April 17, 1872.

The meeting was an immense success, in numbers, brains and respectability. The hall was crowded and the outside meeting was several times larger.

Mr. A. T. Stewart had been invited to preside. He had been a warm friend of General Grant, but had then become lukewarm and indifferent, owing to the fact that he had failed to obtain a Custom House promotion for one of his wife's near relations. I had endeavored for several days to soften Stewart's heart and get him to consent to be chairman of the meeting, but he was incorrigible. Finally, I succeeded in extorting a promise from him that if he did not vote for General Grant he would not vote against him, but beyond this it was impossible to mollify him. He was paragon of obduracy when he had once resolved upon any course. Even the recollection that he, though an alien born, had been offered the second highest position of trust in the nation, Secretary of the Treasury, which he could not accept on account of being in business, failed to draw out his feelings of gratitude sufficiently to forget the fancied slight of refusing his wife's relative promotion.

Failing to secure Mr. Stewart, I invited Mr. William E. Dodge to preside. He graciously accepted the invitation and made a very good chairman indeed.

The array of Vice-Presidents was said to excel anything that had ever appeared in a similar list of the proceedings of any meeting in this city.

I had invited Fred. Douglas and P. B. S. Pinchback, the eminent colored orators, to the meeting, but they could not attend, as they were at a New Orleans convention of their own people. Mr. Rainey, a colored gentleman, spoke most eloquently and with telling effect. This was the first time since the war that a colored orator had addressed a meeting of whites on politics in New York, or probably in the North. Prior to this the colored vote for Grant had been in doubt, as Horace Greeley, whose name was a word to conjure with among these people, had recently been swinging around the circle down South, with a view of capturing alike the vote of the colored people, who loved him, and that of the Democrats, who hated him. By a curious fatality he failed to capture either. As Blaine has truly said of him: "No other candidate could have presented such an antithesis of strength and weakness."

There had been no meeting for a long time previous to this that had been the cause of such an enthusiastic awakening in the party and among politicians generally over the whole country, as this great demonstration of the people at the Cooper Union. It crushed the aspirations of the so-called Independents and smothered the lingering hopes of the Democratic party.

In order to show the influence of this mass meeting upon the destiny of political parties in the Presidential election of

1872, it will be necessary to take a retrospect of the impression it made on parties most deeply interested in the result, and to make known their private opinions on the subject. Inside history of this nature is always instructive, and time has clothed with the attribute of public property, what at one time was a very precious political secret.

Among the striking incidents of the night of that meeting I distinctly recollect one that was truly prophetic, in regard to Senator Henry Wilson, of Massachusetts. A number of the speakers and other prominent men took supper with me at the Union League Club after the meeting, and in proposing the health of Senator Wilson, who had spoken so eloquently, I nominated him for the Vice-Presidency, and sure enough he was afterwards elected to that position.

I shall take the liberty in this place of introducing to the reader a few letters hitherto unpublished, which throw considerable light on the value of the political work done by myself and friends at that time, and how it was appreciated by those most deeply interested in its outcome.

The following from the White House shows how anxiously the current of events was being watched from that great centre:

EXECUTIVE MANSION,
WASHINGTON, D.C.,
APRIL 17, 1872.

MY DEAR CLEWS:

I have received your several interesting letters in regard to the great meeting in New York, and have shown them to the President, who read them with deep interest. I have not written any suggestions, because I know you, being on the ground, could judge so much better of the situation, and the temper of the New York people. You have done a great work, and this evening's success will, I have no doubt, be the reward of your efforts. We shall look anxiously for the reports. What you say is curious about the use of Dix's name and others. Our people are at work in Congress getting up telegrams signed by the Republican members of all the State delegations endorsing the administration of General Grant. I wish we had thought of these sooner, but still we can get them all in time, I hope. I have just come from the House, where I was looking after this matter. Wishing you every success,

I remain yours very sincerely,

HORACE PORTER,

(Sec'y to President Grant)

After the meeting the President's Secretary writes as follows:

EXECUTIVE MANSION,
WASHINGTON, D.C.,
APRIL 19, 1872.

MY DEAR CLEWS:

I have only a moment before the mail closes to say how earnestly we all congratulate you upon the great success of the meeting.

It was glorious and genuine. We read the proceedings in full in the *Times* last night. It has created a marked effect in Congress and elsewhere. Nearly every Republican in the House would have signed the congratulatory telegrams, but the movement was started so late in the day that the paper was not presented to any one.

Yours very truly,

HORACE PORTER.

The following, from the Hon. Roscoe Conkling, is a very flattering reminiscence, which I highly appreciate:

UNITED STATES SENATE CHAMBER,
WASHINGTON,
APRIL 19, 1872.

MY DEAR SIR:

As a New Yorker and a Republican, I want to thank you for the great service you have rendered our country and our cause in conceiving and carrying forward the great meeting of night before last.

The effect of it will be wholesome and widefelt; it was most timely, and its whole management was a success. Our friends all, I think, know and appreciate the large debt due you in the premises.

Noting your suggestions as to the future, I lay them to heart.

Yours sincerely,

ROSCOE CONKLING.

HENRY CLEWS, ESQ.

The New York *Herald's* special from Washington next day after the meeting said:

"The President, in conversation with Senators who called upon him this morning, expressed himself as much pleased with the demonstration in New York last night, which he regards only as evidence of the popularity of the Republican party. He has been assured, from reliable sources, that the leading Democratic merchants and bankers in different parts of the country are anxious that the Republican party may completely triumph at the coming Presidential election, as the surest way of maintaining our credit, and resisting anything like a financial crisis, which they regard as certain if their own party should succeed."

Following are the address and resolutions expressed through the representatives of a grateful people in favor of the hero who had saved the country:

Grant Meeting at Cooper Institute, March 17, 1872.—Address and Resolutions.

ADDRESS.

Hon. E. Delafield Smith, on behalf of the Committee of Arrangements, read the following address, remarking that it was prepared by one of the most eminent and substantial of our business men:

The administration of public affairs under the government of President Grant has been eminently wise, conservative and patriotic; our foreign relations have been conducted with a scrupulous respect for the rights of other nations, a jealous regard for the honor of our own; the noble aspiration with which General Grant emphasized his acceptance of his great office, "Let us have peace," has been happily realized; the Union has been completely re-established on such principles of justice and equity as to insure its perpetuity; the Constitution, with all its amendments, has been adhered to with rigid fidelity; domestic tranquility has been restored; a spirit of humanity has been infused into our Indian policy; the revenues of the country have been faithfully collected and honestly disbursed, so that, while the burdens of taxation have been materially lightened, the public debt has been largely reduced, and the national credit appreciably strengthened; all branches of industry have been stimulated to healthy activity; and throughout the length and breadth of the land security, prosperity and happiness reward the perils and sacrifices by which the rebellion was suppressed and the Union preserved.

It is an act of poetic justice that the soldier whose victories in war, and the statesman whose triumphs of peace have made the last decade the most glorious in the annals of American history, should receive an earnest of the gratitude of his countrymen by his re-election to the Presidency.

It is an auspicious circumstance that the people are evidently awakening to a higher sense of the duties and responsibilities of public officials. There is a general disposition to hold men entrusted with place and power to a strict accountability for their acts, and to demand that honesty and capability shall be the inflexible conditions of appointment to office. The recommendations of the president in favor of the principles enunciated in the report of the Civil Service Commission, were timely and apposite, and deserve universal endorsement.

Numerous investigations have been set on foot during the present session of Congress, having for their object the discovery of corruption in the public service. Disaffected Republicans and partisan Democrats have made common cause in the endeavor to elicit evidence tending to show acts of wrong doing, and to implicate the President in knowledge or toleration of such acts. As in the days of Daniel, "they sought to find occasion against him." But, like the enemies of Daniel, *"they could find none occasion nor fault, forasmuch as he was faithful, neither was there any error or fault found with him."*

The more incisive the scrutiny, the more palpable the demonstration of his purity. The cost of pursuing these investigations has exceeded the aggregate loss incurred by the Government through the dishonesty of its subordinates since the administration came into power.

A record so clear and honorable challenges the admiration, and compels the approval of citizens whose only aim is to secure a stable and beneficent Government—to preserve inviolate the faith of the nation—to give security to capital, adequate reward to labor, and equal rights to all.

With the grievances of disappointed office seekers, the masses who thrive by their own toil, cannot be expected to find time or patience to sympathize. Whether this Senator has had more or that Senator less than his share of patronage, are insignificant questions compared with the grave issues involved in a Presidential canvass. It is the constitutional prerogative of the President to make appointments to office. That he has not exercised these functions unwisely, the success of his administration abundantly proves.

Believing that General Grant's civic career fitly supplements his military greatness, that he has brought to the discharge of his duties to the State the same energy, foresight and judgment which marked his achievements in the field, and made his campaigns from Donelson to Appomatox for ever illustrious; and that he possesses and deserves the confidence of the American people, we pledge to him our united and hearty support as a candidate for re-election.

RESOLUTIONS.

Hon. E. Delafield Smith, Chairman of the Committee on Resolutions, presented the following:

First. That the merchants and mechanics, the bankers and business men of New York, represented in this meeting and in the call under which it is assembled, are satisfied with the wisdom, ability, moderation and fidelity with which the national government is administered, and in common with the bulk of our brethren throughout the Union favor the continuance of its distinguished head in the office which he holds with usefulness and honor.

Second. That the practical result of the coalition movement, if successful, would be to restore the Democratic party to power.

Third. That such a restoration, after the late glorious triumph over rebellion, would read in history like the record of a Tory resurrection at the close of our revolutionary war.

Fourth. That Republicans elected to office mainly by those who assailed the Union at the South and at the North embarrassed its defenders, would inevitably become serviceable to the powers that sustain them, like those northern presidents who were chosen by the South and did its bidding better than its own statesmen.

Fifth. That the patriotism that made Grant President of the Republic he saved, is akin to that which placed Washington at the head of the nation he created. The trust was accepted by each at a manifest sacrifice of interest and inclination, with modest misgiving as to civil experience and qualification. But having been well and wisely administered, the confidence implied in a re-election is an appropriate reward for faithful services, and accords with the broadest views of public policy.

Sixth. That against hostile criticisms and unfounded imputations, against alluring promises and prismatic theories,—we array the practical reforms constantly inaugurated and the substantial results already achieved by the present administration. The chronic vices of existing systems, unfairly paraded to its injury, have been placed in a course of amelioration or removal. The reduction of the national debt has elicited the admiration of the world. Our diplomacy has made peace the ally of national honor. And our President has been in deed as in name a kind and "great father" to the Indian tribes still lingering within our borders.

Seventh. That while honorable opposition is entitled to respect, every effort to blacken, for political purposes, the character of President Grant, is a crime against truth which vindicates him, and an insult to the American people who honor and exalt him. Pure in private as irreproachable in public life, with strong convictions yet deferential to the popular will, patient under attack, more ready to listen than to speak, with no display and no ostentation—those who know him best bear testimony to the sense, the sagacity, and the power of analysis by which his utterances are characterized and impressed.

Eighth. That in the judgment of this meeting a majority of the people of the country expect, desire, and decree the re-nomination and re-election of Ulysses S. Grant.

SPEECH OF HON. E. DELAFIELD SMITH

Mr. E. Delafield Smith said:—Fellow Citizens:—It is manifest to us all that President Grant will be re-nominated at the Convention in Philadelphia. It is equally clear that such is the wish of the American people. This is due to a confidence reposed in him by the "plain people" of the country, which no misrepresentation seems able to impair. His opponents assert that the public declarations in his favor are influenced by the office holders. But this cannot well be, for the office *holders* are always far outnumbered by the office *seekers*. With regard to executive patronage, it is as true now as when Talleyrand first said it, that every office conferred makes one ingrate and forty-nine enemies. The truth is, possession of the offices is a source, not of strength, but of actual weakness to any political party. In spite of this, General Grant is so strong and popular that a coalition is frantically sought as the only and forlorn hope of defeating him. It is thought that the Democratic masses can be carried over bodily to the few Republican seceders. But the moment the Democratic organization is relaxed, it will lose its hold upon thousands of its own members, and they may and will prefer in voting for a Republican to make the choice themselves, and they will rally in large numbers to the hero of our patriotic armies. The coalition meeting, lately held in this city, recalls the old arrangement as to colored troops, where the officers were white men, but the rank and file negroes. So here, the platform was covered with Republicans, but the audience was made up of Democrats. In thus acting with their old opponents our disaffected friends boast of their independence, and impute servility to us. But they are wrong. That man is most independent who is at once loyal to his country, true to his party, and faithful to his friends! With these brief observations, I move the adoption of the address and resolutions.

My only apology for inserting the above address and resolutions is, that I believe they constitute a valuable epitome of a very important chapter, yet to be more fully written, of the political history of the United States.

A greater criterion of the success of the meeting, however, was the editorial opinion of the *Evening Post* next day, which had been for a long time previously very bitter in its attacks upon General Grant. It said:

The meeting held last evening at the Cooper Institute was, we believe, without precedent in our political history. It was expressly called as a gathering of that branch of the Republican party which desires the nomination and re-election of President Grant. Yet, when it came together, the officers and speakers assumed that it was a mass meeting of the Republicans of New York. This is to say, according to the organizers and promoters of this gathering, the one test of Republicanism now is the political support of one man's aspirations, and that before any nomination has been made by that party. This is a singular position to receive the approval, at least, by their acquiescence, of such men as some scores of those whose names are prominent in the report of the meeting, and who, as we know, would prefer some other candidate than General Grant, if they could hope to control the Philadelphia nomination.

The power of this meeting was wholly in its organization. The list of officers chosen by it is, on the whole, the best, most reputable, and most influential commanded by any partisan meeting within our recollection. There are a few names on it which disgrace their fellows; there are many which carry no weight, but an unusually large proportion of the very long list are eminent and representative names in this city. The audience assembled was in many respects in keeping with the officers. It consisted mainly of reputable, thoughtful voters.

The good work was continued until November with the result that is now historical.

The New York *Sun* said: "We believe that Henry Clews did more, in a pecuniary way, to promote the success of Grant, than any Republican millionaire of the Union League Club."

Another mass meeting was held late in the fall. Referring to it, and other events of that period, the President's Secretary writes a few days prior to the election as follows:

WASHINGTON, D.C.,
NOV. 2, 1872.

MY DEAR CLEWS:

We are all greatly obliged for the documents and information which you have sent us during the campaign. The President says the list of vice-presidents of the last Cooper Institute meeting is the most remarkable list of prominent names he has ever seen upon one paper. It will of itself do great good.

Our news is charming from all quarters, and all our hopes will, without doubt, be fully realized on Tuesday next.

If the defeat of the enemy is overwhelming, it will be sufficient reward for all our labors.

Your very truly,
HORACE PORTER.

To show still further the interest which the leading merchants, bankers and business men of this city took in the movement to re-elect General Grant at that time, the following circular furnishes an excellent and historical record. It constitutes, in a small compass and compact form, a valuable chapter of financial history:

CIRCULAR

Of the Business Men of New York on the Financial Condition of the National Debt of the United States. Further Reduction October 1, 10,327,000 Dollars.

The undersigned, merchants, bankers and business men of New York, respectfully submit the following statements for the information of all parties interested therein:

The Republican candidate for President of the United States is Gen. Ulysses S. Grant, who was unanimously named for re-election at Philadelphia, in May last.

At the commencement of Gen. Grant's first term of office, March 4, 1869, the national debt was $2,525,000,000. On the first day of September, of the present year, there had been paid and cancelled of the principal of this debt, $348,000,000, leaving a balance of principal remaining unpaid at that date, in accordance with the official statement of the Secretary of the Treasury, the sum of $2,177,000,000.

Of this amount, $1,177,000,000 are represented in a funded debt, bearing interest in gold, while $400,000,000 remain unfunded in Treasury circulation.

Up to the close of the last session of Congress, the annual reduction of taxes, as measured by the rates of 1869, had been as follows:

Internal revenue tax, ...	$82,000,000
Income tax, (repealed,)	30,000,000
Duties on imposts, ...	58,000,000
Making a total reduction of	$170,000,000

The reduction of the yearly interest on the public debt exceeds the sum of $23,200,000, of which $21,743,000 are saved by the purchase and cancellation of the six per cent. public securities.

A careful consideration of these results of a prudent and faithful administration of the national Treasury, induces the undersigned to express the confident belief, that the general welfare of the country, the interests of its commerce and trade, and the consequent stability of its public securities, would be best promoted by the re-election of Gen. Grant to the office of President of the United States.

New York, Oct. 4, 1872.

PHELPS, DODGE & CO.,
GEORGE OPDYKE & CO.,
A. A. LOW & BROTHERS,
JOHN A. STEWART,
VERMILYE & CO.,
JAY COOKE & CO.,
JOHN STEWARD,
HARPER & BROTHERS,
JOHN TAYLOR JOHNSTON,
FREDERICK S. WINSTON,
PEAKE, OPDYCKE & CO.,
MORRIS FRANKLIN,
SCHULTZ, SOUTHWICK & CO.,
J. S. ROCKWELL & CO.,
ROBERT H. McCURDY,
WILLIAM M. VERMILYE,
R. W. HOWES,
WILLIAM CULLEN BRYANT,
C. L. TIFFANY.
SPOFFORD BROS. & CO.,
JOHN C. GREEN,
H. B. CLAFLIN & CO.,
MOSES TAYLOR,
WM. H. ASPINWALL,
ROBERT LENOX KENNEDY,
S. B. CHITTENDEN & CO.,
JAMES G. KING'S SONS,
HENRY E. PIERREPONT,
EMIL SAUER,
BOOTH & EDGAR,

WILLIAM ORTON,
ISAAC E. BAILEY,
SHEPHERD KNAPP,
WILLIAMS & GUION,
EDWARDS PIERREPONT,
RUSSELL SAGE,
PETER COOPER,
ANTHONY, HALL & CO.,
GARNER & CO.,
J. S. T. STRANAHAN,
E. D. MORGAN & CO.,
DREXEL, MORGAN & CO.,
AUGUSTINE SMITH,
WM. H. VANDERBILT,
MORTON, BLISS & CO.,
JONATHAN STURGES,
J. & W. SELIGMAN & CO.,
J. & J. STUART & CO.,
JOHN A. PARKER,
BENJAMIN B. SHERMAN,
JOHN D. JONES,
J. D. VERMILYE,
SAMUEL T. SKIDMORE,
HENRY F. VAIL,
LLOYD ASPINWALL,
JACOB A. OTTO,
GEORGE W.T. LORD,
SAMUEL McLEAN & CO.,
HENRY CLEWS & CO.

CHAPTER 18

THE TWEED RING, AND THE COMMITTEE OF SEVENTY

THE RING MAKES ITSELF USEFUL IN SPECULATIVE DEALS. — HOW TWEED AND HIS "HEELERS" MANIPULATED THE MONEY MARKET. — THE RING CONSPIRES TO ORGANIZE A PANIC FOR POLITICAL PURPOSES. — THE PLOT TO GAIN A DEMOCRATIC VICTORY DEFEATED AND A PANIC AVERTED THROUGH PRESIDENT GRANT AND SECRETARY BOUTWELL, WHO WERE APPRISED OF THE DANGER BY WALL STREET MEN. — HOW THE COMMITTEE OF "SEVENTY" ORIGINATED. — THE TAXPAYERS TERRORIZED BY BOSS TWEED AND HIS MINIONS. — HOW "SLIPPERY DICK" GOT HIMSELF WHITEWASHED. — OFFERING THE OFFICE OF CITY CHAMBERLAIN AS A BRIBE TO COMPROMISE MATTERS. — HOW THE HON. SAMUEL JONES TILDEN, AS COUNSEL TO THE COMMITTEE, OBTAINED HIS GREAT START IN LIFE.

THE Tweed Ring had considerable experience in and out of Wall Street for several years during the municipal reign of the famous Boss. I have made some reference to their attempts to manipulate the market through tight money, in my biographical sketch of that Wall Street celebrity Henry N. Smith.

The Ring was often highly subservient in assisting certain operators in speculative deals in stocks, one notable instance being in Hannibal & St. Jo. shares, which resulted in a terrible loss to Boss Tweed & Co. This stock became quite neglected for a long period afterwards, and so remained until the famous "corner" was engineered many years after by John R. Duff, of Boston, through his New York broker, Wm. J. Hutchinson, and by which poor Duff was almost, if not entirely, ruined. It is only justice to Mr. Duff, in this connection, to state that he was not to blame, as an exhaustive investigation by the Governing Committee of the Stock Exchange showed that his trouble chiefly arose through flagrant dishonesty and betrayal of trust on the part of his agent, in whom he reposed too much confidence.

Boss Tweed and his special retainers sometimes made Wall Street instrumental in engineering national and State political movements. About the time of an election, if their opponents happened to be in power, the Ring would produce a stringency in the money market, by calling in simultaneously all the city money, which was usually on temporary loans in the Street.

This the Ring managers would accomplish through some of the banks which were the depositories of the city funds, and were under their control.

By this means they worked up a feeling of antagonism against the Republicans who were in office, by throwing the blame on them, and thus rendering them odious in the eyes of those who had lost money in speculation. The blame was not unnaturally fastened on the party in power, and most men, when they lose money, are credulous enough to believe anything that seems to account for the manner in which the loss has been sustained. It seems to have a soothing effect upon their minds, and furnishes them with a tangible object upon which they may wreak their vengeance and feel satisfied. There is nothing so irritating to the disappointed speculator as the harassing doubt of where to fix the blame.

The Tweed Ring supplied this long-felt want, and filled the aching void in the heart of the man who happened to on the wrong side of the market. When speculators frequently had their margins "wiped out," and were almost beggared of everything except their votes, they found that consolation which Wall Street refused them, in the sympathetic hearts of Tweed's "heelers," who pointed to the poor office-holders of the Republican party, representing them as the sole possessors of Pandora's box, which contained all evils that flesh is heir to.

So these financial disasters were brought about by the Tweed party for the purpose of getting their friends into office, which always paid tribute to the Boss when he was instrumental in elevating a person to a fat position. He, himself, did not want any better office than receiver general of this tribute.

In those days a Presidential election was largely influenced by the way Pennsylvania went, so that it had grown into a political maxim, "As goes the Keystone State so goes the Union."

In the Spring of 1872, the year in which General Grant was the Republican candidate for the second term, when it was decided that Horace Greeley should be the Democratic candidate, great efforts were made to produce a panic in Wall Street. It was arranged by the Tweed party that the panic should take place simultaneously with the State election in Pennsylvania, so as to illustrate the evil results of Republican rule, and turn the influence in favor of Mr. Greeley's election.

I received intimation of this politico-speculative conspiracy, and communicated my information to Senator Conkling, who was stopping at the Fifth Avenue Hotel at the time. I told him that the Democrats were working up a panic to help to defeat General Grant. He said it was the first he had heard of it, but it was so like a move that Tweed and his party would make, that he felt there was just cause for alarm about it, and he requested me to go and see Governor Morgan, and also George Opdyke, on the subject. I found that the Governor was at a church meeting, and I left my card telling him to call upon me at the rooms of the Republican National Committee, as I wanted to see him upon important business. I left word for Mr. Opdyke to call also.

The Governor soon presented himself at the Committee rooms, and I divulged to him my information and suspicions.

He did not exhibit so much interest as I imagined the importance of the case demanded, and he appeared to doubt the correctness of the report of the political intentions of the Tweed Ring, or rather he seemed to imagine that the Ring was hardly capable of a move that invoked such subtlety and depth of design. Therein he greatly underestimated the power, resources and statecraft of Peter "Brains" Sweeney. The Governor was of a phlegmatic temperament, and it was difficult to convince him of anything that was not very clearly demonstrable. I told him that my information was of such a positive and reliable nature that I knew I was right, and that if there should be a panic in Wall Street I had serious apprehensions that it would prove disastrous to the Republicans in the national campaign.

Governor Morgan appointed a meeting for the next day to discuss the matter more fully and obtain further light upon the subject. I took with me to see the Governor, whom I had now convinced of the reality of the political plot, Mr. George Opdyke and Mr. H. B. Claflin.

In the meantime the Governor had seen Travers, who, being an inveterate bear on the situation, had an inkling of what was in progress to break the market. The Governor had satisfied himself that my representations were correct, and that trouble was really brewing. He then entered with earnestness into the question of the best policy to be adopted to obstruct the schemes, and frustrate the purposes of the Democratic party.

I then suggested, that as the matter did not admit of delay, it was highly essential that some one, or more, of us should go to Washington to see General Grant. The Governor said he could not go. I could not go, and neither could Mr. Claflin. So Mr. Opdyke, who was very ready in such matters, consented to bear the important message in person, provided we all agreed to back him up by writing a strong letter to the President, setting forth the facts in relation to the emergency. This we did, and Mr. Opdyke left at once for Washington. This was on Friday evening, and he transacted his business with more than ordinary despatch, and returned on Sunday morning. He sent for me, and told me that he had explained the matter to the President, who felt exceedingly grateful for the warning which he and our letters had conveyed, and that he had forthwith consulted with the Secretary of the Treasury, and it was resolved to order the purchase, on Monday, of ten millions of bonds, and the sale of ten millions of gold, for the purpose of averting, in advance, any financial disturbance that might arise through the project of the Tweed Ring to create an artificial stringency in the money market.

Then I saw that these men who were engaged in the conspiracy to create a panic, and benefit themselves both politically and financially by its results, were a deeply designing lot, and that under the law, gold could be bid up, the highest bidders obtaining it, having the option of either paying by depositing their money in payment for it in the National depositories, which were the Fourth National Bank and the Bank of Commerce, or else depositing it in the Sub-Treasury. If deposited in the latter it would be locked up, and the effect intended by the Treasury, to make money easy, would be neutralized, in so far as the influence of the money as a circulating medium was concerned.

In order, therefore, to provide for that probable contingency, my firm subscribed for the whole ten millions of gold, the names being the clerks of my office. We were awarded eight millions, and we paid the money into the Bank of Commerce, and the Fourth National Bank, through which it was brought into circulation.

Thus ten millions of greenbacks and also ten millions of gold came fresh from the Sub-Treasury into circulation immediately, promptly anticipating and defeating the machinations of the Ring.

The Tweed Ring being "all broke up" on this deal, the effect was magical on the market. The plans of the conspirators had been entirely upset, and the Pennsylvania election took place a few days afterward with an overwhelming majority for the Republicans.

Had the panic, which was projected by the Ring, taken place, the result might have been otherwise, and the re-election of Grant thus jeopardized.

After this triumph over Tweed and his gang, I set my wits to work to plan their overthrow. I saw that their power was entirely money power, obtained by official position through official theft. I was satisfied that these patriots who had put their hands up to the elbows in the City Treasury of New York were bent upon buying, stealing or otherwise obtaining their way to the National Treasury at Washington.

They had hoped to do there on a large scale what they had accomplished on a smaller scale in the city of New York, where they were becoming restive under their limited resources.

It was with the view of suppressing the dangerous aspirations of this band of political marauders that I originated the well known Vigilance Committee of Seventy, and at the first meeting to organize this committee I nominated sixty-five of its members.

The committee was thus backed at the start by so many prominent citizens as to make it at once a power in the community.

Then for the first time in many years the citizens of New York were emboldened to become outspoken on the subject of political plunder and tyranny, and against the officials who had ruled the city with a rod of iron.

For a long time previous to this there had been grave suspicions that robbery on a large scale was being perpetrated, but no one dared to give utterance to the fact except with bated breath and in half smothered whispers. No one, with the possible exception of a few who were not taxpayers, had the temerity to open his mouth to say a word against the desperate men who controlled the destinies of the city, through fear that on the event of any remark reaching the ears of the Boss or his minions, the property of the person thus offending should be marked up to an artificial value and his taxes accordingly increased. This was one of the most effective methods pursued by the Ring to choke off unfriendly criticism by the rich men of the city. In this way the power of some of the most influential citizens became paralyzed, being held in complete subjection under the terrorism of this subtle system of blackmailing.

The power the Ring possessed of covering up the rascality of its members and bamboozling the public is hardly conceivable at this day except by those who had experience of it at the time. As an instance of this I may state that some time prior to the appointment of the Committee of Seventy certain accusations were ventilated against Richard Connolly, the City Comptroller. He put on a bold front, and insisted upon an investigation of his department by a committee of leading and prominent citizens. He named his committee, who were Moses Taylor, Marshall Roberts and John Jacob Astor. These were men against whom no person could have any objection. They were wealthy and independent citizens, and it might have been difficult at the time to have selected any other three who commanded greater confidence in the community. The investigation, through the unblushing effrontery and audaciousness of Connolly and his "pals," resulted in an acquittal of Mr. Connolly, which gave him a new lease of political life, and rendered it more dangerous than ever for any one to utter a word of hostile criticism against his methods of managing the city finances.

Results showed, when the Ring was exposed, that Connolly had made the very best use of this investigation in appropriating additional sums out of the City Treasury.

The Ring was now supreme in city affairs, and the city was under a reign of terror. This state of things existed until the summer of 1872, when the Committee of Seventy got into harness, after which the despotic thieves that had ruled the roast so long, were driven from power one after another in rapid succession, and scattered to the four corners of the globe.

The task of ousting this brazen band of plunderers, root and branch, was attended with considerable difficulty, as their resources were so numerous and powerful. When they were no longer able to exercise their arbitrary power they stooped to every form of cajolery and bribery in order to adhere to the remnant of their official authority. As an illustration of this, I may state that at the beginning of my efforts in connection with the Committee of Seventy I was waited upon by a member of the Ring and asked if I would not accept the position of City Chamberlain. I said: "That is a matter, of course, which I could not decide upon at once, as there is no vacancy at present. It will be time enough for me to consider the matter when a vacancy occurs, and then when the position is offered to me."

This answer carried with it an intimation, which I had intended, with a view of drawing out some of the internal methods of procedure in such cases, that I would probably accept the position and help to smooth over impending revelations. I thought that the end which the Committee had in view justified this means of mildly extorting an important secret in methods of Ring management, that was calculated to aid us in the work of municipal reform.

Next day I was again waited upon by one of Tweed's most trusty friends, who graciously informed me that the City Chamberlain had resigned, and that there was a vacancy which I could fill to the entire satisfaction of the then appointing power. I desired him to convey my feelings of deep gratitude to the powers that were then on the point of being dethroned, and to say that I very respectfully declined the flattering offer. I said that I had thought earnestly over the matter since the previous day, and as I was a member of the Committee of Seventy, which was a reforming organization, I felt that I could not conscientiously accept the position.

It was necessary that the office should be filled immediately, and it was next offered to Mr. F. A. Palmer, President of the Broadway Bank, which had been one of the Ring's depositories of the city funds.

Soon after this the majority of the city officials had resigned and taken their flight to parts unknown. They were scattered broadcast over the world. Some had gone to Europe, some to Cuba, and others to that favorite and paradisiacal colony of defaulters, the New Dominion, leaving the Committee of Seventy, as a reform and revolutionary body, in complete control of the city.

Tweed remained, but was not quite so audacious in putting his pet interrogative, "What are you going to do about it?" He seemed to be convinced that the Committee of Seventy meant business. Mayor Oakey Hall also remained, and facetiously protested that as far as he was concerned everything was "O.K."

The Hon. Samuel J. Tilden began to loom into prominence about this time. Through the influence of William F. Havemeyer, he was chosen one of the three legal advisers of the committee. Abraham R. Lawrence and Wm. H. Peckham were the other two. Mr. Tilden was quick to seize this opportunity of sudden prominence to bring himself to the front and pose as a great reformer. Had it not been for the Committee of Seventy, I believe it is very doubtful whether this great reformer would ever have been known as such, and it is also exceedingly problematical whether he would have ever got the chance of being counted out, or attempting through the magic of his occult cyphers, to count anybody else out of the Presidency of the United States.

CHAPTER 19

DANIEL DREW

DREW, LIKE VANDERBILT, AN EXAMPLE OF GREAT SUCCESS WITHOUT EDUCATION.—CONTROLLED MORE READY CASH THAN ANY MAN IN AMERICA.—DREW GOES DOWN AS GOULD RISES.—"HIS TOUCH IS DEATH."—PREDICTION OF DREW'S FALL.—HIS THIRTEEN MILLIONS VANISH.—HOW HE CAUGHT THE OPERATORS IN "OSHKOSH" BY THE HANDKERCHIEF TRICK.—THE BEGINNING OF "UNCLE DANIEL'S" TROUBLES.—THE CONVERTIBLE BOND TRICK.—THE "CORNER" OF 1866.—MILLIONS LOST AND WON IN A DAY.—INTERESTING ANECDOTE OF THE YOUTH WHO SPECULATED OUTSIDE THE POOL, AND WAS FED BY DREW'S BROKERS.

O NE of the most singular and eventful careers in Wall Street was that of Daniel Drew, familiarly called "Uncle Daniel." This man affords another remarkable instance of the possibility of attaining great success by stubbornly following up one idea, and one line of thought and purpose. His life also shows that education is not necessary to success in the acquisition of money, but, as I have attempted to show in another chapter, may be a great hindrance.

This fact is abundantly illustrated in the lives of both Drew and Vanderbilt. In fact, everybody who knew these two men were of the opinion that with a fair or liberal education they would never have cut a prominent figure as financiers. It is also questionable whether either of them, with all their ability in other respects, would have been capable, with their pecu-

liar predilections for other pursuits, of receiving a common
school or college education. They, probably, had not the
capacity for that kind of acquisition. Perhaps it might have
been impossible for any teacher to make Drew pronounce the
word shares otherwise than "sheers," or convince Vanderbilt
that the part of a locomotive in which the steam is generated
should not be spelt phonetically, "boylar."

It is more than probable that professors in grammar would
have found it a hopeless task to convince the Commodore
that there was anything wrong in the expression, "Never tell
nobody what yer goin' to do, till you do it," or Drew that it
was improper to say to his broker, "Gimme them sheers,"
when he desired his stocks reduced to possession. Both men
seemed to think with the character in Shakespeare, that reading and writing, like their other attributes, came by nature.
They evidently thought that their abilities for financiering
emanated solely from that source, and results largely bore
them out in that interpretation. Both had supreme contempt
for persons of less ability than themselves in the speculative
arena, yet they were terribly jealous of rivals who essayed to
compete with them in their own peculiar methods of making
money. Cunning and shrewdness were the leading characteristics of Drew. Though illiterate himself, he, however, showed
that he appreciated education in others, by erecting and
endowing a seminary in his native place.

Some people who were not inclined to give Drew any
credit for the finer and more generous and genial feelings of
man's nature, said that his motive for this endowment was
merely popularity, and a morbid desire, like that of Vanderbilt,
to perpetuate his name.

Another motive, however, less ennobling to man's nature,
seemed to be the true one. He saw that the religious element
in society was then influential, and that many religious people
of his acquaintance were in good circumstances, and he
sought to ingratiate himself with them in order to make use
of them in his speculations.

This appears clearly to have been at the bottom of his precious gift of a seminary to his native county. It was a curious

illustration of retributive justice, if I am right about his motive, that he was obliged to default in the payment of that gift, with the exception of the interest.

Daniel Drew, at one time, could command more ready cash at short notice than any man in Wall Street, or probably than any man in America. His wealth was estimated at thirteen million dollars. He made a very large part of this out of his speculations in Erie stock, of which corporation he was then managing director and treasurer. Being thus on the inside, he was enabled to leave everybody else on the outside in the ups and downs of the market, which he himself generally engineered.

The Street was frequently amazed by fluctuations of 20 or 30 per cent. in Erie stock, sometimes in the course of a day or two, through the able manipulation of Mr. Drew.

It was a sorry day for Drew when Jay Gould took his place in the control of Erie, and it was equally disastrous for the Erie property.

From this period Gould began to grow rapidly to the full stature of speculative manhood, while Drew moved as quickly in a downward direction, until he found himself again at the lowest rung of the financial ladder. It was no wonder that he said of Gould, "his touch is death."

Drew's losses followed one another in quick succession, until his thirteen millions had melted away like snow off a ditch, and eventually he died in debt and broken hearted. His last days stand out as a sad, but eloquent warning to the avaricious. And this reminds me of a festive event, the chief incidents of which, I think, are worthy of reproduction.

I remember being at a dinner party ostensibly given to the old gentleman when in the very zenith of his financial fame and prosperity. It was a kind of mutual admiration society, Drew being the king-pin of the social coterie. On account of his thirteen millions he was the centre of cringing admiration, and was by a number of the assemblage almost deified.

As is usual on such occasions, speechmaking was in order, the oratorical talent being called out by the toasts as they went the round of the board.

When it came my turn to speak, I followed suit, to some extent, in picking up the thread of the general glorification extended to the honored guest, to whom I paid marked deference.

"We are honored," I said, "on this festive occasion, by a gentleman of vast wealth, one who can control more ready money than any man in America, and be it said to his honor, it has all been of his own creation. He is a true representative of American thrift and enterprise. His money and his genial disposition together combined make all men his friends, and I know of only one antagonistic spirit to the continued growth of this already marvellous fortune; but that one, in all probability, may yet work his ruin. I refer to our honored guest, Mr. Drew, and his one enemy which I have in mind is 'Avarice.'"

In five years from that memorable dinner Daniel Drew was a ruined man, and his thirteen millions had vanished like the baseless fabric of a vision, leaving nothing but the miserable wreck of an avaricious spirit behind.

The manner in which Drew was supposed to make religion the handmaid to speculation was satirically touched in the following verses published in the New York *Tribune* about fifteen years ago:

He was a long, lank countryman,
   And he stoppeth one of two.
"I'm not acquaint in these yeere parts,
   An' I'm a lookin' fur Dan'l Drew."

"I'm a stranger in the vineyard,
   An' my callin' I pursoo
At the institoot at Madison,
   That was built by Dan'l Drew."

"I'm a stranger in the vineyard,
   An' my 'arthly wants are few;
But I want sum p'ints on them yer sheares
   An' I'm a lookin' fur Dan'l Drew."

Again I saw that laborer,
   Corner of Wall and New;

lie was looking for a ferry boat,
    And not for Daniel Drew.

Upon his back he bore a sack,
    Inscribed "Preferred Q. U."
Some Canton scrip was in his grip,
    A little Wabash, too.

At the ferry gate I saw him late,
    With his white hat askew,
Paying his fare with a registered share
    Of that "Preferred Q. U."

And these words came back from the "Hackensack"
    "Ef yew want ter gamble a few,
Jest git in yer paw at a game o' draw,
    But don't take a 'and with Drew."

Mr. Drew was negligent in his attire, even to the verge of slovenliness. He dressed like a drover, having originally been employed in that capacity. By the way, the significant term of "watering stock" originated in the practice of Uncle Daniel giving his cattle salt in order to create a thirst in them that would cause them to imbibe large quantities of water, and thus appear bigger and fatter when brought to market. Until he met with Gould and Fisk, it was difficult for anybody to get the best of him in a deal.

He was wonderfully prolific in resources for the purpose of getting advantage of those who attempted to overreach him.

A good story, illustrative of this trait in his speculative character, is told of the time that he was so severely squeezed in Northwestern stock. He was greatly grieved at his ill luck, while the brokers and operators who had been prosperous at his expense were highly elated. They considered it a great thing to have caught the wily old Daniel napping. He was accordingly made the victim of much ribaldry and jesting for several days in Wall Street. Some of the young men carried the joke so far as to meet him and laugh significantly and irritatingly in his face. He seemed to take it all in good part, for he had a happy flow of animal spirits, but he had a terrible rod in pickle for these young men who were

making him an object of ridicule. He watched for his opportunity, and one evening as several of them were enjoying
themselves in an uptown club, Uncle Daniel walked in, *sans
ceremonie*. He appeared to be looking after some man, and
though invited to remain, seemed to be in a great hurry to
get away, and was apparently excited and warm. He seemed
to have something important on hand. He drew a big white
handkerchief out of his pocket a few times and wiped the
perspiration from his heated brow. When he was about to
depart there came out of his pocket with the handkerchief a
small slip of white paper which floated around apparently
unseen by him, and alighted at the feet of one of the
bystanders, who quickly set his foot upon it. When Mr. Drew
made his exit the white scrap of paper was instantly scanned.
It contained these ominous words in his own handwriting:
"Buy me all the Oshkosh stock you can at any price you can
get it below par."

Here was a speculative revelation for the boys, for everybody believed at the time that Oshkosh had already gone too
high, and the point had been circulated to sell it "short." The
mysterious words written on this erratic slip of paper, however, convinced these operators that there must be a new
deal to give Oshkosh another "kiting." There was no time to
be lost in taking advantage of the unexpected and highly
valuable information. They formed a pool to purchase 30,000
shares the next day. They bought the stock according to prearrangement, and a new broker of Daniel Drew's was the
man who sold it to them. They only discovered how badly
they themselves had been sold by Mr. Drew's handkerchief
trick when Oshkosh began to decline at the rate of a dozen
points a day, and Uncle Daniel soon raked in from the jokers
and their friends more than he had lost in Northwest.

Mr. Drew first entered the Board of Directors in Erie
about the year 1852, and remained there until he was
squeezed out, and almost ruined, in 1868. He held the office
of treasurer to the corporation.

Drew was born in the town of Carmel, Putnam county, in
the year 1797, and was three years younger than Vanderbilt.
As I have intimated above, in early life he drove cattle from

his native town to New York. He afterward became proprietor of the Bull's Head tavern in this city.

He never changed his style of dress from that to which he was accustomed to wear when he was a drover, and when he was worth thirteen millions, instead of sporting a gold beaded cane, he went around Wall Street with the handle of an old broken umbrella in his hand. While treasurer of Erie he used every opportunity to manipulate the stock to his own advantage, irrespective of the rights or interests of any other person. He was the leading bear of the market for many years. Like Vanderbilt, he was interested to some extent in steamboats, but he made Erie stock the great medium of acquiring his vast wealth. He got the name of the speculative director, and at the outbreak of what was known as the Erie war he was supposed to be almost financially impregnable.

The "corner" of 1866 was the beginning of Uncle Daniel's troubles. Up to that period all had gone merry as a marriage bell with him, and he was piling up the millions at a rate which no other financier or speculator had ever dared to imitate. Erie stock was selling at 95 in the spring of that year. The company was badly off for money. It made application to its treasurer for the needed relief. He was ready to serve it in that way at all times, but he wanted security for the loan. There were then 28,000 shares of unissued Erie stock. The company also claimed the right to raise money by the issue of bonds convertible into stock at the option of the holder.

This was an old trick in the management of Erie matters. It had saved Jacob Little on one occasion, as I have mentioned in a former chapter, during the earlier history of speculation in Wall Street. It was, therefore, not original with the Drew management of Erie, as some people have supposed.

The 28,000 shares of unissued stock then, and three millions of dollars of convertible bonds, were placed in the hands of Mr. Drew as security, and he advanced the loan of $3^{1}/_{2}$ million dollars to relieve the pressing necessities of the corporation.

When Drew found himself thus fortified with the convertible bonds, he laid another trap for the boys in the Street. Erie had been rapidly absorbed for some time, and was very

strong at 95 with anxious purchasers. The stock was, therefore, becoming very scarce. Mr. Drew had a large number of
contracts to fill, and operators were wondering where he
would get the stock to settle. Many of them were laughing in
their sleeves at his impending embarrassment, as they had
done on a former occasion, and were in ecstacies of delight
at the idea of the terrific "squeeze" which the old man was
about to experience. When he seemed on the very horns of
this dilemma, upon which the rampant bulls thought they
would successfully impale him, he converted his three million
bonds into an equivalent amount of stock, threw 58,000
shares on the market, met all his contracts, and fed the voracious bulls with all they wanted.

Hungry as the Street had been for Erie, this was an over-
dose that it was utterly incapable of digesting. The bulls were
paralyzed, and before they could rally their broken ranks
from the demoralizing effects of this unexpected sortie from
the stronghold of Erie, the stock had declined from 95 to 50,
wiping out the broadest margins and putting the whole army
of bulls, reserve forces and all, to utter rout.

Millions were lost and won in a day in this deal.

This was regarded as a grand *coup d'etat,* and one of Drew's
most brilliant exploits in operating. In fact, at the time, it
seemed to throw every prior operation of this nature totally
in the shade, and the other leading operators of the street
were blue with envy, green with jealousy, and raging mad
over their losses and the way they had been entrapped and
almost ruined by the deeply-laid scheme of the Erie treasurer.
Drew was despised, feared and revered on account of this
unparalleled achievement. He then essayed to rest on his oars
for a short time, but his period of repose was but short-lived.

There was a little side-show in connection with the maturing of the operations in the pool just referred to, which is so
characteristic of Daniel's methods that it is worth relating.
There was a young man in the Erie pool, but not in the
wheel-within-the-wheel in that sacred circle, who imagined
that the purpose of the pool was to put Erie stock up, and
accordingly he borrowed money from Uncle Daniel, his credit

being good and having money in the pool funds, to purchase Erie. The accommodating treasurer not only lent him the money, but his private brokers sold the young man the Erie stock desired. He was duly fed from day to day with the quantity which his speculative appetite craved. After the slump just referred to, this unsophisticated youth and some other members of the pool among his friends, went to Uncle Daniel and requested him, as manager of the pool, according to the programme supposed to have been agreed upon, to put Erie again on the line of advance, in order that the young man and his friends might get in and out again, so as to cover their recent losses.

Mr. Drew, however, coolly informed them that the pool had no Erie stock and did not want any, and was not prepared to trade in that security any more at that time.

"I sold all our Erie at a profit," said Uncle Daniel, "and am now ready to divide the money."

So this youthful member had the felicity of discovering that while he was speculating on his own account for a rise, Uncle Daniel was looking after his interests in another direction, and had realized at the most opportune moment.

Thus this amateur operator, whom Uncle Daniel had amused, without letting him into the secret, in the way described, got nearly enough of money back to pay the loss he had sustained experimenting outside the pool on his own account, and upon his own independent but fallacious judgment.

If he had not speculated outside, he would have had very handsome profits from the pool, but he would not have obtained the useful experience which was connected with his losses, and the independent attitude he was ambitious to assume in speculations.

CHAPTER 20

INTERESTING EPISODES IN DREW'S LIFE

INCIDENTS IN THE EARLY LIFE OF DREW, AND HOW HE BEGAN TO MAKE MONEY.—HE BORROWS MONEY FROM HENRY ASTOR, BUYS CATTLE IN OHIO AND DRIVES THEM OVER THE ALLEGHANY MOUNTAINS UNDER GREAT HARDSHIP AND SUFFERING.—HIS GREAT CAREER AS A STEAMBOAT MAN, AND HIS OPPOSITION TO VANDERBILT.— HIS MARRIAGE AND FAMILY.—HE BUILDS AND ENDOWS RELIGIOUS AND EDUCATIONAL INSTITUTIONS.—RETURNS TO HIS OLD HOME AFTER HIS SPECULATIVE FALL, BUT CAN FIND NO REST SO FAR AWAY FROM WALL STREET.—HIS HOPES, THROUGH WM. H. VANDERBILT, OF ANOTHER START IN LIFE.—HIS BANKRUPTCY, LIABILITIES AND WARDROBE.—HIS SUDDEN BUT PEACEFUL END.— CHARACTERISTIC STORIES OF HIS ECCENTRICITIES.

I had intended at first to give only a sketch of the salient points in the speculative career of Drew, but, on reflection, I find that the lives of great men all remind us that people want to know a great deal of minutiae concerning men who have made their mark in this world. Our enterprising newspapers are encouraging this laudable curiosity more and more every day. So in the case of Drew, I must try to furnish answers to questions that may be asked about him in order that popular expectation may not be disappointed. I shall endeavor to anticipate what the reader may naturally want to know when he comes to the end of Drew's great speculative ventures. One of these questions will probably be, what kind of a boy was Daniel Drew, and how did he begin to make money?

It goes without saying that Drew was the most unique figure that Wall Street has ever seen, and a characteristic specimen of one kind of American thrift, enterprise and speculation. Every side of his many-sided and peculiar character, therefore, is of interest as the representative of a class to the reader who sets his heart on making money, and the majority of readers have this weakness. He is of special interest to all speculators not only in this country, but throughout the civilized world. These facts constitute my apology for dwelling so long and minutely on his characteristics. I have an idea that his life and adventures will be read with deep interest many years hence, and help to prolong the existence and reputation of this book. They will also assist to immortalize the man who was one of the most wonderful products of American civilization, and who could hardly have been evolved from any other soil or clime. Such prodigies of success cause the members of the older social fabrics to stare with astonishment at the stupendous capabilities of our great country.

There is nothing interests people so much as the start in life, probably because there are so few who consider themselves able to get a good start. So far as I can learn, in the case of Daniel Drew, the boy was father to the man. He worked on a farm, going to school at intervals, where he was unable to learn anything, except that he obtained a notion of the current theological ideas of that day, until he was fifteen years of age, when his father died, leaving him, a younger brother and their mother to shift for themselves on a poor, small farm. His father was of English and his mother of Scotch descent.

In his seventeenth year young Drew enlisted as a substitute in the State Militia, which had then been called into service on account of the second war with England.

The regiment was placed at Fort Gansevoort, on the Hudson, opposite New York. Hostilities ceased between this country and England a few months after his enlistment, and the regiment was mustered out. Daniel returned home. His mother had taken charge of his substitute money, which probably did not exceed a hundred dollars, the amount with which his great rival, Commodore Vanderbilt commenced life, and which he earned from his mother by ploughing and planting a field.

"I want my substitute money," said Drew to his mother, one day shortly after his return. "What are you going to do with it?" queried the old woman, for being of Scotch descent, she was quite as thrifty in looking after the pennies as her American contemporary, old Mrs. Vanderbilt. They both had the gripping sense by nature, and to this transmissible quality may probably be attributed, in a large degree, the financial success of both of their sons.

"I am going to buy cattle, and sell them in New York," replied Daniel.

"Are you sure you will not lose money by it?" rejoined his mother.

"I am sure I will make money," he said.

He started to purchase cattle in the country and to sell them in New York. His profits were at first very small, especially as his capital was so limited. He soon discovered that if he could purchase his cattle in Ohio he would be able to increase his profits largely, and he applied to Henry Astor, a butcher in Fulton Market, and a brother of the great millionaire, John Jacob Astor, for a loan to speculate in Ohio cattle. Astor accommodated him, though he at first thought he was running a considerable risk. He was mistaken, for Drew made money and soon established his credit on a solid basis. He bought cattle throughout Ohio, and drove them over the Alleghany mountains. He is said to have been the first drover who attempted this daring experiment. It required sixty days then to make the journey. He suffered great hardship and privation, and would sometimes lose a third part of a drove of 600 or 1,000 in crossing the mountains. Yet, as cattle were very cheap in Ohio, his profits were still very large.

One terrible night, in a terrific thunderstorm, the tree under which he took shelter was shattered to splinters, his horse was killed under him, and he himself was struck sense-less for a time. But no hardship or privation could deter him in the pursuit of making money. He afterwards extended his operations to Kentucky and Illinois.

In 1829 Drew opened a cattle yard at Twenty-fourth street and Third avenue and ran the Bull's Head Tavern. He went into the steamboat business in 1834. Vanderbilt had then been seventeen years in the business. *Westchester* and *Emerald* were the names of his first two boats, and they ran between New York and Albany, in opposition to the Vanderbilt Line. Drew reduced the fare from three dollars to one, and attempted to freeze out Vanderbilt. The war of rates became so fierce that people were carried 100 miles between these two cities for a shilling. Drew added the *Knickerbocker,* the *Oregon, George Law, Isaac Newton* and the *New World* to his river fleet, and became quite a formidable competitor of the Commodore.

In 1840 Isaac Newton organized the People's Line on the Hudson, of which Drew became the largest stockholder. The boats *St. John, Dean Richmond* and *Drew* were built. The *Isaac Newton* was burned and the *New World* was sunk.

When the Hudson River Railroad was opened, in 1852, Drew refused to sell out his stock. "You can regulate your fares as you choose," he said to the President of the Railroad Company, "but the only way you can regulate my steamboat fares is to buy the People's Line, and this I don't believe you have money enough to do." The railroad line merely stimu-lated traffic, as the elevated railroads have done in our day, and Drew was only a gainer instead of a loser by the appar-ent competition. He also controlled the Stonington Line for twenty years.

Drew made his debut in Wall Street in 1844, just thirteen years prior to my first appearance on the boards of this finan-cial theatre, and he was quite a war horse in speculation when I entered the arena. He formed a partnership with his son-in-law, a Mr. Kelly, and Nelson Taylor, as stock brokers and bankers. Their business was large and their credit good. The firm continued for ten years, until it was dissolved by the death of his partners. Drew then became one of the most daring and successful operators in Wall Street.

Drew was married at the age of 25 to Roxana Mead, a farmer's daughter, by whom he was the father of three children, William H., Josephine, who died in infancy, and Catharine, who was married to the Rev. W. I. Clapp, a Baptist clergyman, who died and left his widow in good circumstances. So there were very little grounds for "Uncle Daniel's" dread that he should probably die in miserable destitution, as it seems that his two surviving children were very kind to him. His wife died in 1876.

Drew was a member of St. Paul's Methodist Episcopal Church of New York for several years. He contributed large sums to various religious and educational institutions, but like Wilkins Micawber, he usually paid the money in notes, which appeared in the schedule of his liabilities when he had lost his large fortune, and had become bankrupt. He founded the Drew Seminary at Carmel, for young ladies, at a cost of $250,000. He built the Drew Theological Seminary, at Madison, New Jersey, also at a cost of $250,000, and endowed it with a similar amount. He only paid the interest on the latter. He increased the endowment fund of the Wesleyan University, at Middletown, Conn., and the Concord Biblical Institute. He added $100,000 to the endowment fund of Wesley University, but only paid the interest on that also. These appear in the schedule, in the list of his unsecured claims. He owned several large grazing farms in Putnam county, but they were heavily mortgaged.

Drew had some intention of returning to his old home after the bankruptcy proceedings in 1876, to spend the remainder of his days there among his grandchildren. This desire shows that there was something inherently soft and good, after all, in his avaricious nature, and reminds me of the touching lines of Cowper on the same subject:

> "Be it a weakness, it deserves some praise,
> We love the play place of our early days,
> The scene is touching, and the heart is stone,
> That feels not at the sight, and feels at none."

He went out to Putnam county in 1876, when he was sick, but he was soon glad to get back to the city. He said: "I was

troubled with visitors, some of 'em well on to 100 years old.
Some of them said I bought cattle from them when I was
young, on credit, and they wanted their bills. I kept no
books, and how was I to know I owed 'em for them critters?
It was dull outen thar," he continued, "and yer never can tell
till the next day how 'sheers' is gone."

So Uncle Daniel came back and stopped at the Hoffman
House, where he could have ready access to the ticker, and
kept constantly posted on the price of stocks. His principal
broker was Mr. David Groesbeck.

The city still seemed to have certain fascinations for him
that the country was unable to afford. He often spoke regret-
fully, in his latter days, of being too old to retrieve his fortune. He said he longed for rest. Nothing seemed to weigh
more heavily upon his mind than his inability to carry out
the plans connected with his religious endowments, and he
grieved deeply that he had not the means to return to Wall
Street that he might have another lucky turn that would
enable him to fulfil these religious obligations according to
the original intention.

In the bankruptcy schedule his personal property is item-
ized as follows: watch and chain, $150; sealskin coat, $150;
wearing apparel, $100; Bible, hymn books, &c., $130.

Although he was economic in his domestic expenses, he
entertained friends liberally, and his house at the southwest
corner of Seventeenth street and Union Square was always
open to Methodist ministers, free of charge, from all quarters
of the world.

Some years prior to his death Mr. Drew gave the following
candid, succinct and pathetic account of his embarrassment to
a journalist who interviewed him:

"I had been wonderfully blest," said Uncle Daniel, "in
money making. I got to be a millionaire before I knowed it
hardly. I was always pretty lucky till lately. I didn't think I
could ever lose money extensively. I was ambitious of making
a great fortune, like Vanderbilt, and I tried every way I knew,
but got caught at last. Besides that, I liked the excitement of
making money, and giving it away, and am glad of it. So
much has been saved anyhow. Wall Street was a great place

for making money, and I could not give up the business when I ought to have done so. Now, I see very clearly what I ought to have done. I ought to have left the Street eight or ten years ago, and paid up what I owed. When I gave $100,000 to this institution and that, I ought to have paid the money, and I ought to have provided better for my children, by giving them enough to make them rich for life. Instead of that I gave my notes, and only paid the interest on 'em, thinking I could do better with the principal myself. One of the hardest things I have had to bear has been the fact that I could not continue to pay the interest on the notes I gave to the schools and churches."

"I gave my son the old homestead," continued Mr. Drew, "and some other small property up in Putnam, where we came from, which I hope will make him independent at least. My daughter married a rich man, and when he died, leaving considerable property to five children, I was made executor of the will. For so great a trust as their property I was obliged to give security, which I did by making over to them this house where we are, and the North River steamboats, the *Drew, Dean Richmond, St. John* and *Chauncey Vibbard.* This security makes them whole, and I thank God that breach of trust is not on my conscience. Their mother, my daughter, is, of course, well provided for, through her children and deceased husband. My son's principal business is now in connection with the management of the boats, by which he is getting on very well."

After Drew's great disaster in the Erie "corner," he became a special partner in the firm of Kenyon, Cox & Co., and when this house failed, after the panic of 1873, Uncle Daniel was compelled to make an assignment. He had been for years on the losing side, having dropped between two and three millions in the Erie "corner" through the machinations of Gould and Fisk. Horace F. Clark and Gould had also cornered him in Northwestern to the tune of $750,000. After the panic he had made an assignment to Wm. L. Scott, of Erie, Pa., but was not legally declared a bankrupt until 1876. His liabilities were $1,074,131.83, and his assets were estimated at $746,499.46.

Like Vanderbilt, Drew kept his accounts in his head, and considered the whole paraphernalia of book-keeping a confounded fraud.

His failure, which at one time would have induced a panic, did not cause a ripple on the surface of speculation. After his discharge in the bankruptcy proceedings, he appeared to pluck up fresh courage, and said, "The boys think I'm played out, but I'll give 'em many a turn and twist yet." He was interested in Toledo & Wabash, Canada Southern, Quicksilver Mining Company and Canton (Land) Company stock.

Wm. H. Vanderbilt, who had received his early financial training as a clerk in Drew's office, still retained a kindly feeling for his old employer, and sometimes gave him "pints" as Drew called them, on which he made a little turn. It was said that Mr. Vanderbilt had intended to give him another start in life about the time Drew passed suddenly over to the majority. He died at 10.45 P. M., September 18, 1879, at the residence of his son, Wm. H. Drew, No. 3 East Forty-second street.

His death came without any prior warning. He had been apparently in his usual health during the day, and had dined with Mr. Darius Lawrence, of Lawrence Brothers, brokers in Broad street, at the Grand Union Hotel, at six o'clock in the evening. After dinner he returned to the house of his son. About nine o'clock he complained of feeling ill, but refused to permit anybody to sit up with him, saying he would call Mr. Lawrence, who slept in an adjacent room, if he should feel worse. About ten o'clock he went into Mr. Lawrence's apartments and said he felt much worse. Dr. Woodman, his family physician, was immediately summoned, but before his arrival Mr. Drew had expired. The cause of his death was apoplexy.

Among the numerous stories related of Uncle Daniel's eccentricities, one is noteworthy in relation to his habit of getting in a mellow mood when prayer failed to soothe him, and covering himself up in bed after any speculative disappointment. He was found in this condition one day at the Sturtevant House, the year in which he died, by two Wall Street acquaintances who called upon him, and were conversant with his peculiar habits. He had all the windows closed, so that the atmosphere in the room was stifling, and was enveloped in several pairs of double blankets. His friends called for a bottle of champagne, of which he refused to partake. When this was drunk they called for another, and left it with him, believing that when he was left alone he might be inclined to imbibe without any feeling of embarrassment.

Another story is related characteristic of Uncle Daniel's methods of making the best use of a secret, and any confidence that a person might foolishly repose in him, in a speculative deal. During the war a young man known as California Parker, who had more money than brains, began to buy Erie in the vicinity of par, and put it up to 120. He went to Drew and told him that he would let him in at fifteen per cent. below the market, if he would only aid him with a little money to carry the price higher. Mr. Drew blandly appeared to entertain the young millionaire's proposition favorably and Parker, on the strength of that, continued the struggle until he had almost reached the end of his California gold. The next morning when he met Drew the latter told him that he was unable to raise the money, and appeared to be grieved at his disappointment. In the meantime Drew had instructed his brokers to sell Erie "short," knowing that Parker was unable to absorb any more of that precious paper, Erie stock. The market went down, Drew made a "scoop," and Mr. Parker retired from Wall Street a ruined, but a wiser man.

In personal appearance Drew was tall, strong and sinewy, and in his latter days his face was seamed with deep lines, indicating intense thought and worry. He had restless twinkling eyes, with a steady cat-like tread in his gait. His general demeanor was bland, good-natured and insinuating, with affected but well dissembled humility, which was highly calculated to disarm any resentment, and enable him to move smoothly in society among all shades and conditions of men. He has often been mistaken for a country deacon.

So, now, having revived and collated the chief incidents in the chequered career of this great speculative celebrity, I close this sketch with the ardent hope that he may have found that peace beyond the tomb which the ordinary speculator in Wall Street can seldom or never hope to achieve on this side of "that beautiful shore."

CHAPTER 21

WILLIAM H. VANDERBILT

A BUILDER INSTEAD OF A DESTROYER OF PUBLIC
VALUES. — HIS RESPECT FOR PUBLIC OPINION ON THE
SUBJECT OF MONOPOLIES. — HIS FIRST EXPERIENCE IN
RAILROAD MANAGEMENT. — HOW HE IMPROVED THE
HARLEM RAILROAD PROPERTY. — HIS GREAT EXECUTIVE
POWER MANIFESTED IN EVERY STAGE OF ADVANCE
UNTIL HE BECOMES PRESIDENT OF THE VANDERBILT
CONSOLIDATED SYSTEM. — AN INDEFATIGABLE WORKER. —
HIS HABIT OF SCRUTINIZING EVERY DETAIL. — HIS
PRUDENT ACTION IN THE GREAT STRIKE OF 1877, AND ITS
GOOD RESULTS. — SETTLED ALL MISUNDERSTANDINGS BY
PEACE AND ARBITRATION. — MAKES PRINCELY PRESENTS TO
HIS SISTERS. — THE SINGULAR GRATITUDE OF A BROTHER-
IN-LAW. — HOW HE COMPROMISES BY A GIFT OF A MILLION
WITH YOUNG CORNEEL. — GLADSTONE'S IDEA OF THE
VANDERBILT FORTUNE. — INTERVIEW OF CHAUNCEY M.
DEPEW WITH THE G. O. M. ON THE SUBJECT. — THE GREAT
VANDERBILT MANSION AND THE CELEBRATED BALL. — THE
IMMENSE PICTURE GALLERY. — MR. VANDERBILT VISITS
SOME OF THE FAMOUS ARTISTS. — HIS LOVE OF FAST
HORSES. — A PATRON OF PUBLIC INSTITUTIONS. — HIS GIFT
TO THE WAITER STUDENTS. — WHILE SENSITIVE TO PUBLIC
OPINION, HAS NO FEAR OF THREATS OR BLACKMAILERS. —
"THE PUBLIC BE DAMNED." — EXPLANATION OF THE RASH

EXPRESSION. — THE PURCHASE OF "NICKEL PLATE." — HIS
DECLINING HEALTH AND LAST DAYS — HIS WILL AND WISE
METHOD OF DISTRIBUTING 200 MILLIONS. — EFFECTS OF
THIS COLOSSAL FORTUNE ON PUBLIC SENTIMENT.

IN treating of the family in the order of descent, I shall now
make a brief survey of the life of William H. Vanderbilt,
especially in its relation to Wall Street affairs and the management of his great railroad system, the two being closely
connected. William H. Vanderbilt was not much of a speculator in the Wall Street sense of the term. He was more of an
investor than a speculator, and his investments had always a
healthy effect upon the market. Unlike Woerishoffer and others of that ilk, he built up instead of pulling down values,
but was at the same time careful to avoid the error of inflation. He paid due deference to public opinion also, in striving
to allay its alarm in regard to the dangerous overgrowth of
monopolies. A grand illustration of this was seen in the sale
of the large block of New York Central. His first experience
in railroad matters was in connection with the Staten Island
Railroad, thirteen miles in length. The road had been mis-
managed and was deeply in debt, and became bankrupt. As
he and his father had considerable interest in the road
William H. was appointed receiver. It seems this was done
secretly at the suggestion of the Commodore, who wanted to
discover by this experiment if his son had any capacity for
railroad management. The receivership of the Staten Island
Road was crowned with signal success. In two years the
entire indebtedness of the road was paid, and the stock,
which had been worthless, rose to 173. William H. Vanderbilt
was then elected President of the road. It was at this time, it
is said, that the Commodore began to correct his judgment
regarding the "executive ability of William H.," and the latter
relaxed no effort to please his exacting father in everything,
taking all his abuse without complaint or anger. After the

Commodore secured control of the Harlem road, which was his first great railroad venture, he made William H. Vice-President. As a co-worker with his father the latter further demonstrated his capacity for railroad management, and Harlem stock, which had been down to nearly nothing, in a few years became one of the most valuable railroad properties in the country. So, it is a fact, although not generally known, that William H. Vanderbilt had proved himself to be a competent railroad manager before his eminent father had fairly begun that line of business. It was almost entirely owing to his individual exertions and sound judgment that, in a few years, the Harlem road was double-tracked, and such other improvements made as sent the stock from 8 or 9 to above par. The Commodore was so highly pleased and agreeably surprised with his son's management of the Harlem road that he made him Vice-President of the Hudson River Railroad also, and at a later date associated him in the same capacity with the management of the important consolidation of New York Central & Hudson River. The great executive power of William H. was manifested in every successive movement which his father directed, and unparalleled prosperity was the result in every instance. After William H. was fully installed in the Vice-Presidency of the consolidated system of the Vanderbilt railroads he became an indefatigable worker, taxing his physical and mental powers to their utmost capacity, and it was doubtless this habit of hard work, persisted in for many years, that resulted in so sudden and comparatively premature death for a member of a family famous for its longevity throughout several generations. He insisted on making himself familiar with the smallest details of every department, and examined everything personally. He carefully scrutinized every bill, check and voucher connected with the financial department of the immense railroad system, and inspected every engine belonging to the numerous trains of the roads. In addition to this general supervision of everything that pertained to the railroads, he was in the habit of going over a large amount of correspondence which the majority of other men not possessing the hundredth part of his wealth hand over to their clerks, and he answered a great number of letters with his own hand which financiers of comparatively moderate means are in the habit of dictating to their stenographers. When his father died, at the age of 82, in January, 1887, William H. Vanderbilt, then 56 years of age, found himself the happy possessor of a fortune variously estimated at from 75 to 90 million dollars. The remainder of the Commodore's bequests amounted to 15 millions.

After the death of his father the executive powers of Wm. H. Vanderbilt, in the management of the vast railroad interests bequeathed to him, were called into active play. The great strike of 1877 among the railroad employes threatened to paralyze business all over the country, and came pretty near causing a social revolution. In this emergency a cool head and prudent judgment were valuable attributes to a railroad manager. Mr. Vanderbilt proved that he possessed both in more than an ordinary degree. Just prior to encountering the knotty problem of the strike, he had been highly instrumental in bringing about suspension of hostilities in the freight war, and the course which he advised led to an arrangement that produced harmony among the trunk lines for a considerable period. As a consequence of the rate war the railroad companies were obliged to cut down the wages of their employes, and this was the chief element in causing the strike. There were 12,000 men in the employ of the New York Central and Harlem. Their wages had been reduced ten per cent. and they had threatened to annihilate the Grand Central Depot. Instead of making application to have the militia called out, as had been done in Pennsylvania, Mr. Vanderbilt—although a man possessed of far more than ordinary courage—with keen foresight proposed a kindly compromise with his employes. He telegraphed from Saratoga to his head officials an order to distribute $100,000 among his striking employes and promising them a restoration of the ten per cent. reduction as soon as business improved to a point justifying such an advance. This prompt and prudent action had the desired effect, and the consequence was that while there was a small insurrection in Pittsburgh, and bloody war to the knife, at great cost to Allegheny County, calmness reigned in the prominent railroad circles of New York, and the taxpayers escaped the burden that might otherwise have been put upon their shoulders, and the demoralizing effects of violence and bloodshed were prevented. Over 11,500 of the 12,000 men returned to work, thus showing their gratitude to Mr. Vanderbilt and faith in his promise, which was afterwards duly fulfilled. The policy of Wm. H., in the management of his great railroad system, unlike that of his father, was entirely pacific in its character. He was disposed to settle all misunderstandings by reason and arbitration, and had no inclination for fighting and conquest, after the manner of the Commodore. Although a very close calculator in business matters, a habit to which he adhered even to the precision of striking out superfluous items which should not have been charged in his lunch bill, Mr. Vanderbilt was in many respects generous to a fault. He compromised the suit with his brother, "Young Corneel," allowing him the interest on $1,000,000, whereas his father had only left him the interest on $200,000, with a forfeiture clause in the event of "Corneel" contesting the will. Wm. H. also made a present of $500,000 in United States bonds to each of his sisters, out of his own private fortune. A good story is related in connection with the distribution of this handsome gift. Mr. Vanderbilt, it is said, went around one evening in his carriage, taking the bonds with him and dispensing them to the fortunate recipients from his own hands. One of his brothers-in-law having observed by the evening papers that the bond market had declined a point or two on that day, said, "William, these bonds fall $150 short of the $500,000, according to the closing prices of this day's market." "All right," replied Mr. Vanderbilt, with assumed gravity, "I will give you a check for the balance," and he wrote and signed it on the spot. It is related that another brother-in-law followed him to the door, and said, "If there is to be anything more in this line I hope we shall not be forgotten." It is said that these remarkable instances of ingratitude, instead of irritating him, as they would have in the case of an ordinary individual, only served to arouse his risible faculties and that he regarded the exhibitions of human weakness as a good joke.

One of the greatest works of Mr. Vanderbilt's life was the building of the beautiful palace on Fifth avenue, between Fifty-first and Fifty-second streets, which he adorned extensively with paintings selected from the great masterpieces of the most renowned artists of the world.

One reason assigned for his disinclination to speculate was that he regarded the property left by his father in the light of a sacred trust, and while he considered it a filial duty to look after its increase and accumulation, he was careful not to do anything that might risk its dissipation.

Mr. Chauncey Depew, who succeeded to the presidency of the New York Central & Hudson River Railroad Company, was upon one occasion, while visiting in London, a guest at a dinner given to the Hon. Wm. E. Gladstone, then Premier of England, and was honored by a seat on the left of Mr. Gladstone, with whom he discussed the differences between American and English railroad and financial management. In the course of conversation Mr. Gladstone said, "I understand you have a man in your country who is worth £20,000,000 or $100,000,000, and it is all in property which he can convert at will into cash. The Government ought to seize his property and take it away from him, as it is too dangerous a power for any one man to have. Supposing he should convert his property into money and lock it up, it would make a panic in America which would extend to this country and every other part of the world, and be a great injury to a large number of innocent people." Mr. Depew admitted that the gentleman referred to—who was Mr. Vanderbilt—had fully the amount of money named and more, and in his usual suave and conclusive way, replied,

"But you have, Mr. Gladstone, a man in England who has equally as large a fortune."

Mr. Gladstone said, "I suppose you mean the Duke of Westminster. The Duke of Westminster's property is not as large as that. I know all about his property and have kept pace with it for many years past. The Duke's property is worth about £10,000,000 or $50,000,000, but it is not in securities which can be turned into ready cash and thereby absorb the current money of the country, so that he can make any dangerous use of it, for it is merely an hereditary right, the enjoyment of it that he possesses. It is inalienable, and it is so with all great fortunes in this country, and thus, I think, we are better protected here in England than you are in America." "Ah, but like you in England, we in America do not consider a fortune dangerous," was the ready response.

The best proof of Wm. H. Vanderbilt's great ability as a financier is the marvellous increase in the value of the estate which he inherited from his father during the seven years which he had the use and control of it, and in which he did more than treble the value at which it was estimated on the death of the Commodore.

The weakest financial operation on his part, known to the public, was the purchase of the Nickel Plate Road, as regards the time of the transaction, in which he was rather premature. It is now positively known that if he had waited about a month longer the road would have gone into bankruptcy and have fallen into his lap on his own terms. In that case the West Shore would have followed suit.

In such an event I believe Mr. Vanderbilt would have been saved an immense amount of money, remorse and mental strain, which, no doubt, aggravated the malady which was the cause of his sudden death. He realized his error when it was too late, and it was a source of great mental anxiety to him in his latter days. He was very sensitive, and nothing afforded him more gratification than a clean and successful transaction, which drew forth public approval, and in the purchase of Nickel Plate he was caught napping. It was a mistake for which the Commodore, had he been alive, could never have forgiven him.

The syndicate that built the road had solely for their object to land it upon either Gould or Vanderbilt, and it was upon its last legs at the time it made the transfer to Mr. Vanderbilt. The syndicate laid a trap for him. It had been coquetting with Mr. Gould in reference to the purchase, and had made it to appear, through the press and other channels of plausible rumors, that he had an eye upon the road. Mr. Gould had occasion to go West about this time and the syndicate invited him to make his homeward trip over the road, taking particular pains that all these rumors and reports should reach the ears of Mr. Vanderbilt, who was impressed with the idea that Mr. Gould's trip was one of inspection, with the intention of buying the road if he did not anticipate him. This was just what the syndicate desired, and the successful consummation of their financial plot.

The purchase was made solely in the interest of Lake Shore, as it was a parallel road, and the road was afterwards turned over to the Lake Shore Company.

The conception of the scheme was to build the road at a nominal price and sell it to Mr. Vanderbilt as high as possible, and this was duly accomplished. I am quite satisfied that if this road had not been sold at this particular time it would then have gone into the hands of a receiver, while a number of the syndicate, who had built the road, would have failed, and a general crash would have ensued. This Mr. Vanderbilt's purchase averted for the time, and served to prolong the period of its coming until May, 1884.

For a few years prior to his death Mr. Vanderbilt was in a weak condition. This cause of mental annoyance came upon him at a time when he was not robust enough to bear it and had not sufficient strength to throw it off. He had been seized with a slight paralytic stroke, the only visible effect of which was a twitching of the lower lip. Shortly after this he lost the entire sight of one eye, about a year before his death. This was not generally known to the public, however, and it was the principal cause of his giving up his favorite pastime of driving, which was one of his greatest pleasures and the chief source of mental diversion from the heavy weight of his worldly cares and responsibilities.

The day after Mr. Vanderbilt's death I sent the following circular to my customers:

As Mr. Wm. H. Vanderbilt was a very important factor in Wall Street business, I feel it incumbent upon me to issue a letter to my friends and clients on the subject of his decease, especially as the loss to the Street is a most important one, and certainly will be felt for some time to come. Mr. Vanderbilt undoubtedly, at the time of his death, was the largest holder of American securities in the world, and had innumerable followers, who were also vast holders of similar properties as those he controlled, who acted more or less in concert with him, and who were at his beck and call. When he told them to buy or sell they would do so. Those parties have now lost a valuable friend and counsellor, and a leader in whom they believed implicitly. In such quarters, for some time to come at least, more or less of a dazed condition will prevail, precisely the same as would exist in an army in the event of the general in command having been killed. Mr. Vanderbilt was a bolder and larger operator than his father ever dared to be, as he spread out over more interests. The market has lost an able leader, who was usually a builder-up of the interests of the entire country, and unlike many other large operators, who, at times, are on that side, but quite as frequently on the wrecking side. It will be a long while before so conspicuous and valiant a leader as Mr. Wm. H. Vanderbilt will be forthcoming, and the market will, for a protracted period, have cause to mourn its great loss. It is, indeed, fortunate that Mr. Vanderbilt lived long enough to see the completion of the consolidation of the West Shore and New York Central roads; since both roads are under the able direction of Mr. Depew, they are now secure from future harm; but the same cannot be said of the South Pennsylvania enterprise, as negotiations remain in connection therewith unfinished, which will suffer by Mr. Vanderbilt's death, and it will be found difficult, I fear, for any other man to knit the discordant elements together that at present exist in that quarter. There is enough in this for some ground of apprehension, and this matter may, therefore, disturb the harmony of the great trunk lines, as this speck of trouble may yet prove a cancer in the body of the stock market. As it is capable of infusing its poison elsewhere, beyond where it is at present located, it is certain that there will be required skillful surgery to prevent inoculation therefrom.

The stock market started off to-day as if held by concerted action, and the appearances indicating that such attitude might prevail to bridge over the Vanderbilt shock. While prices had a moderate break, it was scarcely adequate as a fitting tribute of respect to Mr. Vanderbilt's memory, as the great General of the Army of Finance of this country. It was unmistakable, however, that the large selling was mostly of long stock, coming from numerous frightened holders who were shaken out, and it was very evident that the bears were more conspicuous as buyers than as sellers, to cover their short sales made during the previous several days. I do not think that the market had, considering the power it has lost in the death of Mr. Vanderbilt, as much of a break as should have occurred; still, it must be remembered, that the dealings have been so enormous during the past month, which represent the immense number of operators now interested in the market, that it has taken from it a character which previously existed as a one man market, and therefore it is owing to this fact that the removal of any one man, or a half dozen of them, by death or otherwise, could not bring about, at the present time, any very wide and lasting disaster to Wall Street. This market, as I have repeatedly stated, can fairly be now considered the market for the world, and beyond the permanent reach of any one man doing it any lasting harm. As Mr. Vanderbilt invented pegging stocks, and stood his ground when taken better than any one that will survive him in that plan of strategic movement, he will, in that particular alone, be sorrowfully missed. I am of the opinion, now that Mr. Vanderbilt is no more, that Mr. Gould's plan of leaving the Street will undergo a modification, at least by his remaining for some time longer at the helm. This will prove, in such an event, an important factor in the future, especially as the bulls of the Street have for at least a year past recognized Mr. Gould in the light of a benefactor. To them he has proved a brave and able leader, and the field is now clear for him to become commander-in-chief of all the forces, without any one to dispute his right thereto. This should be enough to fire his ambition and keep him in our midst, and probably will.

Among the popular and erroneous impressions entertained regarding Wm. H. Vanderbilt, the one that he was no judge of pictures seemed to have taken deep root in the public mind, except among the few who knew him intimately, and the celebrated artists whom he visited and from whom he purchased many of the works of art which adorn his great gallery in Fifth avenue, now in charge of his youngest son, George. That Mr. Vanderbilt had an intimate knowledge and correct appreciation of true art has been amply proved by the highest authority. I am well aware that some years ago this statement would have been ridiculed by the majority of the newspapers; but Mr. Vanderbilt never bought a picture that he did not fully understand in his own simple, unaffected method of judgment. He may not have been capable of the highest flights of fancy, necessary to follow the poetic imagination of the artist to its extreme height, but he was equal to the task of grasping all the material essentials from a common-sense point of view.

So far from making any pretence of being a lover of art, he was in the habit of saying, when a handsome painting was shown him, "It may be very fine, but until I can appreciate its beauty I shall not buy it."

Apropos of his modesty and judgment, in regard to the fidelity to nature of a picture, a circumstance is related of his visit to Boucheron, a French picture dealer, where he wanted to see a painting by Troyon, with the object of buying it. A yoke of oxen turning from the plough to leave the field is the subject. Experts in art had taken exception to the manner in which the cattle left the field. When Mr. Vanderbilt's opinion was asked, he said, "I don't know as much about the quality of the picture as I do about the truth of the actions of the cattle. I have seen them act like that hundreds of times." The artists present submitted to his judgment, as he knew more about the oxen than they did. When in France he visited the celebrated Rosa Bonheur, at Fontainebleau, who was about his own age, and gave her an order for two pictures, which she painted to his entire satisfaction. He had his portrait painted by the celebrated Meissonier, to whom he paid nearly $200,000 for seven pictures. He purchased in Germany this artist's masterpiece, "The Information—General Desaix and the Captured Peasant," for $40,000, giving Meissonier, who had not seen it for many years, a great surprise, and filling the heart of the enthusiastic artist with unbounded gratitude for rescuing the picture from Germany and bringing it to America.

Mr. Vanderbilt's taste for music, especially operatic music, was refined, and he had a keen sense of the humorous.

Neither Mr. Vanderbilt nor any of his family ever displayed any anxiety to hobnob with those people who are known as the leaders of society, although possessed of more wealth than the greatest of them. The celebrated fancy dress ball, given by Mrs. Wm. K. Vanderbilt, at the suggestion of Lady Mandeville, in March, 1883, seemed to have the effect of levelling up among the social ranks of upper-tendom, and placing the Vanderbilts at the top of the heap, in what is recognized as good society in New York. So far as cost, richness of costume and newspaper celebrity were concerned, that ball had, perhaps, no equal in history. It may not have been quite so expensive as the feast of Alexander the Great at Babylon, some of the entertainments of Cleopatra to Augustus and Mark Antony, or a few of the magnificent banquets of Louis XIV, but when viewed from every essential standpoint, and taking into account our advanced civilization, I have no hesitation in saying that the Vanderbilt ball was superior to any of those grand historic displays of festivity and amusement referred to, and more especially as the pleasure was not cloyed with any excesses like those prevalent with the ancient nobility of the old world and frequently exhibited among the modern "salt of the earth" in the mother country. The ball had the effect of drawing the Astors and the Vanderbilts into social union. The *entente cordiale* was brought about in this way, as the story goes:

Several weeks before the ball Miss Carrie Astor, daughter of Mrs. William Astor, organized a fancy dress quadrille, to be danced at the ball. Mrs. Vanderbilt, it seems, heard of this and said, in the hearing of some friends, that she was sorry Miss Astor was putting herself to so much trouble, as she could not invite her to the ball, for the reason that Mrs. Astor had never called on her. This was carried to Mrs. Astor, who immediately unbent her stateliness, called on Mrs. Vanderbilt, and in a very ladylike manner made the *amende honorable* for her former neglect. So the Astors were cordially invited to the ball, where Miss Astor presented a superb appearance with her well trained quadrille.

All Mr. Vanderbilt's other attachments vanished in presence of his love for his horses. When any company, of which he formed a part, began to talk horse his tongue was immediately loosened and he became eloquent. Although generally a man of few words and diffident as a talker, he could throw the eloquence of Chauncey M. Depew in the shade when the subject was horse. He not alone admired the speed of his horses; he seemed possessed of the fondness of an Arabian for them, and, like old John Harper of Kentucky, would probably have slept with them only though fear of the newspapers criticising his eccentricity. It was he who introduced the custom of fast driving teams, first with Small Hopes, purchased by his father, and Lady Mac, purchased by himself. With this team, in a top road wagon, he made the then remarkable time of 2.23^1/$_4$.

A host of rivals immediately sprang up, of whom Mr. Frank Work was the most formidable. Mr. Vanderbilt procured faster teams, and with Aldine and Early Rose, under the spur of competition, reduced the time to 2.16^1/$_2$. Mr. Work, however, was a daring and persistent rival, and soon beat this record, although only by a fraction of a minute, which in trotting or racing counts just the same as if it were an hour. Mr. Vanderbilt then purchased the famous Maud S. in Kentucky for $21,000, and with her and Aldine made the mile in Fleetwood Park in June, 1883, in 2.15 1/2.

He afterwards reduced this time to 2.08 3/4, leaving Mr. Work and all other rivals hopelessly in the distance. Eventually he sold Maud S. to Mr. Robert Bonner for the comparatively small amount of $40,000, on condition that she should never be trotted for money. Other men would have given $100,000 for her without this condition.

On the 12th of August, this year, Murphy, the famous jockey, drove Maud S. in single harness, at Tarrytown, a mile in 2.10 1/2, and declared he did not push her. He said he was confident he could make her do the mile in 2.06 or 2.07 if Mr. Bonner would permit him, thus smashing all trotting records.

It has been said by experts in driving that Mr. Vanderbilt was the best double-team driver in America, either amateur or professional.

Mr. Vanderbilt's bequests were liberal and numerous. He added $300,000 to the million which his father gave, through the wife of the Commodore and Dr. Deems, to the Nashville University. He gave half a million to the College of Physicians and Surgeons, and his sister, Mrs. Sloane, added a quarter of a million to this generous donation. It cost him over $100,000 to remove Cleopatra's Needle from Egypt to Central Park. He offered to cancel the $150,000 check which he gave to General Grant to relieve him from the Ward-Fish embarrassment, and his munificent gift to the waiter students in the White Mountains will long be remembered.

Although Mr. Vanderbilt was very courageous, as was proved by the fact that no matter how many threatening letters he may have received—and their name was legion—from cranks, socialists and others, he never made any change in his programme or his routine of business for the day, and

never absented himself from the place where he was
expected at any particular hour on account of such letters.
Yet he was peculiarly sensitive to public opinion, and sought
in various ways to correct its hasty judgment in regard to
himself and his enormous wealth.

It was this sensitive feeling, together with his profound
respect for popular opinion against monopolies, which induced
him to sell a controlling interest, 300,000 shares out of
400,000, at from 120 to 130, ten points below the market
price, of New York Central stock in 1879 to a syndicate, the
chief members of which were Drexel, Morgan & Co., Morton,
Bliss & Co., August Belmont & Co., Winslow, Lanier & Co.,
L. Von Hoffman & Co., Cyrus W. Field, Edwin D. Morgan,
Russell Sage, Jay Gould and J. S. Morgan & Co. of London.
The amount paid for the stock was $35,000,000. As the
syndicate largely represented the Wabash system, the stock
of that property, as well as New York Central, had an important advance.

The reasons assigned for this stupendous and unprecedented stock transaction are briefly condensed by Mr.
Chauncey M. Depew as follows: "Mr. Vanderbilt, because of
assaults made upon him in the Legislature and in the newspapers, came to the conclusion that it was a mistake for one
individual to own a controlling interest in a great corporation
like the New York Central, and also a mistake to have so
many eggs in one basket, and he thought it would be better
for himself and better for the company if the ownership were
distributed as widely as possible. The syndicate afterwards
sold it, and the stock became one of the most widely-distrib-
uted of the dividend-paying American securities. There are
now about 14,000 stockholders. At the time he sold there
were only 3,000."

That hasty expression, "The public be damned," which Mr.
Vanderbilt used in an interview with a reporter for a Chicago
newspaper, has received wide circulation, various comment
and hostile criticism. Although the expression is literally correct, the public at first, and many of them to this day,

received a wrong impression in regard to the spirit in which it was applied. It was represented as if Mr. Vanderbilt was a tyrannical monopolist, who defied public opinion. A true and simple relation of the interview is a sufficient answer to this. The subject was the fast mail train to Chicago. Mr. Vanderbilt was thinking of taking this train off, because it did not pay, and did not appear to him therefore to be a necessity, and he did not propose to run trains as a philanthropist. As part of the interview which relates to this point has become so widely historic, I think it will bear reproduction here, literally:

"Why are you going to stop this fast mail train?" asked the reporter.

"Because it doesn't pay," replied Mr. Vanderbilt; "I can't run a train as far as this permanently at a loss."

"But the public find it very convenient and useful. You ought to accommodate them," rejoined the reporter.

"The public," said Mr. Vanderbilt. "How do you know, or how can I know that they want it? If they want it why don't they patronize it and make it pay? That's the only test I have as to whether a thing is wanted or not. Does it pay? If it doesn't pay I suppose it isn't wanted."

"Are you working," persisted the reporter, "for the public or for your stockholders?"

"The public be damned!" exclaimed Mr. Vanderbilt, "I am working for my stockholders. If the public want the train why don't they support it?"

This, I think, was a very proper answer from a business standpoint, and the expression, when placed in its real connection in the interview, does not imply any slur upon the public. It simply intimates that he was urging a thing on the public which it did not want and practically refused. The "cuss" word might have been left out, but the crushing reply to the reporter would not have been so emphatic, and that obtrusive representative of public opinion might have gone away unsquelched. As it was, however, he and his editor exhibited considerable ingenuity in making the best misrepresentation possible out of the words of Mr.

Vanderbilt, thus giving them a thousand times wider circulation than the journal in which they were first printed, and affording that paper a big advertisement. This is the correct account of that world-renowned expression, "The public be damned!"

The mausoleum at New Dorp, Staten Island, is another outcome of the genius of Wm. H. Vanderbilt. Mr. Richard M. Hunt was the architect. Pursuant to the instructions of Mr. Vanderbilt, it was built without any fancy work, but at the same time on such a grand and substantial scale that it is said there is nothing among the tombs of either European or Oriental royalty to excel it, in solidity of structure and grandeur of design. It is forty feet in height, sixty in breadth and about 150 in depth. It is situated on an eminence commanding the largest prospect of the bay, and one of the finest views all around in the State of New York. The tomb and the twenty-one acres of land, upon the highest part of which it stands, cost nearly half a million dollars, and when the grounds are finished, in the style intended, beautiful roads and walks made, flower gardens planted with the requisite adornments, the entire expense of the mausoleum and its surroundings will not fall far short of a million dollars.

The precautions taken by the family against resurrectionists is one of the best that has ever been adopted. There is a guard at the tomb night and day. Each of these must put on record his vigilance every fifteen minutes by winding up a clock, which is sent to the office at the Grand Central Depot every morning.

In May, 1883, Mr. Vanderbilt, finding that his railroad duties were too heavy for him, resigned the presidencies of his roads and took a trip to Europe. James H. Butter was elected President of the Central, and on his death was succeeded by Chauncey M. Depew, the present President, who so ably fills that office. About a year before his death Mr. Vanderbilt gave unmistakable notice of his approaching dissolution when he stopped driving his fast teams, and went out riding with some other person to drive for him. He must have keenly felt his growing weakness when he was obliged to resign the reins which he so fondly desired to hold, and which he had handled with such inimitable skill. The death of Mr. Vanderbilt was a great surprise, especially to Wall Street, as very few brokers were aware even of his failing health. On the 8th day of December, 1885, he arose early, apparently no worse in health than he had been for a year previous. He went to the studio of J. Q. A. Ward and gave that artist a sitting for the bronze bust ordered by the Trustees of the College of Physicians and Surgeons. Mr. Depew called upon him at one o'clock, but finding that Mr. Robert Garrett, President of the Baltimore & Ohio Railroad Company, had also called to see Mr. Vanderbilt, Mr. Depew waived his opportunity in favor of Mr. Garrett. Mr. Garrett was conversing on his project of getting into New York by way of Staten Island and a bridge over the Arthur Kill. They were in the study. Mr. Vanderbilt sat in his large arm chair and Mr. Garrett sat on a sofa opposite to him. It seems that Mr. Vanderbilt was in perfect harmony with the plans of Mr. Garrett. While he was replying to the remarks of Mr. Garrett the latter observed that his voice began to falter and there was a curious twitching of the muscles about his mouth. Soon he ceased to speak and had a spasm. In a moment he leaned forward and would have fallen on his face on the floor, but Mr. Garrett caught him in his arms, laid him gently on the rug and put a pillow under his head. This was only the work of a few moments, but before it was accomplished the greatest millionaire in America had ceased to breathe. When Dr. McLean, the family physician, arrived be said a blood vessel had burst in the head, and so death, according to the frequently expressed wish of Mr. Vanderbilt, was instantaneous.

On the announcement of Mr. Vanderbilt's death, (which was after Board hours), a panic was predicted in the stock market. A pool was formed of the most wealthy leading operators, with a capital of $12,000,000, to resist such a calamity. It was not required, however. There was a reaction of a few points in the morning following, which was recovered before

the close of the market. The stocks of Mr. Vanderbilt's properties, as well as the properties themselves, had been so well
distributed that such a disaster could hardly have occurred
without a strong outside combination to help it, and the
prevalent desire there was to assist speculation in the very
opposite direction. The remains of Mr. Vanderbilt were conveyed to New Dorp and deposited in the tomb without any
ostentation.

In the chapter on the young Vanderbilts a brief account
of the disposition of the mammoth fortune of $200,000,000
is given.

CHAPTER 22

"YOUNG CORNEEL"

THE ECCENTRICITIES OF CORNELIUS JEREMIAH VANDERBILT,
AND HIS MARVELLOUS POWER FOR BORROWING MONEY. —
HE EXERCISES WONDERFUL INFLUENCE OVER GREELEY
AND COLFAX. — A DINNER AT THE CLUB WITH YOUNG
"CORNEEL" AND THE FAMOUS SMILER. — "CORNEEL"
TRIES TO MAKE HIMSELF SOLID WITH JAY COOKE. —
THE COMMODORE REFUSES TO PAY GREELEY. — "WHO THE
DEVIL ASKED YOU?" RETORTED GREELEY. — "CORNEEL'S"
MARRIAGE TO A CHARMING AND DEVOTED WOMAN.
HOW SHE SOFTENED THE OBDURATE HEART OF HER
FATHER-IN-LAW.

CORNELIUS J. VANDERBILT, the brother of Wm. H., popularly known by the name of "Young Corneel," is entitled
to a place in this book, as he was prominent among the many
financial friends I have had, in his own peculiar line.

"Corneel" was eccentric, and was possessed of some astonishing peculiarities that made him a genius in his way. He led
a charmed and adventurous life in his own circles.

He had a wonderful facility for getting into scrapes, and
"banked" on the Commodore to extricate him therefrom,
which the latter did on many occasions. The mere fact, however, that he had such a father, was in itself sufficient, very
often, to get him out of his troubles, without any effort on
the part of the Commodore in that direction. "Corneel," however, worked this "racket" for all it was worth, and in time it
became almost exhausted. Still, he went on making new

acquaintances without limit, and to many of them the name of the Commodore was a sufficient guarantee of security for sundry loans, that were promised to be paid on the fulfilment of certain expectations which only existed in the borrower's imagination.

But it was not very safe for "Corneel" to rely upon his father, or to bank upon his credit in any case. If he had depended solely on the paternal security, he would often have found, when in his worst straits, that he had leaned upon a willow cane for support. "Corneel" had a peculiar fascination in his ability to catch the ear of prominent men, who would listen attentively to his tale of woe, and some of them were so thoroughly under the spell of his persuasive powers that they would "fork" out the required amount without hesitation, to relieve his pressing necessities.

It is sad to relate that the money thus sometimes piteously solicited, and really required to pay a board bill or room rent, was often thrown away in the first gambling den that the borrower happened to be passing, while the landlady and the washerwoman would be obliged to extend their bills of credit indefinitely.

Amongst the special friends upon whom he was in the habit of exercising his alluring magnetism were the Hon. Schuyler Colfax and Horace Greeley. Over both of these eminent gentlemen he seemed to have perfect control. So hopelessly were they under the charm of his occult power that they seldom said "no" to any request that he made, especially when he wanted to borrow money. No sorcerer ever had his helpless victims more completely at his mercy, nor had greater power by the touch of his mysterious wand, than "Corneel" had over these and certain other men, when he would entertain them with a list of imaginary wrongs which he had suffered at the hands of his father and brother. In their ears this story never seemed to become stale, though it was the same old story every time, with hardly any attempt at variation. To them and others, over whom he exercised this unaccountable influence, the thing did not seem to become monotonous like other twice-told tales, related by ordinary people.

To the man of average intellect and common business capacity "Corneel" was a shocking "bore" and a victim of morbid melancholia, but these men of genius were won by the impression which he had made upon them, and thoroughly imbued with the deepest sympathy for the wrongs which his strange hallucinations conjured up. Unlike most men who borrow money from friends and don't pay, instead of exhausting his credit by this business delinquency, he made it the basis for increasing it, and it generally seemed to be a potent means of enabling him to borrow more. Hence his obligations to Mr. Greeley were persistently cumulative until they exceeded $50,000.

I have been told by a person familiarly acquainted with him that years after Greeley's death he would sometimes sit in deep meditation, with the tears welling up in his eyes, especially when in a great financial strait, and sighingly say: "When Mr. Greeley died I lost the best friend in the world." Be it said to his credit, however, in spite of all his shortcomings, he exhibited his honesty by paying every cent of the debt, with interest, to Mr. Greeley's daughters. He also paid the greater part of all the other debts which he had contracted under similar circumstances, after making a settlement with Wm. H. and receiving a much larger amount than he had been left by the will of his father, who bequeathed him merely a decent competence for his rank and station in life, without any surplus for the policy shops and faro banks.

One of the qualities possessed by "Corneel" in a remarkable degree, and which enabled him to be so successful a borrower, was his extreme earnestness. He bent his whole energies to the work in hand, and his requests usually met with ready response. If he had put the same energy and intense enthusiasm into legitimate speculation, he would have been as successful as his father or Jay Gould. He must have been an intuitive judge of character, for he showed that he generally knew his man in advance of making application for sundry little loans. In that respect he was not unlike the famous huntsman who was a dead shot every time.

My first acquaintance with "Corneel" was through one of his special friends, the Hon. Schuyler Colfax, whom he

brought to my office for the purpose of having himself introduced by Mr. Colfax. He informed me that he had just then
returned from Hartford, Conn., where he had taken his
friend, Mr. Colfax, for a week's visit at his house. It can be
readily imagined, therefore, that at this time Mr. Colfax had
but little control over his own bank account and for a long
time afterwards.

I invited both these gentlemen to dinner at the Club that
afternoon. Although Mr. Colfax was an extraordinarily good
talker he was left far in the distance and almost silenced by
"Corneel." Most of what the latter said, however, had very little in it of a tangible character, and was almost entirely made
up of unstinted praise of his friend Colfax. If ever there was
a man talked up to the skies, or if the thing were possible,
Colfax must have been literally in that elevated position during our dinner.

There was no let-up to the unqualified adulation, yet I must
say that there was none of the uninterrupted stream of ful-
some flattery fell to the ground. Schuyler took it all in as he
did his viands, and as if it were legitimately his due, a proof
positive that "Young Corneel" was not mistaken in his man;
and a further demonstration of his natural sagacity in striking
the man upon whom he could successfully exercise his peculiar charms of persuasion.

When he got tired talking about Mr. Colfax, the object of
his next theme was Mr. Greeley, on whom he was profusely
prolific.

I met Mr. Greeley frequently afterwards, and told him
what a good friend he had in young Cornelius Vanderbilt.
"Yes," he said, with a knowing smile, "I think he is a good
friend of mine. I have heard of his frequently saying nice
things about me. It is a great pity, however," he added significantly, "that he is so frequently short of funds. If he had
more money he would be a very good fellow."

It was generally in the way above referred to that he
would steal a march on Mr. Greeley and impose on his good
nature. He would say nice things about him to some one who
would quote him to Mr. Greeley, and thus pave the way for

an additional loan. In a few days afterward "Corneel" would call on his tried and trusty friend, and never fail to obtain the needed relief, or a large portion of it.

"Corneel" had great tact in utilizing his various advantages for borrowing, and was imbued with a thorough devotion to his object, worthy of a better cause. The day following his first visit to my office, he called again and told me that his friend Colfax had left by the early train for Washington, and had urged him to go along, but as he had some matters to attend to he had postponed his departure until the night train.

He said to me, "By-the-bye, you know Jay Cooke very well." I said, "Yes."

Then he replied, "I have some matters to look after in connection with the Treasury Department, and I think he could be of some service to me. Will you be good enough to oblige me with a letter of introduction to him? I may not need it," he added with a business air of *sang froid,* "but I should like to have it in case of need."

I wrote him a brief and non-committal introduction, somewhat as follows:

This will introduce to you Mr. Cornelius Vanderbilt, Jr., son of the Commodore. I take the liberty of making you acquainted with him through this medium, at his own request.

Truly yours,
HENRY CLEWS.

There was certainly nothing on the face of this document, except the Commodore's name, to justify any person in utilizing it as a bill of credit.

Yet the financial genius of "Young Corneel" was equal to the task of an indirect negotiation of this character, and after the lapse of a few days his drafts from Jay Cooke began to pour into my office like April showers. None of them was very large, but when put together they aggregated a pretty fair amount, and were so cumulative in their character that, had I not wired Mr. Cooke to stop the supplies, it is difficult to say what figure the sum total would have reached.

The last time I saw "Young Corneel" was at Long Branch, where he took a drive with me one fine warm afternoon. He spoke feelingly about his wasted life, and concerning the many good friends who had come so often to his rescue, and had got him out of his numerous holes, into which, through misfortune, he had been thrown. He said all there was of life for him was to live long enough to pay up old scores. He had fully determined to do this, and then, he thought, a prolongation of existence would have no further charms for him. It must be said to his credit that he accomplished this work, and then laying himself sadly down, died by his own hand.

Let us, therefore, throw the mantle of charity over that tragic scene in the Glenham Hotel, and hope that his soul may elsewhere have found the rest which in its poor, afflicted body it vainly sought for here.

That portion of the Commodore's will in which he makes provision for Cornelius J. is thoroughly characteristic of the old man, in its iron-clad provisions. It says: "I direct that $200,000 be set apart, the interest thereof to be applied to the maintenance and support of my son, Cornelius J. Vanderbilt, during his natural life. And I authorize said trustees, in their discretion, instead of themselves making the application of said interest money to his support, to pay over from time to time, to my said son, for his support, such portions as they may deem advisable, or the whole of the interest of said bonds. But no part of the interest is to be paid to any assignee of my said son, or to any creditor who may seek by legal proceedings to obtain the same; and in case my said son should make any transfer or assignment of his beneficial interest in said bonds or the interest thereof, or encumber the same, or attempt so to do, the said interest of said bonds shall thereupon cease to be applicable to his use, and shall thenceforth, during the residue of his natural life, belong to my residuary legatee. Upon the decease of my said son, Cornelius J., I give and bequeath the last mentioned $200,000 of bonds to my residuary legatee."

Though a portion of this provision is rather whimsical, yet it was ably designed to force "Corneel" to desist from his besetting sin, the gaming table.

If the trustees were permitted to pay him the whole of the interest at whatever period they should choose, it seems harsh that the beneficiary should forfeit it entirely, if he should seek to relieve present and pressing necessities, by borrowing on his future income. It showed that the Commodore, even at the hour of his death, thought that "Corneel" was not fit to be treated otherwise than as a child, and that it was necessary he should be kept under the guardianship of his brother.

This circumstance hurt "Corneel's" feelings greatly, as he imagined himself a bigger man, mentally, than Wm. H. This opinion, however, no other man could conscientiously endorse, except it might have been Greeley or Colfax.

"Corneel," though always exclaiming against the old man's hard-heartedness, had an intense admiration for his father's abilities, and he was as sensitive as a sunflower when any other person would say a word to disparage the Commodore. While railing constantly at the parsimony of his father, he was as devoted a hero-worshipper of the Commodore as Thomas Carlyle ever was of the greatest of his heroes, and he never grew tired talking of his achievements, with the history of which be was thoroughly familiar. He had even a more intense hatred against Gould than his father had, and solemnly believed that Gould and Fisk had, during the manipulation of the Erie "corner," conspired to assassinate the Commodore.

Of course this was one of his many hallucinations, and there was not the least ground for it, but he had got it indelibly on the brain, and he would not tolerate contradiction in that notion any more than in any other opinion which he had got fixed in his morbid mind. He once went into an epileptic fit in the presence of a friend of mine who attempted to reason with him on the improbability of such a man as Gould contemplating murder.

He never forgave his father for having him arrested and incarcerated in Bloomingdale Lunatic Asylum. He had run off to California the time of the gold fever, and shipped as a sailor. He was then in his eighteenth year. When he returned, which was pretty soon, as he had no ability to enter into the terrible mental and physical struggle for wealth on the gold coast, his father had him arrested. It was soon discovered that he was no lunatic, however eccentric he might be, and he was released, but he took the matter dreadfully to heart, and it had a melancholy and demoralizing effect upon all his future life. He was petulant, and still complaining, and often acted like a crazy man in that the more any of his intimate friends tried to please him he seemed the more dissatisfied; yet it was impossible to get along with him without humoring him, and it was almost next to impossible to humor him. In this way he could work on the minds of the strongest of his friends, so as almost to put them into a fit as bad as one of his own.

Dr. Swazy's patience was often put to a very severe test in his attempt to please this eccentric invalid.

"Corneel" was a miser everywhere except at the gaming table, and would cling to a cent with greater tenacity than ordinary people display in holding on to a ten-dollar bill. But among the gamblers either a ten-dollar bill or a hundred-dollar bill was less valuable in his eyes than a cent in the common transactions of every day life. "Faro" and "keno" had terrific power over him. He has often been known to have had an epileptic fit at the gaming table, get a doze afterwards which seemed like the sleep of death, so cadaverous did he look on those occasions, and then awake up and go on with the play, whose fascination he appeared utterly powerless to resist.

When it came to the ears of the Commodore that Greeley was lending his son hundreds and sometimes thousands of dollars at a time, he visited the office of the *Tribune*. He rushed without ceremony into the sanctum, where Greeley was busy at his high desk, grinding out a tirade against some political or social abuse, and thus addressed the Sage of Chappaqua: "Greeley, I hear yer lendin' 'Corneel' money." "Yes," said Greeley, eyeing the monarch of steamboat men through his glasses, with an air of philosophic contempt mixed with commiseration; "I have let him have some." "I give you fair warning," replied the Commodore, "that you need not look to me; I won't pay you." "Who the devil asked you?" retorted Greeley. "Have I?"

This closed the interview. The Commodore retraced his steps down the rickety stairs into Spruce street, and Greeley continued to grind out his illegible chirography for the profane printers. There is no record, I believe, that the subject was ever reverted to between them. Soon after the death of Greeley the Commodore sent a check for $10,000 each to his two daughters.

The Commodore was well satisfied with the marriage of young "Corneel" to Miss Williams, of Hartford, Connecticut, and he had hoped that his son would begin then to lead a new life, but he was doomed to disappointment.

There is a good story told about an interview between the Commodore and Mr. Williams prior to the marriage.

Mr. Williams called upon the Commodore at his office in Fourth street, near Broadway, and informed him that his son, Cornelius Jeremiah, had asked his daughter in marriage, and she was willing if the Commodore had no objection to the union.

"Has your daughter plenty of silk dresses?" asked the Commodore, sententiously.

"Well," replied Mr. Williams, showing some sensitiveness at what he at first considered assumption of superiority and purse-pride on the part of the Commodore, "my daughter, as I told you, is not wealthy. She has a few dresses like other young ladies in her station, but her wardrobe is not very extensive nor costly."

"Has your daughter plenty of jewelry?" continued the Commodore, without appearing to take much notice of Mr. Williams' explanation.

"No, sir," replied Mr. Williams, becoming slightly nettled, and showing a laudable pride in opposition to what he considered a slur on account of his moderate means, "I have attempted to explain to you that I am in comparatively humble circumstances, and my daughter cannot afford jewelry."

"The reason I ask you," pursued the Commodore, "is, that if she did possess these articles of value, my son would take

them and either pawn or sell them, and throw away the proceeds at the gaming table. So I forewarn you and your
daughter that I can't take any responsibility in this matter."

The nuptials were duly consummated, however, in spite of
the Commodore's constructive remonstrance.

After the marriage "Corneel" asked his father for some
money to build a house. "No, Corneel," he said emphatically,
"you have got to show that you can be trusted before I
trust you."

His wife made application to her father-in-law with better
success, however. He gave her a check for $10,000. In a few
months afterward she paid another visit to the Commodore,
who received her cordially, but expected she had come for
another loan, and he was attempting to work up his courage
to the point of refusal; for, strong and almost invincibly obdurate as he was in the general affairs of life, in the presence of
the fair sex, like Samson when he got his hair cut, he was
weak and like another man.

"Well," said the Commodore, addressing his daughter-in-law
with a kindly smile, "what can I do for you now?"

"Well, papa," she replied in her exceedingly candid and
agreeable manner, "we did not need all the money, so I
brought you back $1,500."

The Commodore could hardly believe his ears and eyes,
and thought for a moment that he must be under some mysterious delusion, superinduced by the spiritual seances which
he then was in the habit of attending. But when the cash was
put in his hand he found it was a material reality. This sealed
a warm friendship between him and his worthy and economical daughter-in-law, which was only severed by her premature
death about ten years before that of her unfortunate husband.

The sympathy that some people manifested for "Young
Corneel" was, like his own maladies, of the most morbid or
delusive character. He had $200 a week from his father all
the time that he was whining to the public about his pinching
poverty and denouncing the old man's niggardliness. This
would have been ample, with fair economy, not only for all

the necessaries of life, but, under judicious management, would have afforded the recipient many of its luxuries.

With his irresistible propensity for gambling, he would not have been any better off physically, but worse, with the entire income from his father's 75 or 100 millions. The only difference that should have arisen was that he would have been instrumental in carrying out in part the socialistic and communistic idea of a wider distribution of private property, amassed by thrift, privation and industry, among the drones, lazy "loafers" and criminals of society.

The Commodore's judgment, therefore, in limiting his prodigal son to $200 a week, was not only comprehensive, but beneficent in its results both to his son and to society at large.

CHAPTER 23

DREW AND VANDERBILT

VANDERBILT ESSAYS TO SWALLOW ERIE, AND HAS A
NARROW ESCAPE FROM CHOKING.—HE TRIES TO MAKE
DREW COMMIT FINANCIAL SUICIDE.—MANIPULATING THE
STOCK MARKET AND THE LAW COURTS AT THE SAME
TIME.—ATTEMPTS TO "TIE UP" THE HANDS OF DREW.—
MANUFACTURING BONDS WITH THE ERIE PAPER MILL
AND PRINTING PRESS.—FISK STEALS THE BOOKS AND
EVADES THE INJUNCTION.—DREW THROWS FIFTY
THOUSAND SHARES ON THE MARKET AND DEFEATS THE
COMMODORE.—THE "CORNER" IS BROKEN AND BECOMES A
BOOMERANG.—VANDERBILT'S FURY KNOWS NO BOUNDS.—
IN HIS RAGE HE APPLIES TO THE COURTS.—THE CLIQUE'S
INGLORIOUS FLIGHT TO JERSEY CITY.—DREW CROSSES THE
FERRY WITH SEVEN MILLIONS OF VANDERBILT'S MONEY.—
THE COMMODORE'S ATTEMPT TO REACH THE REFUGEES.—
A DETECTIVE BRIBES A WAITER AT TAYLOR'S HOTEL, WHO
DELIVERS THE COMMODORE'S LETTER, WHICH BRINGS
DREW TO TERMS.—SENATOR MATTOON GETS "BOODLE"
FROM BOTH PARTIES.

O NE of the most interesting episodes connected with the
speculative life of Drew, in the somewhat sensational history of Erie affairs, was the interposition of Commodore
Vanderbilt in one of the famous deals of the Erie clique. His
object was to swallow up the corporation, and it came pretty
near swallowing him. He was only saved by the skin of the

teeth, after one of the most prolonged and desperate financial struggles of his life.

In order to explain clearly the manner in which the Commodore became involved in the Erie matter with Drew and his partners, it will be necessary to take a brief resume of the history of a few of his other prominent deals, more fully dwelt upon elsewhere.

In 1860 Harlem stock had sold as low as eight or nine dollars a share. In January, 1863, when Vanderbilt got full control of the property, the stock had advanced to 30, and in July of the same year it had bounded to 92. In August, when the "corner" was effected, it went to the remarkable figure of 179.

It was put through a similar operation the succeeding year, and the stock, which sold in January below 90, was settled for in the following June at 285. Drew had been drawn into one of these transactions, and his losses reached nearly a million.

Vanderbilt's prospects with the Harlem property were seriously menaced by the competition of the Hudson River Railroad. He bought up the competing line, and thus destroyed the competition. He made this purchase when the stock was at par. He soon manifested his superior power in management, and displayed his skill in the art of "watering," which he had invented. He had the stock advanced to 180 in a very short time.

Seeing his great success with these two properties, through his novel and unique methods of financiering, the managers of the New York Central, thinking that discretion was the better part of valor, and perceiving that they could not hold out against the edicts of manifest destiny very long, offered their property to him almost at his own price, which he very cordially accepted, approving their good judgment and keen perception.

He obtained full control of New York Central early in 1867. As soon as this triple amalgamation was complete he set his insatiable and avaricious heart upon Erie, and essayed to compass his designs and effect his purpose of reducing it to possession through the speculative machinery of Wall Street.

It was through this channel that he had obtained Hudson, and in defiance of the scientific maxim that lightning never strikes twice in the same place, he was inspired with full confidence in his ability to "scoop" Erie in the same manner. He tried first to arbitrate and consolidate, but his efforts in that direction failed.

With all his marvellous foresight and almost unerring judgment in speculative affairs, the Commodore was greatly at fault in his calculation regarding the magnitude of the task he had now undertaken in Erie. He had no idea of the immense volume of the stock which, after the speculative battle began to rage, seemed to spring out of the ground, spontaneously, as the reserve troops of Wellington were said to appear to do in the eyes of Napoleon when the struggle waxed warm at Waterloo. He had to contend with the ablest generals in speculation and finance that ever Wall Street had produced. His first bold, flank movement was an attempt to "corner" Drew. He knew how to manipulate the courts almost as well as the Erie Ring did. Accordingly, he made use of the services of Frank Work to obtain an injunction from Judge Barnard, of Tweed Ring notoriety, restraining Drew from the payment of interest on $3^{1}/_{2}$ million bonds, pending an investigation of his accounts as treasurer of Erie. This was followed up in a few days by another application to the court for the treasurer's removal from office.

These measures were resorted to by Vanderbilt to prevent the issue of this stock, into which these $3^{1}/_{2}$ million bonds were convertible, and thus enable him to get a "corner" in the stock with greater facility. He thus attempted to make the court instrumental in forcing Drew into a position where he would be obliged to commit financial suicide.

The Erie Ring had managed to get legally around what in reality was an over-issue of Erie stock and bonds in the following subtle manner:

There was a statute of New York which authorized any railroad to create and issue its own stock in exchange for the stock of any other road under lease to it. The Ring had obtained the Buffalo, Bradford & Pittsburgh road, which was comparatively worthless, for carrying out this scheme. The Erie management then set about supplying themselves with the amount of Erie stock required, by leasing their own road to the road of which they were directors. They then created stock and issued it to themselves in exchange under the authority vested in them by law.

The nominal price of the road with which they worked this game of legerdemain was $250,000. They issued bonds in its name for two millions of dollars, payable to one of themselves as trustee.

Vanderbilt, before he could get a "corner" in Erie, had to place a limit to the issue of the stock. Otherwise he would have been throwing away millions, like pouring water into a sieve, in his attempt to make a "corner."

Drew was enjoined by the Commodore to return to the Treasury 68,000 shares of the capital stock of Erie. This was the amount that was said to remain in the unsettled trans-actions of the Erie corner of 1866. This was the sword of Damocles which Vanderbilt had suspended over Drew's devoted head.

Vanderbilt thus undertook to play the double game of manipulating the courts and the stock market at the same time, and against wily opponents, who were experts in both operations.

There were at this time three competitors for the posses-sion of Erie in the field. The Drew party, the Vanderbilt party, and the Boston, Hartford and Erie party. Drew had tried to appease Vanderbilt to some extent, and had an inter-view with him at Vanderbilt's own house prior to the election of the Erie directors. He agreed to "let up" on Vanderbilt, and offered him greater swing in purchasing Erie, while, on the other hand, Vanderbilt consented not to press the proceed-ings in court against Drew.

Before this, the Boston party and Vanderbilt had been fixing matters to oust Drew from the Erie directory. Now, Vanderbilt changed his tactics, and resolved to let Drew remain. The Boston party was with him, but to keep up the appearance of what had been formerly determined, the new board was to be elected ostensibly without Drew, and a vacancy created after-wards by which he could be chosen in the board. This method of whipping the Devil around the stump was adopted to put public opinion off its guard, and help to forward Vanderbilt's purposes of consolidation. The election scheme was successfully effected, but the ruse, though well conceived, fell far short of accomplishing its designs.

There were wheels within wheels during this speculative deal. Drew and Vanderbilt entered into a secret alliance to exclude the Boston party, who was Vanderbilt's ally. The new board was elected, leaving Drew out. This was a surprise to Wall Street, but a greater surprise was in store for it when a vacancy was created the next day, and Drew was re-elected to the Erie Board of Directors. The Street was confused and confounded, and at a loss to know how to act, and the Boston party was groping around to find out where it stood. Frank Work was elected to the Erie Board in the Vanderbilt interest. A pool was then formed to put up Erie, as it was in a very depressed condition. Drew was to manage the pool and manipulate the market.

The proposed plan for consolidating with the Vanderbilt interests failed because the Erie people said that the great railroad king would only consent to give them one-third of the earnings, while they contributed more than half to the pool. So, when this scheme collapsed, Vanderbilt went on the speculative war path, and determined to snatch Erie from the hands of the Ring in the way he had obtained Hudson. He began his operations about the middle of February, 1868, and pursued his policy in the courts for the purpose of limiting the apparently unlimited supply of Erie stock.

In the leasing process above referred to with the Buffalo, Bradford & Pittsburgh, the Erie clique added $140,000 a year to its income.

Mr. Work got an additional injunction to prevent Erie from issuing stock in addition to the 251,058 shares which had appeared in the previous report of the road, and forbidding a guarantee by Erie of the bonds of any other road, and Drew was further restrained from any transactions in Erie until he should return the 68,000 shares of capital stock to the treasury.

It will thus be seen that Vanderbilt had taken very rigid measures to "tie up" the hands of the veteran speculator.

The case was set down for hearing in the court of the immaculate Judge Barnard, on the 10th of March. When

Vanderbilt thought he had everything fixed to force Drew to ruin himself by the return of these shares, which would enable Vanderbilt to effect his "corner," he was checkmated by a counter injunction issued in the interest of the Erie people by Judge Balcom, of Binghamton, which stayed all proceedings in Barnard's court.

Richard Schell then applied to Judge Ingraham and got out another injunction in the interest of the Vanderbilt party, staying all proceedings before Judge Balcom.

In the meantime the Erie directors were busy preparing their new issue of stock, despite the injunctions, in order that the bulls of the Vanderbilt party might be generously fed with Erie when the opportunity should arrive.

The Executive Committee of Erie resolved to issue bonds for improvements, extensions and steel rails. The bonds were convertible into stock at not less than $72^{1}/_{2}$. Five millions of these were manufactured by the Erie paper mill and printing press, to be exchanged for Vanderbilt's good, solid cash.

A great difficulty presented itself at this juncture, which, even to the majority of clever speculators, would have been insurmountable. The genius of "Jim" Fisk was called in to cut the Gordian knot. The certificates of the new Erie shares were in the hands of the secretary of the company, but he was enjoined from issuing them. They had been made out on Saturday night. On Monday the secretary directed a messenger, in the Erie office in West street, to take the books containing the certificates to the transfer office in Pine street. The messenger took the books and walked out. He was hardly a minute absent when he returned, apparently frightened, without the books. He stated that Mr. Fisk, who had been standing at the door, took the books from him, and ran away with them!

The certificates were then where no injunction could molest them. The next day the convertible bonds were found upon the secretary's desk. In a day or two afterwards the certificates appeared in Wall Street. An order was obtained from Judge Gilbert enjoining all the previous orders of that legal luminary, Judge Barnard. Mr. Drew then threw 50,000

shares of Erie stock on the market. The boldness of the operation threw the Vanderbilt brokers off their guard, for it never
struck them for a moment that Drew would risk contempt of
court, and use the new issue of Erie in the face of an injunction, so they eagerly devoured the fresh bait before they got
time to examine the quality of it or suspect its origin.

Erie had opened at 80, and advanced to 83. When the facts
became known the stock broke, and declined to 71; but
under heavy purchases by the Vanderbilt party, soon recovered to 78. The "corner," however, was broken by the large
blocks which Drew had thrown on the market, and Vanderbilt
was signally defeated, and had a narrow escape from being
completely swamped. The corner proved a boomerang to
Vanderbilt. In his wrath he again applied to the courts. As
the result, the Erie clique were obliged to fly and take refuge
in Jersey City. Drew crossed the ferry heavily loaded with a
big carpet bag, which contained seven millions, which had
recently changed hands from Vanderbilt to himself in the cornering operation.

Gould and Fisk decamped by different routes. When the
party had taken refuge in "Fort" Taylor (Taylor's Hotel), safe
from the laws of New York, they determined that no papers
should be served upon them, and gave strict orders to the
host that they would not receive anything in the shape of letters or notes. Communications of all kinds were prohibited
except through persons well known to the clique, and the
waiters at the hotel were strictly enjoined to observe this
rule, on pain of being discharged.

While Vanderbilt was working hard to reach the refugees
through the courts, the Legislature and his detectives, he discovered a method of communicating with Drew in spite of
the precautions with which the latter was surrounded. The
Commodore's scheme would have done honor to a first-class
Nihilist of the present day. He instructed a person in his
service to play temporary detective, to go to the Taylor Hotel
in the garb of a commercial traveler from the Far West, and
to watch the movements of Drew, so as to get a note slipped
into his hand in a way that he would be certain to read it.

The amateur detective watched for a day or two, and saw that his only chance of success was when Drew was at lunch, and that the person who waited on him must hand him the note. He saw the waiter, and told him what he wanted, and that when he should be discharged the Commodore would find him a better place.

The waiter agreed to hand Mr. Drew the note. Drew was enraged, sent for the host, and the waiter was instantly discharged, only to enter Vanderbilt's service, according to agreement, at much higher remuneration. The note of the Commodore, however, had the desired effect. What that note contained, probably, nobody but Vanderbilt and Drew ever knew. Though the friends of Drew attempted to frighten him from going by arousing his suspicions of being kidnapped, he came over to New York on the following Sunday and had an interview with the Commodore. The matter was fixed up between them, and while Gould and Fisk were fighting Vanderbilt tooth and nail at Albany, and Gould was arrested and arraigned for contempt of court and other high crimes and misdemeanors in the eyes of the Vanderbilt lawyers, Drew was left unmolested to pursue the even tenor of his way.

As treasurer of Erie, however, Drew took an active part in the progress of legislative matters. He was the first to see that Senator Mattoon, who was chiefly instrumental in organizing the Investigating Committee, wanted tangible recognition of his services before the Committee made its report. He thought he was using Mattoon, but the Senator used him, and gave his casting vote in favor of Vanderbilt, whom he used also, after the most approved method of Albany legislators. Mattoon was also found on the winning side at the end of the legislative farce, when the bill in favor of the Erie clique and its over-issue of stock was passed, and no doubt got his fair share of the half million with which Drew fortified Gould from the Erie treasury when this gentleman went to Albany to conduct the war in the Legislature against Vanderbilt concerning the extra issue of Erie stock.

CHAPTER 24

JAY GOULD

His Birth And Early Education.—Clerk in a Country Store.—He Invents a Mouse Trap.—Becomes a Civil Engineer and Surveys Delaware County.—Writes a Book and Sells It.—Gets a Partnership in a Pennsylvania Tannery and Soon Buys his Partner Out.—He Comes to New York to Sell his Leather, Falls in Love with a Leather Merchant's Daughter and Marries Her.—Settles in the Metropolis and Begins to Deal in Railroads.—Buys a Bankrupt Road from his Father-in-law, Reorganizes it and Sells it at a Considerable Profit.—Henceforth he Makes his Money Dealing in Railroads.—His Method of Buying, Reorganizing and Selling Out at a Large Profit.—How he Managed Erie in Connection with Fisk and Drew.—His Operations on Black Friday.—Checkmated by Commodore Vanderbilt and Obliged to Settle.—He Makes Millions out of Wabash and Kansas & Texas.—His Venture in Union Pacific.—His Construction Companies.—Organization of American Union Telegraph, and His Method of Absorbing and Getting Control of Western Union.—The Strike of the Telegraphers and his Great Encounter with the Knights of Labor and Trades Unionists.—Gould's First Yachting Expedition.—An Exceedingly Humorous Story of his Early Experience on the Water.—His Status as a Factor in Railroad Management.—His Acquisition of Baltimore & Ohio Telegraph, &c.

IF Fenimore Cooper, Sir Walter Scott, Charles Dickens or Dumas, in the height of the popularity of any of these great writers of fiction, had evolved from his inner consciousness a Jay Gould as the hero of a novel, its readers would have found serious fault with the author for attempting to transcend the rational probability allowed to the latitude of fiction. Few novel readers, in fact, would have patiently submitted to such a strain on their credulity prior to the era in the financial development of this country which produced some of the leading characters which Wall Street has brought to the front, as stern realities of every day life, since my advent in the great arena of speculation.

Among these Jay Gould is conspicuous, and of all the self-made men of Wall Street he had probably the most difficulty in making the first thousand dollars of the amazing pile which he now controls.

Jay Gould was born at Stratton Falls, Delaware county, New York, about the year 1836. He was the son of John B. Gould, a farmer, who kept a grocery store. At the age of sixteen young Gould became a clerk in a variety store belonging to Squire Burnham, about two miles from the Falls. Here, in his leisure hours, he assiduously improved the little learning he had received at the village school, by applying himself to the study of book-keeping in the evenings.

It was when he was at this store, according to the most reliable accounts, that he manifested his natural aptitude for making sharp and profitable bargains. His employer, the Squire, had his eye on a piece of land in Albany, which he expected to obtain cheap and so make a profit. He whispered his intention to some friend in the store and his young assistant overheard him. When he went to put his design of purchasing the land in execution he found that young Mr. Gould had been there before him, and had secured the title.

About this time there was a firm which had undertaken to survey the county and make office maps of it, and young Gould was employed to assist them. Having mastered the elementary principles of geometry, and being naturally quick and correct at figures, he soon became a fair expert in common land surveying, and made himself exceedingly useful to his employers. But the idea of not only being his own boss but an employer of other people's brains and muscles was one of his ruling propensities, and he used every effort to attain this object. In a short time he bought out the firm, wrote a history of the county to accompany the maps and peddled his book among the residents.

This natural inclination to buy out every concern with which he has been connected has been the ruling passion of his life, and still tenaciously adheres to him. Prior to his negotiations with the firm of surveyors, he had invented a mouse trap in his intervals of leisure in the store, and with the proceeds of this and the bargain in the land, out of which he had outwitted his employer, he was enabled to make himself master of the situation with the surveyors. Shortly after this Gould became interested in a Pennsylvania tannery with Zadoc Pratt, who was the capitalist. Through the advice of Israel Corse, the Commission Merchant of the firm, Col. Pratt proposed to dissolve the partnership. Gould induced Charles M. Leupp & Co. to purchase Pratt's interest for $150,000. The business did not meet the expectations of Leupp, who in a fit of despondency committed suicide. After his death Gould failed to retain possession of the property, which was sold to H. D. H. Snyder, thus terminating Mr. Gould's career as a Pennsylvania tanner.

On his visits to New York Mr. Gould was attracted by the greater advantages which the Empire City afforded for extending his business, and came here to reside. He had ingratiated himself in the favorable esteem of one of the grocery merchants with whom he had done business. The merchant took him to his house to board and Mr. Gould fell in love with his handsome daughter. It was a mutual affair of the heart, like that of his son George and Miss Edith Kingdon, and a speedy marriage was the result. The results of the happy union seem to have been all that could be desired, and the domestic felicity of Mr. and Mrs. Gould, so

far as the public have been able to ascertain, has never suffered the slightest jar or interruption.

The father-in-law owned shares in a railroad which was in
a bad financial condition. He employed his new son-in-law to
see what he could do to extricate him from a position in
which he was likely to become embarrassed, and he wanted
to sell his shares. Mr. Gould examined the road, (with the
locality of which he had been well acquainted in his boy-
hood,) saw the favorable possibilities of its future, under
good management, and instead of selling his father-in-law's
shares to a stranger, he took them at their market value
himself, purchased more, finally obtained control of the
entire property, and sold it to a rival company at a large
profit. This, I believe, was Mr. Gould's first transaction in
railroad matters, and from that day to this his great speculative forte has been buying and selling railroads. It was in
that kind of business, and not in the stock market, as is
popularly supposed, that he made the great bulk of his enormous fortune.

On his entrance to Wall Street he began business alone.
Afterwards he formed a partnership with Henry N. Smith and
_____ Martin, the firm taking the name of Smith, Gould &
Martin. Martin is now in a lunatic asylum, and Henry N.
Smith, who was the chief cause of the failure of Wm. Heath
& Co. for a million dollars, is now a poor pensioner on
the bounty of his wife. But Mr. Gould still towers aloft, in the
full enjoyment and the continued progress of his speculative
prosperity, without being dismayed by any competitor, however powerful, and overcoming all obstacles, no matter
how gigantic.

As I have noticed pretty fully some of Mr. Gould's greatest speculative transactions, mostly behind the scenes in
the chapter on Black Friday and also in the account of the
"Commodore's Corners," it will be unnecessary to repeat
them here.

There was one clever transaction in the Black Friday affair
that should be put on record to the credit of the able man-

agement of that great deal. One prominent individual connected therewith was personally responsible for $4,500,000.
This was a pretty heavy load at that time even for him to
carry, but it did not weigh very heavily upon him for any
appreciable length of time. He adroitly managed to shift it
over on to the shoulders of that broad-backed, soulless creature called the Erie Corporation, making it responsible by
simply signing himself "T. R.," instead of "J. G.," the large letters representing the ordinary contraction "Tr." for Treasurer.
By this simple and ingenious device this shrewd gentleman
got rid of the burdensome legacy on the negative side,
bequeathed to him by the "Black Friday corner."

There is a story told, with several variations, in regard to a
sensational interview between Mr. Gould and Commodore
Vanderbilt. The scene is laid in the parlor of the Commodore's
house. It was about the time that the latter was making desperate efforts to get a corner in Erie, and at that particular
juncture when, having been defeated in his purpose by the
astute policy of the able triumvirate of Erie—Gould, Fisk and
Drew—he had applied to the courts as a last resort to get
even with them.

They had used the Erie paper mill to the best advantage,
in turning out new securities of Erie to supply the Vanderbilt
brokers, who vainly imagined that they were getting a corner
in the inexhaustible stock. Mr. Vanderbilt was wild when he
discovered the ruse and had no remedy but law against the
perpetrators of this costly prank. These adroit financiers usually placed the law at defiance, or used it to their own advantage, but this time they were so badly caught in their own
net that they had to fly from the State and take refuge at
Taylor's Hotel in Jersey City.

It seems that during their temporary exile beyond the
State Gould sought a private interview one night with
the Commodore, in the hope of bringing about conciliatory
measures.

The Commodore conversed freely for some time, but in
the midst of his conversation he seemed to be suddenly

seized with a fainting spell, and rolled from his seat unto the carpet, where he lay motionless and apparently breathless.

Mr. Gould's first impulse was to go to the door and summon aid, but he found it locked and no key in it. This increased his alarm and he became greatly agitated. He shook the prostrate form of the Commodore, but the latter was limp and motionless. Once there was a heavy sigh and a half suffocated breathing, as if it were the last act of respiration. Immediately afterward the Commodore was still and remained in this condition for nearly half an hour. Doubtless this was one of the most anxious half hours that ever Mr. Gould has experienced.

If I were permitted to indulge in the latitude of the ordinary story teller, I might here draw a harassing picture of Mr. Gould's internal emotions, gloomy prospects in a criminal court and dark forebodings. His prolific brain would naturally be racked to find a plausible explanation in the event of the Commodore's death, which had occurred while they were the sole occupants of the room; and at that time, in the eyes of the public, they were bitter enemies.

I can imagine that, in the height of his anxiety, he would have been ready to make very easy terms with his great rival, on condition of being relieved from his perilous position. It would have been a great opportunity, if such had been possible, for a third party to have come in as a physician, pronouncing it a case of heart disease. No doubt Mr. Gould would have been willing to pay an enormous fee to be relieved of such an oppressive suspicion.

The object of the Commodore's feint was evidently to try the courage and soften the heart of Mr. Gould, who never seemed to suspect that it was a mere hoax. His presence of mind, however, was equal to the occasion, as he bore the ordeal with fortitude until the practical joker was pleased to assume his normal condition and usual vivacity. If Mr. Gould had been a man of common excitability he might have acted very foolishly under these trying circumstances, and this doubtless would have pleased his tormentor intensely.

The *modus operandi* of Mr. Gould, in the purchase and sale of railroads, has been to buy up two or more bad roads, put them together, give the united roads a new name, call it a good, prosperous line, with immense prospects in the immediate future, get a great number of people to believe all this, then make large issues of bonds and sell them at a good price, for the purpose of further improving and enhancing the value of the property. After these preliminaries had been gone through, if profitable purchasers came along, they could have the road at a price that would amply compensate Mr. Gould for all his labor and acute management. If these purchasers should be unable to run the road profitably and were obliged to go into liquidation after a year or two, as frequently happens, then Mr. Gould or his agents would very likely be found on hand at the sale to take back the road at a greatly reduced price. Mr. Gould would then get a fresh opportunity of showing the superiority of his management. He would be able to demonstrate that the road had left his possession in excellent and progressive condition, but through loose management had been run down. He would then set about the work of reorganization again and go through the same role substantially, with slight variations, as before, realizing a handsome profit on each successive reorganization.

It would take too much time, and swell this volume far beyond the space which I have laid out for it, to go minutely into the history of all Mr. Gould's great enterprises. In fact, it would take a large volume in itself to do justice to the various schemes which have been put under way by him directly and indirectly and carried to a successful issue during his busy life of a quarter of a century in Wall Street. This seems a long time for a man who is still so young, although he is a grandfather, and enjoying the use of his mental faculties more vigorously than ever.

Owing to my own busy life I have only time to sketch the most salient points of Mr. Gould's prosperous career. Some future historian of Wall street is destined to make a big "spread" upon him, as the newspaper reporter would say. He will have ample material if he only begins his work soon; but whoever undertakes the job should not forget the maxim of that great veteran of literature, old Dr. Samuel Johnson, about material for biography having a general tendency to become scarce, and, in some instances, eventually to vanish. While the reliable material for Mr. Gould's biography may be subject to the common fate of growing less, as time advances, there is no danger of utter oblivion in his case. He has impressed his footprints on the sands of time too firmly for that.

I don't for a moment mean to insinuate the reason for this, which is given by Shakespeare as applicable to similar cases, although some ill-natured and envious people might use the well-known quotation in this connection:

"The evil that men do lives after them,
The good is often interred with their bones."

I have no hesitation in saying that Mr. Gould will leave a large amount of good after him, and, indeed, it seems now as if the Shakespearian adage was to be reversed in his case. The evil that he may have done is likely to be forgotten. He bids fair to outlive most of it, if he only goes on to the end as he has been doing for the past few years. He is now showing a decided disposition to become more of a builder up than a wrecker of values.

Through his great executive ability in railroad management and construction he has been instrumental in making many blades of grass grow where none had grown before, causing the desert to blossom like the rose, assisting thousands who had formerly been poor and almost destitute, pent up either in European hovels or New York tenement houses, to find happy homes in the West and South. He has been a great factor in improving the value of the land, and thus, while he was enriching himself, adding materially to the wealth and prestige of the nation and thereby elevating it in the appreciation of the world at large.

The correspondent of the London *Times* recently sent over here to write up a description of the country, dwells emphatically on this characteristic of Mr. Gould and other great millionaires and railroad magnates, who contribute so largely to the general prosperity of which they seem to be the indispensable mediums.

It was as the managing power in the Erie Railroad that Mr. Gould laid the broad foundation of his fortune. His speculative connections with Erie are more fully dealt with in the lives of Daniel Drew and Commodore Vanderbilt. The money and influence which he gained, in connection with the Erie corporation, enabled him to extend his operations in the acquisition of railroad property until, through Union Pacific and its various connections, Wabash and a number of Southwestern roads, it seemed probable, at one time, that he was in a fair way of grasping the entire control of the trans-continental business in railroad matters. And this was prior to the time when he obtained his present hold on telegraph facilities.

Some of the able schemes in which Mr. Gould has had credit for playing an important part, and sometimes a role that was considered rather reprehensible, were managed, so far as the outside business was concerned, chiefly by one or more of his wicked partners. In one of the most noteworthy of those projects, namely, the attempt to capture the Albany & Susquehanna Railroad, Mr. Gould seldom or never appeared in person before the public. His partner, James Fisk, Jr., was cast in that role and played it with great ability. With the essential aid of those two shining lights of the New York bar, David Dudley Field and Thomas G. Shearman, the Prince of Erie, (as Jim Fisk was called,) came pretty near snatching possession of 142 miles of a very important railroad, with the control of only 6,500 out of 30,000 shares of the stock, and 3,000 shares of these 6,500 had been illegally obtained, as was eventually decreed by the court.

Mr. Fisk, though the silent member of the Erie firm, had also control of Judge Barnard, of the Supreme Court of the City and County of New York.

The Albany & Susquehanna road would have been a valuable prize for Erie. It runs from the eastern extremity of the New York Central at Albany to a junction with Erie at Binghamton. At that time Erie aspired to be a successful competitor with Central for New England business, and had determined to monopolize the coal trade between that section and Pennsylvania. This connecting link of 142 miles was therefore regarded as a very valuable acquisition by both the large roads. Hence it was worth a desperate effort, and Jim Fisk showed that he had a true appreciation of its value, for he organized a company of New York roughs, placed himself at their head, and being armed with bludgeons and pistols and an injunction from Judge Barnard, obtained from him in New York City—while he was really in Poughkeepsie at the time—went to Albany and took forcible possession of the offices of the railroad. He had the President, Secretary, counsel and receiver of the road arrested and put under $25,000 bonds each. Mr. Fisk went through the farce of an election of Erie candidates for the offices which he had forcibly made vacant in the Albany & Susquehanna, bringing his roughs up to vote as stockholders.

The President of the road, Mr. Joseph H. Ramsey, fought stoutly for his rights and ousted the intruders. He had spent eighteen years building the road, and was naturally attached to it. He also found a Judge to aid him. Justice E. Darwin Smith, of Rochester, eventually rendered a decision in favor of the Ramsey party, with the opinion that "Mr. Fisk's attempt to carry the election by his contingent of 'toughs' was a gross perversion and abuse of the right to vote by proxy, tending to convert corporation meetings into places of disorder, lawlessness and riot." Costs were decreed to the Ramsey directors, and a reference made to ex-Judge Samuel L. Selden, of the Court of Appeals, who fixed the allowance to be paid by the Fisk board to the Ramsey board at $92,000. It is worthy of note that the Fisk board consisted of the unlucky number of thirteen.

The Erie party appealed, but long before the appeal could be heard the Albany & Susquehanna was leased in perpetuity to the Delaware & Hudson Canal Company, against whom the Erie party was not strong enough to go to law. Thus ended the struggle for this great connecting link.

It is worthy of remark that this was one of the few cases in which, where Mr. Gould made up his mind to obtain the control, possession or ownership of property, he did not succeed.

The methods of acquiring the control and the possession of other people's property have been raised to the dignity of a fine art by Mr. Gould. This art has been prosecuted, too, through "legitimate" means. He has had the law at his back every time, and been supported in his marvellous acquisitions by the highest Court authority.

The manner in which he managed to get Western Union into his hands affords a very striking illustration of his methods and the great secret of his success.

When first laying his schemes to obtain the control of the telegraph property he got up a construction company to build a telegraph line. This was a company of exceedingly modest pretensions. It had a capital of only $5,000. It built the lines of the Western Union Telegraph Company, with which Mr. Gould paralleled most of the important lines of Western Union, and cut the rates until the older and larger corporation found that its profits were being reduced towards the vanishing point. Then it was glad to make terms with its competitor; a union of interests was the result, and Mr. Gould obtained control of the united concern.

"Impossible," said Norvin Green, in high dudgeon, when the insidious intentions of Mr. Gould were broached to him a few months before the settlement took place. "It would bankrupt Gould and all his connections to parallel our lines, and to talk of harmony between him and us is the wildest kind of speculation." The genial Doctor was then master of the situation in Western Union, or imagined himself so at that time, and regarded with contempt the efforts of Gould and his colleagues to bring the company to terms. In a few months afterward the Doctor tamely submitted to play second fiddle to the little man whom he had formerly despised.

The arrangement in reference to the cable companies followed the capture of Western Union. The struggle is still pending for the entire monopoly in the cable business, and it now seems only a question of time when the Bennett-Mackay party will have to succumb, leaving Gould in the supreme control of the news of the world. If this should happen he would become an immense power for either good or evil both in speculation and politics. In fact it would be too great a monopoly to be entrusted to the will of one man. Although it might be judiciously managed, as the cup of his ambition would then be surely full, yet the experiment would be extremely hazardous.

The controlling interest in the Elevated Railroads of this city, recently achieved by Mr. Gould through his business and speculative relations with Mr. Cyrus W. Field, are of too recent date to require any special notice or comment here. Suffice it to say, that I fear my friend Mr. Field has not come out at the big end of the horn, although everything has no doubt been in conformity with the most approved business principles and in strict adherence to the most honorable methods of dealing in railroad securities. It is significant, however, that Mr. Field has preserved a prudent reticence on the subject.

Mr. Gould, from my point of view, has been a public benefactor in the bold and successful stand which he has maintained against strikers. Though Western Union lost over half a million dollars by the strike of the telegraphers, which greatly alarmed the stockholders, yet Mr. Gould held out until the strikers were obliged to give in. He pursued the same policy, with a similar result, in the case of the Knights of Labor. During the strike of the latter I explained my views on the subject in a circular to my customers as follows:

"The Knights of Labor have undertaken to test, upon a large scale, the application of compulsion as a means of enforcing their now enlarged demands. This has necessitated a crisis of a very serious kind. The point to be determined has been, whether capital or labor shall in future determine the terms upon which the invested resources of the nation are to be employed. To the employer, it is a question whether his individual rights as to the control of his property shall be so far overborne, as to not only deprive him of his freedom, but also expose him to interferences seriously impairing the value of his capital. To the employees, it is a question whether, by the force of coercion, they can wrest to their own profit powers and control which, in every civilized community, are secured as the most sacred and inalienable rights of the employer. This issue is so absolutely revolutionary of the normal relations between capital and labor, that it has naturally produced a partial paralysis of business, especially among industries whose operations involve contracts extending into the future. There has been at no time any serious apprehension that such an utterly anarchial movement could succeed, so long as American citizens have a clear perception of their rights and their true interests; but it has been distinctly perceived that this war could not fail to create a divided if not a hostile feeling between the two great classes of society; that it must hold in check, not only a large extent of ordinary business operations but also the undertaking of those new enterprises which contribute to our national progress, and that the commercial markets must be subjected to serious embarrassments. * * * * * From the nature of the case, however, this labor disease must soon end one way or another; and there is not much difficulty in foreseeing what its termination will be. The demands of the Knights and their sympathizers, whether openly expressed or temporarily concealed, are so utterly revolutionary of the inalienable rights of the citizen, and so completely subversive of social order, that the whole community has come to a firm conclusion that these pretensions must be resisted to the last extremity of endurance and authority."

The manner in which Mr. Gould acquired his great control in some of the Western and Southwestern railroads was pretty fully developed in the recent investigation held in this city, Boston and San Francisco by the Pacific Railway Commissioners. Mr. Gould's testimony, as reported in the daily papers of May, 1887, probably contains almost as correct and succinct an account of his pooling arrangements and schemes in connection with certain railroads and his methods of making money out of them as can be obtained anywhere. His testimony, on the whole, was exceedingly affable, comprehensive and precisely to the point, and has not been contradicted in any material points by any of the succeeding witnesses that have yet been examined on this widely interesting subject. Its substance was as follows:

[From the *Herald*, May 18, 1887.]

A dapper little man in plain pepper and salt (the pepper predominating) business suit entered the Pacific Railway Commissioners offices yesterday morning and sat down quietly with his not over shiny silk hat on his knee.

The natty gentleman, unobtrusive possessor of the small dark and brilliant eyes, was the man of millions.

He had lots of information for the Commission, and he gave them more of the inside facts of the early consolidation deals of the Union Pacific than they hoped to get.

It had been expected that Mr. Gould would prove a wily witness, hard to corral and liable to shy over the fence at the slightest provocation, but at the very outset his manner was a complete surprise. He told the Commission that he was suffering from neuralgia, and said that he could not speak very loud in consequence. There were times during his examination that his tone was faint, and it was only loud two or three times, when he became very much interested in some explanation. At all times, however, it was well modulated, and now and again had a musical cadence about it that was very pleasing. He first became interested in Pacific roads in 1873. He bought Union Pacific stock in the market, but it went down to fourteen cents on the dollar. He held about 100,000 shares. He had a consultation with Sidney Dillon, and finally made a proposition to fund the floating debt in bonds, of which he took a million dollars' worth at above their par value. In 1874 he became a director and served on the executive committee. He continued in the direction during 1874, 1875 and 1876, and went over the road twice a year. He had no interest in the Fisk suit, but knew it was brought. He had no contingent interest whatever in the suit.

He became interested in the Kansas Pacific in 1878, but thought he knew the road in 1874. He remembered a proposition looking toward a unity of interest between the Denver Pacific and the Colorado Central.

Being examined as to the positions of the roads, and as things did not appear to be very clear, Mr. Gould, putting his hand to his inside pocket. said: "I have a little map here if you are not familiar with the location."

The little map was brought out and all hands gathered around it, while Mr. Gould's index finger went on an excursion over States and Territories in absolute defiance of the Inter-State Commerce Law. He recalled the fact that the plan of consolidation was considered as early as 1875, after Mr. Anderson read some extract from a paper, but he said it was not carried out then. He might even have had a talk with Scott about it on further consideration.

The little road connecting with the Colorado Central was built by him, and was the result partly of the contest between the Union Pacific and the Kansas Pacific. Prior to 1878 he could not recollect having owned any stock or securities of the Kansas Pacific. His interest in the Union Pacific has increased to 200,000 shares, the total issue of stocks being 367,000 shares. He kept books of his transactions. Mr. Morosini kept them a part of the time.

Q. Where are the books? A. I have them.

Q. Where? A. In my possession.

Q. Are they at the service of the Commission? A. If they desire them, with the greatest of pleasure.

This was the first sensation of the day, and the witness smiled blandly as he felt the full force of it.

Up to this time he had answered every question promptly. There appeared to be no hesitation on his part, and, indeed, there was none during the entire day's session. Almost every preceding witness had taken refuge behind "I don't know," or "I cannot remember," or "Really I am not sure," but there was none of this from Gould. And the apparently full and free offer of his books capped the climax.

After this whenever his memory was in any way at fault the witness fell back on the books. In asking him what he had bought certain stocks for he said the books would show.

"Will your books also show who the broker was?" "Oh, yes; certainly, certainly, certainly." In the matter of the St. Louis pool he had conversed with a number of persons.

Q. With whom did you converse? A. I presume with all the signers of the agreement.

Q.Will you tell us all about the preliminary measures leading up to this? A. I would have the neuralgia a good deal worse than I have if I undertook to tell you all of the details.

This was the original proposition of consolidation, which was a stock instead of a bond agreement, and it was soon demonstrated that it would not work.

Q. How soon after this was the new arrangement entered into? A. Almost immediately afterward, I think. The object was the funding of a heterogeneous mass of securities into one class of securities.

Q. Did you confer with others? A. I conferred with myself as well as others. What I thought was a fair price for me was a fair price for the others.

Q. To whom did you deliver your bonds? A. I suppose to the committee, but I do not know.

Q. But you would not deliver $2,000,000 to a man in whom you did not have confidence ? A. Probably not.

Q. Who kept the accounts? A. I don't know.

Q. You don't remember? A. I don't charge my memory with these things after they are over, but my books will show, and they are at the service of the Commission.

Mr. Gould's manner in saying this was unusually suave and polite, and the lines of his mouth relaxed just enough to suggest a smile.

In speaking a few moments later of the securities bought by Mr. Gould from the "St. Louis parties" he was asked of whom he bought them.

"I cannot tell about that off-hand, but my books will show it."

"Which of the St. Louis people did you confer with?"

"I think they came on here to see me. They were tired out and wanted to sell, and came over to do it."

"Then you bought all the securities first and tried to get some other gentlemen to go in with you afterward?"

"Yes, several gentlemen whom I thought would be of service to the road. There ought to be some books. Somebody must have kept accounts of the transactions. My recollection is that these people came on and told me they wanted to sell. I asked them how much they thought they ought to have and they gave me the price quoted in the agreement."

"I simply said, 'I will take them,' and that was all there was to it. That is my recollection. In 1879 I owned about $4,000,000 worth."

The examination led into the stamped income bonds of the Kansas Pacific, and Mr. Gould was asked as to the condition of the road. He thought it was poor. The road had a large intrinsic value, but it had been badly financed and its securities were way down.

Q. Did you not buy some of your securities abroad? A. I bought two millions of Denver Pacific at seventy-four cents, I think, from some Amsterdam people. I was in London and heard that they wanted to sell. I was afraid to go over, because I had very little time, and thought they would probably take a couple of days to smoke before finding out whether they would sell or not. But I was mistaken. I went over and got to Amsterdam in the morning; washed and had my breakfast. I saw them at eleven, bought them out at twelve, and started back in the afternoon.

When Mr. Gould was asked as to the prices he had paid for the securities with which he had acquired the Kansas Pacific bonds he took out his papers and handed the Commission a series of neatly written reports on these purchases and sales.

He purchased in 1879 St. Jo. and Denver first mortgage bonds, $1,562,886.69, for $603,204.78.

Of these, $617,000 worth he sold to Russell Sage, F. L. Ames, Sidney Dillon, S. H. H. Clark, Ezra H. Baker, F. G. Dexter and Elisha Atkins for $246,800.

On January 24, 1880, he surrendered $956,779.76 in these bonds and scrip in exchange for 9,568 shares of Union Pacific at par.

For St. Jo. and Denver Pacific receivers' certificates to the number of fifty-nine he paid $60,695, and on January 24, 1880, he surrendered them for 590 shares of Union Pacific at par, or $59,000.

Of St. J. and Denver stock during 1879 he acquired 8,819 shares, and sold 3,806 shares to the same persons purchasing the bonds. On January 24 he surrendered the 5,013 shares he had remaining on hand at par for $100,200.

During the same time he bought $784,000 worth of the St. Joseph Bridge bonds for $586,940, of which he sold to Sage and Dillon 150,000 worth for $112,500.

He also bought 4,000 shares of stock for $6,000, making the total cost of $634,000 bonds and 4,000 shares of stock $480,440. Received in exchange for the whole business, 6,340 shares of Union Pacific stock at par, making $634,000.

The gentlemen to whom Gould sold the securities were all directors of the Union Pacific. These gentlemen, the witness thought, retained their bonds until the consolidation, as they were bought with a purpose. "The Denver stock was called trimmings," said Mr. Gould, smiling, "and went with the bonds."

On the consolidation of the company he transferred 27,000 shares of Union Pacific Railroad stock for new stock.

He had transferred his Union Pacific stock at one time to some other parties on account of a peculiar law in Massachusetts, which enables an attachment of stock on a suit, whether there was anything in it or not.

"I found out about that law," said Mr. Gould, "and put the stock in somebody's else's name. "You can't tell anything," he continued, sharply, "about any stock list. There are many shares of stock held by brokers for years."

After the consolidation he had begun to distribute his stock among other holders.

"I made up my mind," he said, "it would be better to have four or five stockholders do a little of the walking instead of one."

Q. That idea was very much stimulated by the rise in the stock after the consolidation, was it not? A. Yes, because the stock went up then so much that there wasn't enough to go round.

The witness told the story of the employing of General Dodge and Solon Humphreys to recommend the consolidation. They were fair men, he thought, and would make a fair report.

He had not talked to them after they went West to make their report.

Q. How is that? A. Well, he naively replied, while they were making their examination my interests had changed.

Q. They had changed? A. Yes, I had bought the Missouri Pacific.

Q. Did General Dodge and Mr. Humphreys look into the past history of the road? A. I consider the future of a road more important than its past.

Q. Yes, but what I want_____ A. The past was no criterion as to the Union Pacific road.

Q. But don't you think that General Dodge and Mr. Humphreys_____? A. "All my life," said Mr. Gould, warming up; "all my life I have been dealing in railroads—that is, since I have been of age, and I have always considered their future and not their past."

"That is the way I have made my money," said he. "The very first railroad I ever bought had a most deplorable past, but its future was fair. I paid ten cents on the dollar for its bonds, and finally sold the stock for $1.25. It was the future of the Union Pacific that drew me into it. I went into it to make money."

"You were not in favor of the consolidation at the time it was made?"

"No, my interests had changed."

"Did you try to stop it?"

"Well," said Mr. Gould, slowly, "my opposition to it was known and they were greatly alarmed."

"Who?"

"Ames, Dexter, Atkins and Dillon. They came on from Boston to see me about it. They had heard that I was going to build an extension to the Denver Pacific and connect the Missouri Pacific. They said I was committed to the consolidation and laid right down on me. I offered my check for $1,000,000 to let me out, and I have offered it since."

"I will pay it now," said the witness, with a strong rising inflection of the voice and looking hard at the Union Pacific people in the room.

"I offered them a million, but they would not let me out of the room until I had signed an agreement to carry out the consolidation."

"Where is that paper?"

"I suppose it is in Boston. If I could have carried out my Missouri Pacific plan I would have a property now that would be worth par."

"I don't think you have any reason to complain of your profits in the matter," replied Mr. Anderson, at which Mr. Gould partly closed his eyes to hide their twinkle, and said nothing.

The paper which he signed was an agreement to carry out the consolidation on certain terms. The consolidation was an assured fact after January 15, because the witness held the controlling interest.

"But I have now ceased to be the tower of the Union Pacific," he said.

In asking Mr. Gould about his connection with Lawyer Holmes at the time of the consolidation, Mr. Anderson asked him whether be was sure about a certain conversation.

"Yes," he said, "for I had it impressed on my mind."

"How was that?"

"Well, I remember parting with a lot of stock at ten cents for which I could have got par a few days afterward. Wouldn't that impress the occasion on your memory, Mr. Anderson?"

Everybody laughed at this, and the witness, although he had lost a million or two, laughed as heartily as the loudest.

As far as the Denver Pacific stock was concerned Mr. Gould said it was worth practically nothing unless the consolidation was made. It was the signature of the Union Pacific that made it good.

"Do you consider that the trustees fulfilled their duty in letting this stock out of trust?" be was asked.

"I consider that it was the only thing to do, and I stand on what was done. I am ready to take the responsibility for it that day, or this day, or any other day."

[From the *New York Times*, May 19, 1887.]

Jay Gould gave another day to the Pacific Railway Commission yesterday. His manner was, as usual, cool and collected, and he was apparently full of a patient desire to tell everything he knew. Yet Mr. Gould told very little, although he answered hundreds of questions, some of them puzzling enough to drive a less long-headed financier into a corner. The Denver Pacific stock and the way it got out of the trust were first taken up. Mr. Gould said he thought the course taken was best for everybody. Naturally he wanted the Denver Pacific to go into the consolidation, holding as he did, $1,000,000 of the securities, and being trustee of over $3,000,000 more. At first it was doubtful if the Union Pacific would take it, but it did for the franchises. "I want to say again," declared Mr. Gould, "that no director or person connected with the Union Pacific ever made a dollar out of Denver Pacific. I am glad to put a final nail in that coffin."

His plan at one time was to build a line from Denver to Ogden, via Salt Lake and Loveland Pass. It would have been shorter than the Union Pacific and obtained more local business, for the Union Pacific ran north of the mineral belt and the Southern Pacific south of it. After he obtained the Missouri Pacific he saw what a good thing he had in it, but he was persuaded to give his pledge to go on with the consolidation of the other roads. The Boston folk became agitated within a month after he bought the Missouri Pacific, and got the pledge from him. If the Missouri Pacific had been put through it would have injured the Union Pacific a great deal.

"According to the ethics of Wall street," Mr. Gould was asked, "do you consider it absolutely within the limits of your duty, while a director of the Union Pacific, to purchase another property and to design an extension of the road which would perhaps ruin the Union Pacific?"

"I don't think it would have been proper. That's the reason I let it go."

"Did you consider your duty to the Government?"

"I had considered it."

"How would the Government claim have been affected by building a parallel line?"

"It would have been wiped out."

After the Thurman bill had been sustained by the Supreme Court Mr. Gould had a plan to build a road from Omaha to Ogden, just outside the right of way of the Union Pacific, and give that road back to the Government. It would give others "a chance to walk." The Government tried to squeeze more out of the turnip than was in it. For $15,000,000 a road could be built where it had cost the Union Pacific $75,000,000.

"You were not devoted to the interests of the Government?"

"I wanted to protect them. Their legislative action hurt their own interests and put those of the stockholders in jeopardy. The Government repudiated their own contracts. Cash was offered to pay the Government the Union Pacific debt. I had the debt reckoned up and offered to pay it. In 1877 or 1878 I made the offer to the Judiciary Committee, of which Mr. Edmunds was Chairman. I made the offer myself. The debt was estimated at $15,000,000 or $17,000,000. But the Government would not concede that interest terminated with the bonds. No action was taken on the proposition."

Mr. Gould thought he wrote his own resignation as Director of the Union Pacific. He resigned because he ought not to deal with the company while one of its directors. He put it in President Dillon's office. Mr. Dillon knew what it meant.

"What did it mean?"

"That if the consolidation went through it involved large transactions with Jay Gould, and if I had staid in it would have complicated things. Before January 10, 1880, no bargain was made to pay par for St. Jo. and Western bonds, nor Kansas Central, nor 239 for Central Branch stock. That came afterward."

The Colorado Central lease was canceled on account of a State law against consolidating competing lines. Mr. Gould did not know that the Dodge and Humphreys letter was to be presented to the meeting of January 24. He was probably informed of the consolidation on the day it took place. He was also probably present at the first meeting of the new company on January 24. Mr. Gould's resignation from the Kansas Pacific Board was gone over, and in summarizing his reasons for resigning Mr. Gould said he did not want to be mixed up with trusteeships and directorships. When he was not a Union Pacific director he felt at liberty to take care of himself. There was a chance that the properties might be made hostile to him, and then it would have been improper for him to be a director. He did not know that Russell Sage was to move the acceptance of his resignation.

"At the Kansas Pacific meeting a list of the branch lines obtained from you was read. President Dillon said the company had bought them. What did he mean?"

"Possibly he referred to the directors' agreement with me."

"But we can find no record of this in the books. Don't you think he referred to the agreement with the Boston gentlemen?"

"Very likely, but it had no authority until it was accepted or rejected."

Mr. Gould was set to explaining some discrepancies between the accounts of his dealings in branch securities, handed in on Tuesday, and the list submitted by Controller Mink. Mr. Mink gave 15,162 shares of St. Jo. and Western stock, and Mr. Gould 8,119. The difference was explained by Mr. Gould's getting some stock for building the Hastings and Grand Island. He retained control of the $150,000 St. Jo. Bridge bonds he sold Dillon and Sage and turned them over with his own. His $479,000 Kansas Central bonds and 2,521 shares of the stock cost him $431,820.25 at the time he bought the Missouri Pacific. They all went into the consolidation for $479,000. Mr. Gould bought the Central Branch of the Union Pacific from Oliver Ames and President Pomeroy, who came to New York and induced him to go and look at the property.

"I thought it was doing a big business," said he. "Afterward I learned they had kept the freight back for a week, to impress me. So I saw a freight train at every station when I got there. I bought the road anyway." Its total cost to Mr. Gould was $1,826,500. Over the Central Branch, whose stock was disposed of by Mr. Gould for 239, there was a little stir in the hearing, but the witness tranquilly explained that the road was practically stocked at only $2,500 a mile, and therefore the stock ought to range way above par.

"Has the road earned dividends?" he was asked.

"I don't think so."

"Have the aggregate earnings exceeded the fixed and Government charges?"

"I never figured it out. Stock doesn't always depend upon dividends altogether. I paid 750 for my Missouri Pacific—4,000 shares at that figure. You pay more for rubies than for diamonds and more for diamonds than for glass."

Then the examination turned to the days just after the consolidation, and the witness was asked if there was any corporate action of the new company before the stock was turned over to him.

"All I know," he said, "is that the stock of the new company was delivered."

"Was the new company bound to carry out the Kansas Pacific obligations of this sort?"

"Well, I suppose it assumed the Kansas Pacific obligations."

"Why were you not paid in Kansas Pacific consols instead of stock?"

"I suppose they preferred stock to bonds. I was clever to them and took stock."

Another turn carried questions and answers to other differences in the accounts, but the commission got little light. "It's safe to say the lawyers got the difference," chuckled Mr. Gould, at the end of the set of questions. He had made large cash advances, at different times, to the Kansas Pacific to meet the floating debt, and very likely these would have to be counted in to explain matters in all cases. There was one point upon which the witness strongly insisted, and that was that all through the negotiations and transactions no class of people nor any particular holders of securities experienced any discrimination in their favor, as compared with the treatment given everybody else.

After the consolidation Mr. Gould said he had few transactions in Union Pacific branch lines. He had an interest in the Denver & South Park, however, a minority interest at first, but subsequently he bought the whole road from Governor Evans. "I'm showing you my whole hand," he said, cheerfully, at the end of the catalogue of the branches. Of the Union Pacific's legal expenses he knew of none which were not perfectly legal.

"Who were the road's counsel in Washington?"

"Messrs. Shellabarger & Wilson were the only ones, as far as I knew."

"Have you ever been to Washington on business of the company?"

"Yes. And I paid my own hotel bills."

"Do you recall persons sent to Washington from other places in the interest of the road?"

"Judge Usher and Mr. Poppleton."

"Who represented the Kansas Pacific?"

"Judge Usher. I don't know that they had anybody in Washington."

"How often did you go to Washington for the road?"

"I was there while the Thurman bill was pending. It passed, and I haven't been there since. No, I take that back. I was down before the Labor Committee. I got rather disgusted."

"Do you know whether anything was spent to influence legislation?"

"No, sir. I know of no such expenditure."

"Where could we find records of such transactions?"

"I don't think such transactions exist."

"Do you remember advising, at a meeting, that Mr. Ordway, of Washington, be employed in the interests of the Kansas Pacific?"

"No, sir."

Mr. Anderson read from the minutes of a Kansas Pacific meeting, in 1876, and Mr. Gould remembered that Senator Rollins, a great friend of Mr. Ordway, asked him to write a letter about it. He knew of nothing coming from the letter.

"Do you remember any talk of fighting the Credit Mobilier?"

"I saw some of their stockholders and they said they would turn in their stock to us. Others wouldn't. The Credit stockholders alleged that the Union Pacific owed their company a great deal of money. I succeeded in getting the great bulk of the stock turned over before a judgment was obtained."

"You remember your address to the Union Pacific president and directors."

"I wanted to put myself in a position to bring a suit."

"Who opposed this proposed action of yours?" asked Mr. Anderson, reading from the minutes of a directors' meeting that Mr. Dexter moved "to decline to bring suit, as requested by Mr. Gould."

"I think the directors declined, and I brought the suits individually."

"There is another letter of yours to the directors, requesting them to begin suit against the Credit for a full accounting of all profits, under certain alleged contracts," etc.

"I think that was on a different set of contracts."

Mr. Frederick L. Ames, the first witness called, testified that he was formerly a stockholder in the Union Pacific Railroad, and is a cousin of the Hon. Oliver Ames, Governor of the Commonwealth. He was familiar with the relations of this road and the Kansas Pacific Road prior to 1877. "I personally attended," he said, "to the affairs of the road under the direction of my father, Oliver Ames. The first dividend of the road was paid in 1875 or 1876. I do not remember the rate paid. I was somewhat familiar with the condition of the Kansas Pacific. I did not think the stock of much value in 1877. Mr. Jay Gould was instrumental in buying up the Kansas Pacific securities in 1876. I understood that he owned a large amount of the funding bonds and unstamped incomes. I never knew what the respective interests of any of the gentlemen interested were. I owned no securities that entered into that pool. I received two certificates for $50,000 each. I have not these in my possession now. They were turned over to somebody. These certificates were probably issued to every member of the pool. I think I paid $100,000 to the Farmers' Loan and Trust Company."

Mr. Anderson—Have you been able to find those certificates, Mr. Mink?

Controller Mink—They are not in our possession, sir.

Mr. Anderson—It is very strange that we cannot get any clue to these certificates.

Continuing, Mr. Ames testified as to the manner in which the business of the pool was conducted, a copy of the consolidated mortgage being introduced in evidence.

"I do not remember," he said, "that I ever contributed the $383,000 funding bonds named in this mortgage. My connection with this pool was limited to the advancement or the $100,000. The pooling rates and mortgage rates were identical. I was a director in the Kansas Pacific Road in 1879. I cannot explain why bonds were issued to persons having claims against the road at a rate which would exaggerate its indebtedness more than $1,000,000. I exchanged my bonds for Kansas Pacific bonds. I do not remember that, in 1880, $2,950,000 of preferred stock was issued to Jay Gould at 75 when the bonds were worth 94. I do not know of any other transaction of the kind. I do not know how the Kansas Pacific Road came to be indebted to Jay Gould for $2,000,000 at this time. All the directors were in favor of the consolidation except Jay Gould. He was unwilling to accede to any such terms as we thought we were entitled to, and seemed very much agitated at the course we had taken. The final consummation was reached at Mr. Gould's house. I do not remember that we would not let Mr. Gould leave the room until he had signed the paper. The paper was signed by all present. The basis of the consolidation was $50,000,000."

When asked how he explained the payment of dividends by the Union Pacific with a condition of affairs which requires a sale of stock for the extinction of a floating debt, Mr. Ames said that the declaration of the dividend was made upon the statement of the net earnings, and the road might very well have earned the dividends several times over and at the same time have been building roads and borrowing money and using its funds for other purposes, in addition to the property, which would not interfere with the right to declare dividends. Mr. Ames also said that the directors of the Union Pacific were largely controlled in signing the agreement read at the forenoon session by the fact that they were cornered by Jay Gould. "I think it has resulted favorably for the Union Pacific," he continued, "and I would not take back the action if I could. I made nothing by the consolidation, as I did not sell my Kansas Pacific stock, but hold it now. Mr. Gould made about $3,500,000."

Judge Dillon cross-examined Mr. Ames, and showed from his evidence that he had no personal ends served by the consolidation. He said that his interest in the Union Pacific is larger now than it was in 1880, and that he is one of the largest stockholders.

JAY GOULD AND HIS SYSTEM.

The following from the *New York Times* of April 27, 1887, contains a graphic account of Mr. Gould's mode of reviewing his system of railroads:

On first thought it seems almost impossible that Jay Gould has only been a railroad magnate of the first class little more than half a decade, yet such is the fact. In 1879 he owned only the nucleus of his present Southwestern system of railroads, and as the rival of the Wabash through considerable territory was the Missouri Pacific, he felt by no means at ease regarding the ultimate fate of his venture. Commodore Garrison owned a controlling interest in Missouri Pacific, which was managed by his brother Oliver. Commodore Garrison did not like Mr. Gould, and would not have objected to make Gould's purchase of Wabash a dear bargain. He probably would have done so had it not been for Oliver Garrison. The latter and Ben W. Lewis, Gould's manager of the Wabash, were close friends, and Garrison, as chief executive of the Missouri Pacific, did nothing to injure Gould's property. But when Mr. Lewis called upon Mr. Gould in New York one day toward the close of 1879, and tendered his resignation on the ground of other interests which claimed his attention, Gould immediately saw breakers ahead, and said so. Lewis suggested that he remove the breakers by buying the control of Missouri Pacific. The suggestion was not allowed to get moldy. Gould called upon Oliver Garrison and offered $1,500,000 for the Garrison interest in the road. Garrison was much surprised, and said it would be necessary to consult with the Commodore. He said, however, that $1,500,000 was at least $500,000 too low. When the Commodore heard of Gould's offer he rubbed his hands, laughed, and put the price at $2,800,000. Gould retorted that he could have bought it on the previous day for $2,000,000. The Commodore explained that the difference between yesterday and today was $800,000. Gould said nothing and retired. He made another effort on the following day. The Commodore been thinking. His thoughts cost Mr. Gould $1,000,000, for his price on the third day of the negotiations was $3,800,000. Mr. Gould did not express his thoughts, but his speech demonstrated that he appreciated the danger and expense of delay. He said, "I'll take it," and he did. Thus from a beginning of less than 1,000 miles he secured control of a system of over 5,000, forming the Missouri Pacific, Iron Mountain, and International and Great Northern and their branches into one compact system. The bargain, in comparison with the present value of the property, was as close a one as Mr. Gould ever managed to make, and from the day it was closed he has lost no opportunity of extending his railroad property, which, with lines that are yet on paper, but are almost certain to be built, is soon likely to embrace at least 6,000 miles of rail.

Though the General Manager's office is at St. Louis, and none of the Gould roads—for the Wabash is not considered in the system—run east of the Mississippi, nothing of importance is transacted there without the knowledge and sanction of Mr. Gould. Private wires run from the St. Louis office to the Western Union Building, in which is Mr. Gould's private office, where he spends some hours each day sitting at a desk that never ought to have cost more than $25.

He has traveled many times over every mile of his railroads. There is an immensity of interest in such a trip when made for the first time, or even the second or third, but it has been made so often by Mr. Gould that he has thoroughly absorbed all the pleasure to be obtained from it except that which smacks of dollars and power. His trips occupy about three weeks from the time his special car, the Convoy, leaves St. Louis until it returns to that hot and dusty city of pageants and conventions.

When word is flashed to St. Louis that Mr. Gould is on his way, every official on the system packs his head full of information, and there is unwonted activity from Omaha to Galveston and from Fort Worth to San Antonio. All of the system's executive force was selected either by Mr. Gould or by trusted officials in whom he had implicit faith, and the heads of divisions who work for Jay Gould could not work harder for anybody else, although in some instances their bank accounts do not show it.

Mr. Gould lately was in the Southwest on a tour of inspection. On his trips he is always accompanied by General Superintendent Kerrigan, a New Yorker by birth, a Southwesterner by education. Physically they are in marked contrast. The cleanly shaven, fair-complexioned Superintendent would make two of his employer. In manner they are much alike, though Kerrigan has a spice of bluffness that is lacking in the other. He has the composed, unexcitable manner of Gould to perfection, and is never known, no matter how great the provocation may be, to speak except in a low-pitched tone. He is a walking railroad encyclopedia, and has the topographical features of the Southwest—every corner of it—at his fingers' ends. He has been employed on railroads of the system for over thirty years. From his Superintendent Mr. Gould obtains such details as the latter gathers from the Division Superintendents and other officials, but in making a trip Mr. Gould insists upon stopping at every point included in one of Mr. Kerrigan's regular trips of supervision, he is always accompanied by a stenographer, who is also a typewriter, and the Superintendent and the heads of divisions follow the same plan.

Upon arriving at a station at which it has been decided to make an inspection, Mr. Gould asks how long a stop will be made. The answer may be "an hour." Mr. Gould looks at his watch. He then accompanies the Superintendent on a part of his rounds, listens quietly to his talk with the railroad officials of the place, and having heard all he cares to listen to, wanders around by himself while the Superintendent picks up the information which later he will give to his employer. Mr. Gould manifests no impatience until the hour has been exhausted. But if the engineer is not ready to start on the minute, and all hands are not in their places on the car, he begins to fidget, and is restless until a fresh start is made.

He is a strong advocate of method. The day's work is laid out in the morning and almost before the train starts in the morning he has settled how many stops can be made during the day and where the night can be spent. He dines and sleeps on board his car from the start to the finish of a three weeks' trip. At night the Convoy is run to the quietest part of the yard, as the owner objects to more noise than he can avoid at night, though he can apparently stand as much as any one else in daylight. His car is always a curiosity along the line, and people come from far and near to look at it as it stands in the evening in a secluded spot, secure in its loneliness. In some parts of the country through which his roads run he is quite as much of a curiosity in the eyes of the country folk as a circus, and were he to stand on the platform after the manner of James G. Blaine, would attract quite as big a crowd as that gentleman. He is never apparently anxious to achieve notoriety in that way, and is quite as modest in his demeanor while on one of his tours as he is in his office or his Fifth Avenue mansion. In the latter, as a few newspaper reporters know, he is more unassuming and far more polite than a majority of his thousand-dollar employees.

Mr. Gould meets some odd as well as prominent people on his trips and occasionally has a peculiar experience. On his first visit to Galveston, Texas, he discovered that it was on an island. Like a good many others be imagined it was on the mainland. On this occasion a number of citizens had been appointed to do him honor and he had promised to take up his quarters at a hotel. The committee had neglected to secure carriages for the party, and made a desperate effort just before the arrival of his car to repair the omission. This it was unable to do. There was an election at Galveston on that particular day. It was a hot one, both the day and the election, and everything on wheels had been bought up by the contending parties. Twenty dollars was offered for a hack and refused. The committee felt forlorn until Mr. Gould laughed at its dilemma and remarked that he saw no hills that he couldn't climb. This is the only joke charged against Mr. Gould by the people who live on the line of his roads, for the highest point of Galveston is only three feet above the sea level. The inhabitants claim four feet, and denounce as a libel the statement made by people who live inland to the effect that tide water is three feet higher than Galveston.

While skimming along over the International and Great Northern, between Houston and Galveston, Mr. Gould cannot look on either side of him without looking at land owned by A. A. Talmage, manager of the Wabash Railroad. Mr. Talmage owns a tract or ranch— though there are but few cattle on it—of 160,000 acres. For this land Mr. Talmage paid 12½ cents per acre. He would probably refuse to sell it to-day for $6 an acre. If Mr. Talmage owned nothing else besides this ranch he might be considered above want. Mr. Gould owns some land in different parts of the country also, but as a proprietor of the soil he occupies a much lower grade than Manager Talmage. George Gould probably owns as much land—railroad land grants not considered—in the Southwest as his father, and is always on the lookout for bargains. These are always to be had at the close of a disastrous agricultural or cattle season. Newcomers in Texas are liable to forget that disastrous years only occur occasionally, and that in three favorable seasons the profits will be large enough to stand one bad season in three. They may hear of all this after they sell out, but the old settler is not offering information that can only be bought with experience until it is valuable as a mournful reflection.

The Iron Mountain Railroad has a station called Malvern. It is 44 miles south of Little Rock. As his car pulls into Malvern Mr. Gould sees on a narrow gauge railroad that also has a station there an engine with a diamond-shaped head-light. The narrow gauge road runs from Malvern to Hot Springs. Mr. Gould has no interest in it, but he knows it was built and is owned—every spike in it—by a man who received his first start in life from the same man who placed him on his feet. The Hot Springs railroad is owned by "Diamond Joe" Reynolds, who was started in business many years by Zadock Pratt, of the town of Prattsville, Greene county, N.Y., when the young man lived in Sullivan county, right across the line of Delaware county, Penn., where Jay Gould was enabled by Mr. Pratt to tan hides with oak and hemlock bark, not after the fashion of Wall Street. Reynolds and Gould were assisted by Mr. Pratt about the same time. Reynolds is not as wealthy today as Mr. Gould, but he owns all the money he wants, and Mr. Gould has often said it did not need fifty millions to secure contentment. "Diamond Joe" Reynolds is a rich man and he spends much of his time between Chicago and Hot Springs. On his first visit to Hot Springs he was compelled to stage it from Malvern. The ride disgusted him as much as the Springs delighted him. He found a man who had obtained a charter for a railroad from Malvern to the Springs and who had no money. The charter and some money changed hands. Reynolds built the railroad and owns it, rolling stock and all. The road is 24 miles long. He made his money in wheat, but not in Sullivan county. After getting a start there he went West and shipped wheat from Wisconsin to Chicago. He shipped it in sacks and marked the sacks with a diamond and inclosed in it the letters "J. O." It was from this circumstance, because the sacks and trade mark became widely known, that he obtained the sobriquet of "Diamond Joe," and not as those who have only heard of him think for a penchant for gems, and Mr. Reynolds is modest as well as rich.

Mr. Gould travels like a rocket while inspecting his roads. In this way he gets a certain amount of exercise, for, as travelers know, a heavy train drawn at the rate of 50 miles an hour will make little fuss in comparison with the antics of a single car tacked to an engine making the same rate. Mr. Gould often travels in the Convoy at a 50-mile gait, and during such a trip he has been known to change seats—from one side of the car to the other—not of his own volition, but without changing countenance. So long as Superintendent Kerrigan keeps his hand off the bell rope Mr. Gould makes no remonstrance, but accepts his shaking without a grumble. He changed engineers on one of his recent trips without knowing it. The engineer had been running slowly, for reasons of his own, in spite of numerous pulls at the bell cord. When, however, he discovered that dinner was under way he pulled the throttle open, and the locomotive darted ahead suddenly as if going through space. The jar cleaned the table like a flash. At the next station the engineer was promoted to a freight train.

A REMINISCENCE OF KANSAS PACIFIC.

There is an interesting piece of information regarding the deal in Kansas Pacific in the testimony of Mr. Artemus H. Holmes, formerly the attorney of that company, showing how the stock made a marvelous leap from two or three dollars to par in seven days. Mr. Holmes testified as follows:

From 1873 to 1877 the market value of all the Kansas Pacific securities was extremely low. The Kansas Pacific stock was $2 to $3 a share and practically valueless. Land grant bonds were worth 10 cents on the dollar, and Denver extension about 40, but ranged from 50 to 70 in 1876 to 1878. The first mortgage bonds were below par, the company's credit was gone and the stock unmarketable. Sidney Dillon, who was then President of the Kansas Pacific Company, was anxious to have the matter settled as quickly as possible. At the former's suggestion a friendly suit was brought on January 17, 1880, before Judge Donohue, in the Supreme Court, in this city, to settle the ownership of the Denver Pacific stock. The trustees said they could not do anything with the stock that would injure it. On January 20, 1880, Horace M. Ruggles, as referee, heard argument, the case was closed in two days, the decision was made January 23 and the decree signed by Judge Donohue on January 24, giving the stock to the Gould party. Mr. Holmes stated: "All the time this was pending the articles of consolidation were being drawn up, but I did not know anything about it until they were signed on January 24." Referee Ruggles decided that 29,000 shares of Denver Pacific stock free from mortgages should pass to the Kansas Pacific. This was put into the Union Pacific and 29,000 shares of the consolidated company's stock given in exchange, which sold at par. The witness was sharply questioned as to what he knew about Referee Ruggles' report. He was asked if he knew who wrote the report, or had any knowledge as to who did.

Q. In order to prepare the decree which was signed on Jan. 24, you must have had the finding before you, did you not? A. No.

Q. How could you prepare it without knowing what the finding was, for the decree was presented the very next day?

A. I must withdraw that answer, and change it to yes.

Gov. Pattison—Do I understand you to say that the stock which was exchanged had risen in a few days from $2 to $3 a share to par. Mr. Holmes said that was a fact, and then this question was put to him:

Q. In other words, Mr. Dillon had sworn on Jan. 17, 1880, that the stock had no financial value, and yet on Jan. 24 it was worth par. A. Yes.

This discloses another of Mr. Gould's valuable secrets of the way to make money rapidly.

GOULD'S FIRST YACHTING EXPERIENCE.

There is a humorous story told of Mr. Gould's first yachting experience, which was recently published in the Philadelphia *Press,* and its veracity vouched for by a living witness to the event. It is characteristic of Mr. Gould in some special respects, and runs as follows:

At the residence of a club man, whose reputation as a *raconteur* is nearly as great as that of his Burgundy, I noticed a pretty model of a jib and mainsail yacht. Replying to my admiring inquiry the club man explained:

"That is the model of a boat upon which were passed some of the sunniest hours of my life. She was owned by one of the Cruger family, of Cruger-on-the-Hudson, and has an added interest from the fact that upon her Jay Gould acquired his first yachting experience, and so eventful a one that I'll bet he remembers it to this day.

"Crugers—one of the oldest and best known families in the State, intermarried as they are with other Knickerbockers like the Schuylers, Livingstons and Van Rensselaers—owned all the land in the neighborhood of the station subsequently named after them. A portion of this property consisted of a brick yard, which was rented to the son of old Schuyler Livingston. It was in 1853 or 1854, and Jay Gould had just failed in the tannery business in Pennsylvania.

"Young Livingston's leased brick yard wasn't paying, and he concluded that it needed a shrewd business man at its head. He advertised for a partner, and one day there appeared in response a small, dark gentleman, looking scrupulously neat in his black broadcloth. He gave his name as Jay Gould. Pending negotiations, Mr. Gould became the guest of the Crugers at the old mansion on the hill. Every effort was put forth to entertain him during his stay, the more as he seemed to regard favorably a partnership with their young friend.

"One day Mr. Cruger invited Gould to a sail to Newburgh, and got ready his yacht, of which that model is the reduction. Several of us youngsters were taken along to help work the boat. Eugene Cruger, a nephew of the yacht's owner, was one of us. Peekskill was reached and the whole party went up to the hotel.

"All the way up the river we had noticed that Mr. Gould was uneasy, shifting about constantly on the deck, where he sat, and squirming and twisting as if seeking to find a softer spot. Nothing was said about it, of course, but when we landed Mr. Gould himself furnished the explanation. From the heat of the sun the yellow paint on the boat's deck had become baked and chalky, and it was not long before the little man discovered that the dry powder was coming off on his trousers. Hence his uneasiness. He concluded by saying he was afraid his broadcloth nether garments would be, if they were not already, ruined, and was determined to abandon the trip and return by rail. This Mr. Cruger would not hear of, and promised to obviate the difficulty. We all adjourned to a general store and Cruger bought, for two shillings and a half, a pair of jean overalls. These Mr. Gould put on when we went aboard the boat and expressed his unqualified satisfaction at the result.

"On our trip back from Newburgh we again called at Peekskill, and once more the party started for the hotel. This time Mr. Gould declined the invitation to take something and preferred to remain on board. About an hour was spent in the hotel, when suddenly Mr. Cruger remembered that he wanted some white lead, and young Eugene Cruger and I went with him to the store to carry it down to the boat.

"'How'd the overalls work, Mr. Cruger?' was the salutation of the storekeeper. Then before answer could be returned, he added admiringly: 'That friend o' yourn is purty shrewd.'

"'Who, Mr. Gould? Yes, he appears to be a thorough business man.'

"'Well, I sh'd say so! He can drive a mighty sharp bargain.'

"'Drive a sharp bargain?' repeated Cruger, all at sea. 'What do you mean?'

"'Why, don't you know he was in here 'bout three quarters of an hour ago, and sold me back the overalls you bought for him.'

"'Thunder, no!' roared Cruger in astonishment.

"'Well, sir, he jest did that. He kem in here, tole me he'd no fu'ther use for 'em, that they was as good as when I sold 'em, an' after we'd haggled awhile he 'greed ter take two shillin' fur 'om, which I paid him. Here's the overalls.'

"I can shut my eyes now," went on the jolly club man, with a hearty laugh, suiting the action to the words, "and call up Mr. Cruger's face with its mingled expression of amazement and incredulity. He left the store in silence. Not until we had nearly reached the boat did he speak. Then he only said, 'Boys, I'll fix him for that!' We reached home without any reference to the incident. On the way back Mr. Gould sat upon his pocket-handkerchief.

"The same night Mr. Cruger perfected his plan. Next day Mr. Cruger proposed a fishing party. Mr. Gould declined to go. He had concluded, he said, not to take an interest in young Livingston's brickyard, and would return to the city on the afternoon train. A business engagement, involving quite a sum of money, had to be kept. His host argued with him, but for a time to no purpose. The saturnine little man had a tremendous amount of determination in his composition. Finally a compromise was effected, it being agreed that he should put Gould off at a station in time to catch the train. That he must catch it without fail, he most emphatically declared.

"The day passed on and we were off Sing Sing, when we saw the smoke of the coming train. We had been running free before the wind, but immediately Mr. Cruger, who was at be stick, shoved it down; we hauled in on the sheets and headed for the Eastern shore. Mr. Gould was by this time on his feet, clinging to the windward coaming, the deepest anxiety pictured on his face. Just there the water shoals rapidly. We were within fifty feet of the shore, opposite the railroad depot. The time had now come for Mr. Cruger's revenge.

"'Let go the main and jib sheets!' he shouted. 'Down with your board!'

"Never was order more eagerly obeyed. The sheets whizzed through the blocks, ready hands slipped out the pin and jammed down the centre-board, and in a second the yacht, with a grating shock and shaking sails, came to a stand, fast on the sandy bottom. There she was bound to stay until the obstructing board was lifted again.

"'What's the matter?' exclaimed Mr. Gould, anxiously. Of course he had not detected the ruse, for he knew no more about the working of a yacht than a sea cow does about differential calculus."

"'I'm afraid we're aground,' replied Mr. Cruger, with a fine assumption of sadness. 'Boys, get out the sweeps and push her off.'

"We struggled with the long oars in a great show of ardor, while Gould watched us in breathless suspense, between hope and fear. But as we had taken care to put the sweeps overboard astern, the harder we shoved the faster we stuck. The little man's suspicions

were not in the slightest degree aroused and he turned in despair to
Mr. Cruger.

"'What shall I do!' he almost wailed. 'I've got to catch
that train!'

"'Then,' replied the joker, solemnly, 'you'll have to wade or swim.'

"Already the train was in sight, two miles away, and whatever was
to be done had to be done quickly. As I have said, there was plenty
of grit in the embryo railroad king, and quick as a wink he was out
of his sable clothes and standing before us clad only in his aggres-
sively scarlet undergarments. Holding his precious broadcloth suit
above his head, he stepped into the water, which, shallow as it was,
reached to the armpits of the little gentleman. Then he started for
the shore, his short, thin legs working back and forth in a most
comical fashion as he strove to quicken his pace. The station platform was crowded with people, and very soon the strange figure
approaching them was descried. A peal of laughter from 500 throats
rolled over the water to us, the ladies hiding their blushes behind
parasols and fans. The men shouted with laughter. Finally the wader
reached the base of the stone wall, and for a moment covered with
confusion—and but little else—stood upon the rock, one scarlet leg
uplifted, looking for all the world like a flamingo on the shore of a
Florida bayou, while the air was split with shrieks of laughter, in
which we now unreservedly joined. Then came the climax of the
joke, which nearly paralyzed the unfortunate victim.

"Haul on your sheets, boys, and up with the board!" was Cruger's
order. As the yacht gathered headway and swept by within ten feet
of the astonished Mr. Gould, we laughingly bade him good-bye,
advising a warm bath when he got home.

"Then his quick mind took in the full force of the practical joke
we had worked upon him and his dark face was a study for a
painter. But the train had already reached the station, taken on its
passengers and the wheels were beginning to turn again for its run
to the city. As Gould scrambled up the wall, his glossy black suit
still pressed affectionately to his bosom, the 'All aboard!' had
sounded and the cars were moving. Every window was filled with
laughing faces as he raced over the sand and stones and was dragged by two brakemen on to the rear platform, panting and dripping.

The last glimpse was as the train entered the prison tunnel. Then, supported on either side by the railroad men, he was making frantic plunges in his efforts to thrust his streaming legs into his trousers as the platform reeled and rocked beneath him."

"Did he ever return Mr. Cruger the two shillings?" the writer inquired.

"Return the two shillings!" echoed the club man. For a moment he was silent. Then, as a retrospective gleam crept into his eyes, he slowly shook his head and, with seeming irrelevancy, said:

"I—guess—you—are—not—very—well—acquainted—with—Mr.—Jay—Gould."

The above story was submitted to Mr. Eugene Cruger at his residence, No. 1211 Livingston Avenue, together with the inquiry as to its accuracy. Mr. Cruger made the following reply: "I must say that I can't imagine who can have furnished these particulars, for most of those who took part in the incidents related have gone forever. Whoever the informant may be, however, it cannot be denied that you have received a true account of what occurred. I enjoyed the affair at that period, but time has softened things and the recollection is not without its unpleasant side."

The success of Mr. Gould in securing the Baltimore and Ohio Telegraph to be consolidated with Western Union, has placed him at the head of the greatest telegraph monopoly in the world, practically beyond competition. It remains to be seen whether or not Congress will take any action towards the creation of a Government telegraph that will afford a guarantee of protection against extortionate rates. It is true that Western Union has lowered its rates, but this is generally regarded as a conciliatory move of a temporary character on the part of Mr. Gould for the purpose of showing that Government telegraphy is not a necessity, and that as soon as the attention of Congress is turned away from the question rates will go up again.

While I should not approve of the Government going so far as to condemn Western Union property, and making a purchase thereof on an appraised valuation, still I do believe that proper Congressional action should be taken to provide supervision and protective control over the telegraphic communication throughout the country. My idea is that the Government should interfere rather as a regulator than an owner, being careful to avoid everything that could be construed into monopoly on its own part, any more than in connection with our railroad system.

Mr. Gould went to Europe late in the fall, and visited several places there ostensibly for health, pleasure, and recreation. What his secret and ultimate designs may be has not yet transpired, although they have been a leading topic of much conjecture among financiers and Wall Street magnates since his arrival on the other side. One of the best things got off on this subject was, that when Mr. Gould sent in his card to one of the Rothschilds, the latter requested the messenger to inform the gentleman that Europe was not for sale.

He returned about the end of March to find some of his railroads, especially in Missouri Pacific system, in a somewhat crippled condition.

With a feeling of deep humility that I have made many important omissions in Mr. Gould's variegated career, although I have surrendered all the space to him that I can very well afford, I now beg to take my leave of him, at least so far as the present edition is concerned.

CHAPTER 25

KEENE'S CAREER

He Starts in Speculation as a California Broker. — A Lucky Hit in a Mining Stock Puts Him on the Road to be a Millionaire. — His Speculative Encounter with the Bonanza Kings. — He Makes Four Millions, Starts for Europe and Stops at Wall Street, Where He Forms an Alliance With Gould, Who "Euchres" Him and Others. — Selover Drops Gould in an Area Way. — Keene Goes Alone and Adds Nine Millions More to His Fortune. — He Then Speculates Recklessly in Everything. — Suffers a Sudden Reversal and Gets Swamped. — Overwhelming Disaster in a Bear Campaign, Led by Gould and Cammack, in Which Keene Loses Seven Millions. — His Desperate Attempts to Recover a Part Entail Further Losses, and He Approaches the End of His Thirteen Millions. — His Princely Liberality and Social Relations with Sam Ward.

ONE of the most remarkable up-and-down lives known to Wall Street is that of James R. Keene. His rise and fall are both of recent date.

Mr. Keene is of English parentage, and was born in London, about 48 years ago. He came to this country at the age of 17, lived in the South and studied law there. He removed to San Francisco in 1853, and became well informed in mining matters through several mining cases that were put into his hands while practising at the bar in that city. I am told he was also connected with a Western newspaper for some time. He caught the speculative fever shortly after his arrival in California, and, as it seems, abandoned both law and journalism to become a broker.

Keene had hard work for some time to make both ends meet, and his struggle for existence in the wild West made serious inroads on his health. His physician told him he must give up work, and advised him to take a long sea voyage if he intended to prolong his life. Acting on this advice, he secured his passage to the East. This was the turning point in both his health and fortune.

Prior to his departure, Mr. Keene was urged to invest a few hundred dollars in a mining stock then selling very low. The length of his journey and the change of scene caused him almost to forget about his investment, and the methods of communication between the far West and the far East in those days were so very slow that he had hardly any chance of being informed of his lucky venture until his return. As an illustration of this slow transit of news at that time, it may be stated that gold was discovered January 19, 1848, but the news did not reach the Eastern States until the following December. It was authoritatively announced in the President's annual message, and created great excitement. Mr. Alfred Robinson, with about twenty companions, were the first to leave New York for the scene of the new El Dorado, on the bark "John Benton."

After nearly a year's absence Keene was surprised to find, on his return, that mining stocks had taken a prodigious bound upward and carried the one in which he had invested with them. The mine had turned out to be a veritable bonanza, and the stock which had cost him only a few hundred dollars was then worth over $200,000.

Had Mr. Keene's health not required his absence from the scene of speculation the chances are that he would have disposed of his stock as soon as it should have realized a few thousand dollars.

This was a wonderful realization for one who had been comparatively poor, and was sufficient to turn the head of any ordinary man; but it only made Keene more anxious for greater success, which he set himself diligently to achieve.

The speculative craze was then intense and epidemic. Waiters and chambermaids bloomed into millionaires with the rapidity of mushroom growth. Mr. Keene secured a seat in the Board, and began to do an immense business.

Flood, Mackay, Fair and O'Brien were then the prominent operators. The speculative contagion spread rapidly over the coast, and soon imparted its influence to the entire continent. Keene' s further investments were crowned with similar success to that of his first venture, and even in a greater ratio of profit.

Seeing the great and rapid advance in the stocks of the Comstock mines, he naturally reasoned, like old Daniel Drew, that what had gone up so high and so fast was bound to come down. There were but few people on the coast at that time, however, in a mood to reason so soberly, and it required more than ordinary nerve to make the experiment of selling "short." Mr. Keene, however, had the courage of his convictions, and made an onslaught upon the market.

There was a strong contingent to oppose him, for the wealthy syndicate just named, with the Bank of California behind them, were his bitter foes, and they did their best to crush him. In spite of their efforts, however, the market began to yield under the pressure of Keene's "short" sales. In a little while the list gave way and stocks began to topple from their dizzy eminence, even quicker than they had climbed to that unprecedented height. Keene netted millions in their fall. He cleared two and a half millions in the Belcher and Crown Point mines, and over half a million in Ophir.

So, in a few years, this poor lawyer, journalist, curbstone broker and invalid, found himself the happy possessor of millions, his name covered with speculative glory, and the fame of his fabulous fortune heralded in every city, town, hamlet and mining camp between the two oceans.

Keene was still found on the right side of the market when the great bubble burst, when the Bank of California went under, and its president, Mr. Ralston, committed suicide while pretending to take a bath in the Pacific Ocean.

In 1877 Mr. Keene started on a voyage for Europe for the good of his health, and made a friendly call in Wall Street to see how business was transacted there. He found the speculative attraction irresistible. Mahomet had come to the mountain and was held by its magnetic power.

Although Mr. Keene had been a grand success in California, he had a good deal to learn when he came to Wall Street. He soon discovered that California tactics would not do here. He began to sell "short," but found the market failed to yield to the touch of his bearish wand as it had done in San Francisco. When he sold ten thousand shares of a certain stock the decline, instead of being a slump, as he expected, was only an insignificant fraction, and the market soon reacted. Mr. Keene quickly discovered that he was throwing water into a sieve, and stopped sacrificing his California gold so lavishly.

A pool was then formed by Mr. Keene and Jay Gould to put down Western Union. Keene and Selover sold the stock in large blocks, but it was absorbed by some party or parties unknown as fast as it was thrown out. It was gravely suspected that Mr. Gould was the wicked partner who was playing this absorbing game behind the scenes. Major Selover brooded over the matter so seriously that his suspicions began to take tangible form and "body themselves forth" in violence.

The Major and Keene met one morning at the rear entrance of the Stock Exchange, in New street, and interchanged intelligent glances on the subject, after the fashion of those passed between Bill Nye and his companion at the card table with the Heathen Chinee. Selover walked down the street with blood in his eye, and meeting Mr. Gould on the corner of New street and Exchange Place, caught him up by the collar of the coat and a part of his pants and dropped him in the area way of a barber's shop.

The little man promptly picked himself up, went quietly to his office, and made a transaction by which Selover lost $15,000 more. This was his method of retaliation.

Mr. Keene next went into the Atlantic and Pacific Telegraph pool, and was again fortunate. It has been frequently asserted that he lost heavily in this deal, but I have it on good authority that he came out ahead. In the deal with Gould in Western Union, he and Gould netted on joint account $1,300,000. It is popularly believed that Gould "euchred" Keene in this pool, but these are the bare facts.

Keene looked over the speculative field, and found that there had been great depreciation in values prevailing here since the panic of 1873. He had arrived in the nick of time to take advantage of the situation. He was backed by four millions of money, and the few losses which he at first sustained were not felt by him, and only seemed to initiate him properly.

This new blood was just what Wall Street then wanted to put the wheels of speculation in motion. Mr. Keene informed himself about the principal stocks dealt in at the Exchange. He did so with remarkable rapidity. They were all down to panic prices, and seeing that most of them were intrinsically cheap, he bought heavily. Soon the turn came which resulted in the high tide of speculation which continued with but slight reactions all through 1879–80.

The advance was immense, as can be seen in the tabular statement at the end of this book, and the profits were enormous.

Keene's millions were doubled and trebled. He must have felt himself a modern Croesus.

Fully nine millions were added to the four which he brought from California. He stood in the centre of that great pile, figuratively speaking, the cynosure of all eyes from Maine to California, and his fame was noised abroad in Europe.

Gould and other old speculators began to grow green with envy at Keene's unprecedented success. He seemed likely to exceed the wildest dreams that ever the avarice of Monte

Cristo or Daniel Drew had conjured up, and with him the imaginary profits of Col. Sellers had become material realities. His investments were nearly all in good, reliable securities. No dubious paper acceptances nor rotten railroad items were mixed up with his tangible fortune, which was without parallel in Wall Street for its size and rapidity of accumulation.

The history of speculation was ransacked in vain for an illustration of such amazing success in so short a period. But here, I regret to say, this marvellous prosperity ends.

In an evil hour Mr. Keene was induced to spread himself out all over creation, while he still retained his immense interest in stocks. He was so flushed with successive victories that he began to regard failure impossible, and thought he was a man of destiny in speculation, such as Napoleon considered himself in war. He speculated in everything that came along—in wheat, lard, opium and fast horses.

Keene's attempt to get a corner in all the grain in the country, however, was a signal failure. The very week that Foxhall won the Grand Prix in Paris he himself was sadly beaten in the speculative race by the steady going farmers of the West, who sent their wheat to market quicker than he could purchase it with his thirteen million dollars, and all the credit which that implied.

All of a sudden, reversal in the tide of speculation set in. Mr. Cammack was quick to perceive that Mr. Keene was extending his lines and his ventures. He had a conversation with Mr. Gould. They became convinced that the Californian must soon be obliged to leave some of his enterprises in a weak and unguarded position. It was impossible that he could take care of them all. These two champion bears united their efforts to upset the market, and each day brought additional force to their aid. By dint of perseverance their efforts commenced to bear fruit, and it was apparent that they would soon be rewarded with success. The bears began to multiply while the bulls diminished, and the remnant of the latter that were left were anything but rampant at that time.

The bankers became timid. The brokers were inspired with the same spirit and were still calling out for more margin. Loans were called in as a part of the programme of a bear campaign, and all the machinery of depression was put in active motion. Prices were torn to pieces. Properties that had been considered good as solid investments for a long turn, were mercilessly raided, and some of them shattered to fragments. In fact, there was a regular panic. In the general slaughter, many of the brokers sold Mr. Keene's stocks out. His wheat was also sold in immense quantities at great sacrifice, and his load was lightened all around, even more quickly than it had been heaped up.

His losses are said to have amounted to seven millions of dollars at this time.

The manly efforts of Mr. Keene to recover these losses, as is usually the case in such instances, only resulted in further misfortune. Disaster followed disaster, and as he became desperate in his efforts to get back something, his losses became constantly greater, until nearly the whole of his immense pile was buried in fruitless efforts to recover a portion of it.

Great sympathy has been felt in Wall Street for Keene since his failure, for the Street had never before found such a liberal man. By general consent he decidedly took the palm in this respect, not only from all his speculative contemporaries, but the archives of Wall Street since the days of the first meetings of the brokers in the Tontine Coffee House, opposite the sycamore tree, early in the century, can furnish no such parallel of princely liberality as that of James B. Keene during the period of his matchless prosperity.

The parasites that waxed fat on his bounty and business are numerous. At least a score of Wall Street brokers were raised from penury to wealth by the commissions which they made out of him. Many of them are to-day living in luxury who started with a desk and a few plain office chairs to do business for the California millionaire, and now he is comparatively poor, and thrown on the slender resources of his wife.

Keene arose from nil to be worth thirteen millions. He is now back where be started.

A full and correct history of Keene's beneficences would fill this volume, and however much I admire him, I cannot afford to give him so much space.

I shall relate one remarkable instance of his unbounded generosity, however, as the object has been so universally known, and was himself such a popular society man.

Long prior to Mr. Keene's advent in Wall Street, Sam Ward had been a conspicuous figure in Washington and Wall Street, and had acquired a society reputation in Europe.

This gentleman was originally forced into prominence by his marriage with Miss Astor.

Mr. Ward had changed from one thing to another until finally he took up his abode in Washington, and became a lobbyist.

When Mr. Keene came to New York with his four millions of dollars, which he had made when the majority of New York investors had been on the losing side, dropping their money almost as fast as water runs down hill, through the unprecedented shrinkage in values, there was a wide field for profitable investment. This shrinkage had been going on from the panic of 1873, step by step downward until 1878, when society had reached a stratum by dint of levelling down that placed almost everybody upon an equality. Property, in many instances, became a serious encumbrance instead of a benefit, and many were glad to be rid of the responsibility of their holdings for what was sufficient to settle the mortgage. Everybody felt poor, and was really so, with a few fortunate exceptions.

Mr. Keene arrived here at the most fortunate moment for investment. Everything was down to bed-rock prices. He, therefore, became an object of actual curiosity, and was as much of a lion in our midst as he had been in San Francisco.

He was not only the favorite of fortune, but a favorite of society, which generally go together with curious inconsistency in our social democracy.

One of the first acquaintances Mr. Keene made on his arrival was this great society man, the celebrated Sam Ward, who at once recognized his social worth, not only in dollars and cents, but in considerable liabilities, genuine representatives of dollars and cents. The more tangibly he realized this fact the more tenacious was his attachment, until Mr. Keene found Mr. Ward the very *beau ideal* of Scriptural fraternity, namely, "a friend that sticketh closer than a brother."

Wherever Keene appeared, though apparently alone, it was safe to bet that Ward's shadow could soon be seen.

It is said of Seneca, when he observed a house falling, and nobody near it, that he asked: "Where is the woman?" So Keene's presence naturally suggested Ward to the mental vision of every Wall Street man and every sporting man.

Whether it was up-town or down-town, at Newport, or in London, at the Derby, or the Grand Prix, it was all the same, where Keene was, there Ward soon appeared with the promptitude of the genius that stood before Aladdin when he touched his wonderful lamp or rubbed his magic ring.

This self-sacrificing friendship and ardent devotion on the part of Mr. Ward was recognized by Mr. Keene in the most tangible manner. He made an investment for his protege, of $50,000 in solid securities, placing them in the hands of trustees, so that his ward received the income therefrom of three thousand dollars, as an annuity, for life.

Mr. Keene bestowed numerous benefits on other newly made acquaintances, of which this is a fair sample.

A Pacific coast biographer draws the following graphic sketch of Keene, some time after his departure from California, which is curious reading in the light of the events which I have related:

No series of sketches of men, prominently identified with the stock interests of the Pacific coast, would be complete without a pen portrait of James R. Keene, the free lance operator of the San Francisco stock market, who dared to beard the Bonanza Kings in their den, and came off victorious with many shekels of gold and silver. Mr. Keene is no longer with us. Some time since, after having realized largely on his stock ventures, he concluded to take a trip East, to be extended to Europe, unless on the Atlantic seashore he regained the health which too active exertions on the Pacific had impaired. And so he went with his family. Those who bade him God-speed expected to see him return within a few months, certainly within a year, with recovered health, new ambitions, new conquests to make. But he comes not. New York has presented more attractions than his old love, San Francisco. Railroad stocks, Jay Gould, Sam Ward, Rufus Hatch, Long Branch, Trenor W. Park, Newport, have been too many attractions for Jim Keene. He fell into the New York market as easily as any man generally falls among thieves—but he seems to have got the best of the thieves in every issue. When it was rumored that Keene contemplated making Wall Street his headquarters, his old San Francisco friends generally wrote out their calendars, and figured up when 'Jim' would be back, bursted out and out, looking for a job. A few who had abiding faith in Keene, who knew his pluck, who had gauged his capacities, who had measured his horse sense, consulted their calendars and said: 'Jim is gone! He never will come back to couch his lance in such a narrow field as ours. New York is big, Wall Street is big—just about the size of institutions that Keene wants to tackle.' The few were right. Keene hasn't come back to look for a job. He has tried conclusions with the smartest of the Wall Street operators, and, novice that he was, came out triumphant. The California goose that was to be plucked wasn't plucked. Even Jay Gould, with all his shrewdness, gave it up as a bad job; and Vanderbilt condescends to confer with Keene on momentous occasions.

Keene started in his career as a stock operator years ago in San Francisco. He first was conspicuous as an impulsive, dare-devil sort of a street broker, acting for big firms, with an occasional dash for liberty and himself. Gradually he worked his way from steerage to cabin, from the private's ranks to the position of the lieutenant of the watch, then to officer of the day, and finally, boss of the stock concern. No man in the stock market exercised so much influence as Mr. Keene. He had hosts of friends, friends whom he grappled with hooks of steel, ready to swear by him on any and every occasion. Generous to a fault, brusque in manner at times, but with the heart of a woman, ready to melt at a moment's notice, open-handed and open-hearted to the appeal of even an acquaintance, no wonder that Jim Keene was the ideal of the market.

It is not generally known that Keene was chiefly instrumental in rehabilitating the Bank of California after the death of Ralston. He raised a large subscription in the Stock Board, and got the Hon. William Sharon, D. O. Mills and "Lucky" Baldwin to subscribe a million each, and he put in a million himself. The bank was thus enabled to meet all immediate demands, and a threatened panic was averted.

At the time of Keene's failure he was chief of a syndicate which had purchased 25,000,000 bushels of wheat, which would soon have netted many million dollars of profit, if it had been firmly held, but one or two of his partners in the pool became timid and sold out. The syndicate went to pieces, and both profits and capital vanished. He laid his misfortune mainly to the newspapers which raised such a universal cry about the immense "corner" that was being manipulated in wheat, threatening a famine in the great staple of human life.

Keene was next shaken out of his stocks. This was done chiefly by an ably concocted scheme of the bears, and he had the mortification of seeing the stocks which he had held advance within a few months' time to a point that would have enabled him to realize ten million dollars, if he had been able to hold them.

CHAPTER 26

VILLARD AND
HIS SPECULATIONS

RETURN OF THE RENOWNED SPECULATOR TO WALL
STREET. — RECALLING THE FAMOUS "BLIND" POOL IN
NORTHERN PACIFIC. — HOW VILLARD CAPTURED NORTHERN
PACIFIC. — PURSUING THE TACTICS OF OLD VANDERBILT. —
RAISING TWELVE MILLION DOLLARS ON PAPER CREDIT. —
VILLARD EMERGES FROM THE "BLIND" POOL A GREAT
RAILROAD MAGNATE. — HE INFLATES HIS GREAT SCHEME
FROM NOTHING TO ONE HUNDRED MILLION DOLLARS. —
HIS UNIQUE METHODS OF WATERING STOCK AS COMPARED
WITH THOSE OF GEORGE I. SENEY.

THE return of Mr. Henry Villard to Wall Street, after two
years' absence in Germany, his native land, renews the
public interest in the career of that bold speculator. My reminiscences of Wall Street affairs would be incomplete without a
sketch of the daring railroad operations of this gentleman,
which so fully illustrate some of the evils to which I have
referred in my chapter on "Railroad Methods."

The culminating point in the speculative history of
Mr. Villard, which covered a period of five years, from 1879
to 1884, was the famous blind pool in Northern Pacific.

Instead of taking up the events of his life in detail, and carrying my readers to this point, I shall depart from the usual
course of biography, and present the more interesting facts of
the career of my hero at the beginning.

In his capture of Northern Pacific he seems to have followed the methods of the elder Vanderbilt very closely, with the important exception that he failed in the consummation of his purpose. Vanderbilt always, eventually, triumphed.

Villard was the chief agent in forming the Oregon Railway and Navigation Company, which was organized for the purpose of consolidating the business of the Oregon Steam Navigation Company with that of the Oregon Steamship Company, and for the purpose of buying, building and operating railroads, as stated in the circular setting forth the objects of the company. The lines of the Oregon Railway and Navigation Company extended from Portland west to Wallula Junction.

The value of this property was seriously menaced by the project of the Northern Pacific to extend its lines west, with a terminus at Tacoma.

President Billings, of the Northern Pacific, rejected a proposition from Mr. Villard to accommodate the Northern Pacific by permitting it to reach the Pacific coast over the lines of the Oregon Railway Navigation Company.

It was at this juncture that Villard resorted to the old Vanderbilt tactics, by attempting to purchase stock enough of the Northern Pacific to enable him to control the property. For this purpose he formed a blind pool, in which Mèssrs. Woerishoffer, Pullman and Endicott, and a host of other solid men, were the original members. A fund of $8,000,000 was subscribed to purchase Northern Pacific stock. During the spring of 1881 the pool kept on buying steadily, and continued their operations until the middle of summer, when it was discovered that the treasury of the pool was almost exhausted without having effected its purpose of acquiring control of the Northern Pacific property.

Mr. Villard then called a meeting, explained matters, proposed to extend the scope of the pool's operations, and to increase its membership. By showing the enormous profits to be gleaned in the future, he succeeded in getting $12,000,000 more subscribed. This secured the control of the road, and in September, 1881, Mr. Villard was elected President of Northern Pacific.

Villard at once emerged from this blind pool into a great railroad magnate, in a manner, to the eye of the general public, as miraculous as the springing forth of Minerva fully armed from the brain of Jupiter.

The stock of Northern Pacific advanced rapidly in price, and Villard and his friends were supposed to be accumulating millions with unprecedented celerity. Villard appeared to have realized all the financial dreams of Monte Cristo, and he was fast looming up into a proud and dangerous rival of Gould, Vanderbilt and Huntington.

He went forward with the building of the Northern Pacific road, which was finished two years after his success in capturing it through the medium of his blind pool. His phenomenal success induced him to enter largely into the extension of other investments. He became lavish in his personal expenses also, although he had formerly been accustomed to the closest economy in his mode of living, and he built a palace at Madison Avenue and Fiftieth street.

When seemingly on the highest tide of prosperity, Villard suddenly became embarrassed, and when an accounting of the cost of finishing the road was made, he was found to be away behind. There was a miscalculation of $20,000,000 somewhere. Villard explained it by declaring that the estimate of the engineers for finishing the road was $20,000,000, whereas the real cost reached $40,000,000.

For the $20,000,000 subscribed by the blind pool the subscribers received the stock of the Oregon & Transcontinental. This company had been organized to build branch lines to the Northern Pacific, as the charter of the latter did not permit it to build such lines.

This is the speculative history, in brief, of Mr. Villard from the time he took hold of the Oregon & California Railroad up to the juncture of his grand collapse. There were several incidents, however, of more than ordinary interest in his railroad history prior to the time he set his heart upon Northern Pacific. As a stock-waterer he had, probably, no superior, and was only equalled by Mr. George I. Seney, in that important department of railroad management. His methods in obtaining control of the Oregon Steam Navigation Company and the Oregon Steamship Company amply illustrate his remarkable ability in this respect. When Villard proposed to purchase these two companies he had no money, but he had unlimited confidence in his own ability. He asked each company to give him an option to run a year for $100,000. They agreed to do this, and Villard forthwith consulted a number of capitalists, who came together and filed articles of incorporation of the Oregon Railway & Navigation Company, a consolidation of the two companies above-named. When this company, with such a high sounding name, was organized, it had no assets, and the prospects of acquiring any seemed exceedingly blue. The names of the incorporators were as follows: Henry Villard, James H. Fry, Artemus H. Holmes, Christian Bors, W. H. Starbuck and Charles E. Brotherton, all of the city and State of New York, and W. H. Corbett, C. N. Lewis, J. N. Dolph, Paul Schulze and N. Thielson, all of Portland, Oregon. The capital was nominally six million dollars, divided into 60,000 shares. This arrangement was made in June, 1879.

The next problem to be solved after the reorganization was how to raise money to run the concern.

The Board of Directors, under the management of Mr. Villard, were equal to the occasion. They met at Portland a few days after the organization and executed a mortgage to the Farmers' Loan and Trust Company of New York, and under this mortgage issued 6,000 bonds of $1,000 each, payable in thirty years after July 1, 1879, with interest at 6 per cent.

Mr. Villard then paid the $100,000 bonus money to the companies which had been incorporated, took his option, stock and bonds and came East to negotiate his securities. It is said he presented them to Jay Gould, who refused to touch them, as he believed there was not much stamina in the scheme, and he wished to avoid trouble with the Northern Pacific, which he plainly saw the project involved. Villard was more fortunate with Mr. Endicott, Jr., of Boston, Mr. George Pullman and others whom they interested in the enterprise.

The property of the two companies, out of which the new company had been formed, whose securities were so boldly placed upon the market, was not in reality purchased until March of the following year.

After the organization was complete, the visible assets of the Oregon Railway and Navigation Company did not exceed $3,500,000, while the total liabilities amounted to $21,000,000. This was made up as follows:

Original stock	$6,000,000
Water	3,000,000
Water	6,000,000
Mortgage bonds	6,000,000

It will thus be seen that there were seven dollars of liabilities for every dollar of assets, and the intrinsic value of the stock was represented by a minus quantity of 20 per cent., having no positive value at all. In other words, it was 20 per cent. worse than nothing.

In spite of these facts, however, Mr. Villard had the stock listed at the Stock Exchange, and through a carefully prepared report, showing immense and unprecedented earnings, he had the stock bulled up to 200. It was when it reached this high figure that the $9,000,000 of water (noted before) were thrown in to prevent it from becoming top-heavy.

This was the preparatory and successful process of watering which preceded the transactions of Mr. Villard on a more magnificent scale in his manipulation of Northern Pacific, as described at the opening of this chapter. Mr. Villard excelled Mr. Seney in one respect which is noteworthy. As I have shown in a former chapter, Mr. Seney poured the water in lavishly at the reorganization, and prior to having his properties listed on the Stock Exchange.

Villard improved upon this process by employing Seney's method liberally in the first instance, and also by a free and copious dilution after the stocks had been inflated to the very point of bursting.

There is probably no instance in the whole history of railway manipulation in which a man has presented to the public, and with such amazing success, such a specious appearance of possessing solid capital where so little existed in reality.

He began with nothing in 1879 and succeeded in the course of a year in possessing himself, by various adroit methods, as described, of $3,500,000 of assets in railroad securities. With this as a basis of operation, in five years he managed to obtain temporary control of property aggregating in value over $1,000,000,000.

CHAPTER 27

FERDINAND WARD

PECULIAR POWER AND METHODS OF THE PRINCE OF SWINDLERS. — HOW HE DUPED ASTUTE FINANCIERS AND BUSINESS MEN OF ALL SORTS, AND SECURED THE SUPPORT OF EMINENT STATESMEN AND LEADING BANK OFFICERS, WHOM HE ROBBED OF MILLIONS OF MONEY. — THE MOST ARTFUL DODGER OF MODERN TIMES. — THE TRUTH OF THE SWINDLE PRACTICED UPON GENERAL GRANT AND HIS FAMILY.

IN making a fair estimate of the part that Ferdinand Ward, of the firm of Grant & Ward, played in the panic of 1884, I can only say that Ward's methods, taken altogether in their conception and execution, constituted a huge confidence game. He built up confidence by deceiving a few eminent men in financial and social circles, who, from his insinuating and plausible demeanor, were induced to place reliance upon his representations.

His presence was magnetic, and his manner deceitfully unassuming. He had the art of dissembling in great perfection and was possessed of extraordinarily persuasive powers, without appearing to have any selfish object in view. So highly developed in him were these social gifts, through the power of cultivation, that he could convince his unhappy victims that he was actuated with a single purpose for their welfare.

By practicing in this way on the credulity of certain people, Ward managed to get into his hands, for his own personal use, sums of money aggregating millions. Some of the richest financiers became his victims, chiefly induced by promises of high rates of interest and large profits on various ventures.

Ward would ascertain the names and circumstances of certain people who had large balances in their banks and were unable to make satisfactory and paying investments with them. He would bring certain influences to bear upon them to take their money out of the bank and invest it through him in "Government contracts," which he said afforded immense returns, but were of a delicate character, and required some secrecy in the manipulation. This circumstance naturally prevented him from going into an explanation of the details of the enterprise, which it was not necessary for the investors to know when their profits were secured through such a stable investment. It was sufficient for them to be assured that the returns would be very large.

As an instance of the successful manner in which Ward's specious pretences worked, I will relate the experience of one gentleman who deposited $50,000 with him, on the strength of these representations—just as an experiment.

This gentleman was going on a trip to Europe and he left the amount stated in the possession of Mr. Ward to be used to the best possible advantage during his absence, and invested in his own way.

About six months after the date of this deposit, the gentleman returned from Europe and called at the office of Grant & Ward to learn what progress had been made with his investment. He saw Ward, and called his attention to the fact.

The young Napoleon of finance recollected the appearance of his customer at a glance, for he is admirably developed in what phrenologists term individuality, and never forgets a face, but in the immense rush of his speculative business he had forgotten the circumstance until he referred to his books. He was but a few minutes absent in the interior office when he returned and informed the gentleman that his $50,000 had been invested with the ordinary turn of luck that usually accrued under his management, and he was very happy to be able to hand him a check for $250,000, after deducting the ordinary commission, as the result of the investment.

The man was overpowered with this unexpected turn of luck, and the enormous profits taxed his credulity to its utmost capacity. This was a speculative mine that he had never dreamed of, and instead of sleeping any that night he set his entire mind to calculate the profits on $250,000 in the same ratio that his $50,000 investment bad been transformed into this amount.

It required very little mathematical knowledge to arrive at the conclusion that with such another turn of speculative prosperity, he would, within the next six months, be a millionaire and have the original investment left intact. Then if he should make this on three turns, which seemed not unlikely, when he should be present to look after his own business, he might pile up millions by the dozen.

The mind of this fortunate speculator being filled with such thoughts as these, he lost no time after breakfast in taking the train on the elevated road and arrived at Ward's office before business had begun. When Ward arrived he met his customer with a gracious smile, took the check in the most handsome manner and made a note of it in his book.

The investor had not very long to wait this time before he knew the result of his venture. It was only a few days prior to the 12th of May, 1884, at which date the failures of Grant & Ward and the Marine Bank were announced in Wall Street, as the *avant courier* of a sudden panic. So, the only thing that interfered with the second check producing similar results to those of the first, was the unfortunate panic, but of course Mr. Ward could tell his customer that he was not responsible for that.

In this connection an important financial question arises. Would there have been any panic had it not been for Ward, Fish, Eno & Co.? However this may be, there is one thing very evident, namely, that Mr. Ward must be accorded the power of ability to control men with whom he came in contact in a remarkable manner, and of being able to get the best of them in all financial matters. Old and astute financiers, who were considered experts in every method of speculation, and who knew all the artifices of making a sharp bargain, became helpless in the mystical presence of Ward, and were completely non-plussed by his superior acumen in taking advantage of every situation that offered the least opportunity of practicing his peculiar methods of chicanery and fraud.

Ward seems to have been very much of a mind reader. He knew when he passed that check over to the gentleman referred to, for $250,000, that it would come back again, that it would keep burning that man's pocket while he kept it there, and that sooner or later he was bound to return it to the mysterious place of its issue. Doubtless this was not the first case that Ward had experimented upon in this way. He had evidently made a regular practice of it, and could calculate the proportion of his victims with as much accuracy as tables of mortality are made out for insurance companies. There was no blind chance about Ferdinand's methods. He worked according to a rule, having calculated to a nicety the exceptions that proved it, and his success showed that he had not wasted much time over stubborn cases.

Ward displayed marvellous tact in discovering, at a glance, those who were sufficiently credulous to be entrapped into acquiescence with his schemes, and manifested great executive ability in pouncing upon his prey at the proper moment. His methods of operation were admirably suited to his purposes. He saw, for instance, that this man would not put the money in any other kind of investment, and would not be likely to operate, except through Ward himself, as no other man could be found anywhere who could make himself the instrument of realizing such stupendous returns for the money invested.

It is marvellous how the idea of large profits, when presented to the mind in a plausible light, has the effect of stifling suspicion.

The specious pretexts of Ward appeared equal to the task of overcoming the most obdurate cases of incredulity. So, it is not so singular, after all, that men utterly unacquainted with business methods and sharp practice in speculation, were so easily victimized by the sinister methods, conciliatory manners and seductive schemes of this consummate imposter.

Ward was so successful in his arts of persuasion that he could not only succeed in getting possession of all the available capital, for his own practical use, of many eminent financiers, but he had the power of transforming them into walking advertisements for the promotion of his nefarious designs, and turned them to the best account in drumming up business and customers for him while they were blissfully ignorant that they were all the time the subservient mediums of swindling projects. In fact, they made themselves the willing instruments of "roping" in others for Ward's purposes, inspired by the purest motives of gratitude toward him as their confidential broker and benefactor.

In this way General Grant and his sons became the helpless victims of Ward's deeply designing duplicity.

People who have blamed General Grant fail to reflect on the fact that the famous soldier and able tactician was no better than a raw recruit in the hands of a disciplined warrior when he was placed in contact with Ferdinand Ward's superior financial tactics.

One great point in the confidence game worked on joint account between Fish and Ward was to obtain men of well known reputation to vouch for the genuineness of the enterprises in which they were engaged. This enabled them to solidify and extend their credit. It was for this purpose that General Grant was inveigled into signing the well-known letter No. 2, addressed to Fish, which has been the subject of so much criticism and comment. Following is a copy of this letter:

No. 2 WALL STREET, ROOM 6,
NEW YORK,
JULY 6, 1882.

My Dear Mr. Fish:—In relation to the matter of discounts, kindly made by you for account of Grant & Ward, I would say that I think the investments are safe, and I am willing that Mr. Ward should derive what profit he can for the firm that the use of my name and influence may bring.

Yours very truly,
U. S. GRANT.

This letter was written in answer to one from Jas. D. Fish, President of the Marine Bank, saying he had negotiated notes for the benefit of Grant & Ward, to the amount of $200,000. He said in explanation: "Those notes, as I understand it, are given for no other purpose than to raise money for the payment of grain, &c., to fill the Government contracts."

This letter, signed by General Grant, was designated by his counsel as "only an ordinary letter in the course of business," and that is all it is where a man placed confidence in another as General Grant did in Ward and Fish.

It was Ward who wrote the letter, through the instruction of Fish, and got General Grant to sign it.

In an interview with a reporter of the New York *World,* in July last, Ward explained the circumstances under which the letter was signed, as follows:

"Do you know anything about that letter addressed to Mr. Fish and signed by Gen. Grant, regarding the Government contracts?" asked the reporter.

"Of course I do," quickly replied Ward. "I made the original draft. It was by Mr. Fish's direction, and he asked me to do it, suggesting what I should write. He had had some trouble in getting Grant & Ward's paper discounted, for he attended to that and raised millions of dollars. He wanted something to show to Mr. Cox, President of the Mechanic's Bank, and others from whom he tried to get money for the firm. The contract business was the great thing, and he said if he only had something from the General to show that he knew about the contracts, it would be easier for him to go to these men. I distinctly remember the circumstances under which this letter was prepared. Fish gave me an idea what it ought to be like and I wrote it. Then Mr. Fish went over it and made some corrections in his own handwriting. It was scrawled on a piece of paper that happened to be handy in the office, and after he had it to suit him he handed it to me and I gave it to Spencer, our cashier, to copy. I am not sure but that I have got that draft somewhere among my papers. I think I have seen it since the failure, and if it is still in existence it can plainly be seen that Mr. Fish knew all about it before it received Gen. Grant's signature. The General was in the habit of signing papers I asked him to without paying much attention to what they were. So when I asked him to sign this one he did so without much if any questioning. I understood well enough what Fish wanted it for, because he told me, and I have no doubt that Mr. Cox and other gentlemen from whom he borrowed money saw the letter."

CHAPTER 28

HENRY N. SMITH

How Mr. Smith Started in Life and Became a Successful Operator.—His connection with the Tweed "Ring," and how he and the Famous "Boss" Made Lucky Speculations, through the use of the City Funds, in Making a Tight Money Market.—On the Verge of Ruin in a Pool with W. K. Vanderbilt.—He is Converted to the Bear Side by Woerishoffer, and Again Makes Money, but by Persistence in his Bearish Policy Ruins himself and Drags Wm. Heath & Co. down also.

I have already had occasion to speak of Henry N. Smith, who was a member of the firm of Smith, Gould & Martin, but I consider him of sufficient importance, speculatively speaking, for a separate biographical sketch.

This gentleman is a native of Buffalo, and had been in the mercantile business there before coming to Wall Street. He was familiarly known as the young man from Buffalo. He had then a decidedly Hebrew aspect; was a strawberry blonde, with full beard of auburn hue, sharp, piercing eyes, and an air of self-confidence. He had made some money in Buffalo, and was lucky in his first ventures in Wall Street, being one of the few who emerged from the panic of 1864 on the winning side. Smith became a bold operator, and accumulated considerable money. He was invariably successful in his transactions whenever he was governed by his own judgment. The first disaster overtook him in the panic of 1873.

Immediately prior to that he had been under the influence of Commodore Vanderbilt, who put him into Western Union, and the loss which he sustained by its terrible fall in that year almost ruined him. He lost all his ready money, being left without anything but his New York residence and a stock farm.

He did not lose courage, however, by this speculative blow, but picked himself up again and soon became quite a power in the Street, and in spite of the ups and downs of speculation and the various panics, Smith kept clearly ahead of the market for many years, and became a successful and comparatively wealthy operator.

He always managed to ingratiate himself with wealthy connections in his various operations, and was able to command an enormous amount of credit in comparison with his actual means.

A few years ago, on his return from Europe, he met W. K. Vanderbilt, and they began to discuss the probable future of the market. Vanderbilt had been a bull for some time previously. They entered into an agreement to operate on the bull side together. The result was that Vanderbilt lost several millions, and came pretty near running the risk of exhausting a large part of his then anticipated share of his father's estate. The deal was disastrous to Smith also.

Soon after this discomfiture, one day, on his way to Long Branch, Mr. Smith met the late Mr. Woerishoffer, who was the great bear on the market, while Smith and Vanderbilt were still then the leading bulls. Woerishoffer succeeded in convincing Smith that his position on the market was wrong that he had better make a clean sweep of it in selling out the stocks which he held, and join hands with him on the bear side.

Smith was impressed with Woerishoffer's advice, earnestness and personality.

The great bear was also in a position to back up his theory by examples of his success, the best and most convincing argument that could possibly be employed, especially by a Wall Street speculator. As the result of this bearish counsel,

Smith soon recuperated from the effect of his former losses, and, in consequence, got bearish notions so badly on the brain that he was prepared to swear by Woerishoffer's judgment, and considered his own equally infallible. He could see nothing but disaster ahead any more than his general, and was recklessly prepared to follow wherever the champion bear should lead in the destruction of values.

Smith seemed to have the same abiding faith in Woerishoffer that Ignatius Loyola reposed in the Pope of his day. "If the Holy Father," said that eminent Jesuit, "should command me to row several leagues into the ocean in an open boat, in the midst of a terrific gale, I should straightway obey his mandate without asking why or wherefore."

Such is hardly an exaggerated illustration of the thorough appreciation which Smith entertained of the perfection of Woerishoffer's bearish discipline, and the exact certitude of his judgment in all matters of a speculative character. It is almost impossible for a man who has had no experience in Wall Street matters to estimate the extremes of fanaticism in speculation to which a man is prepared to go when he is seized with a monomania either on the bull or the bear side, but especially on the latter.

The evidence of his senses counts for nothing, and the evidence of other people's senses, if possible, goes for less. He is a consistent bull or bear, as the case may be, and that settles it. He is Sir Oracle on the stock market, and when he speaks let no dog bark.

This inveterate combination of egotism and fanaticism has ruined many hundreds, to my own knowledge. The disease is contagious, and Smith had a very obstinate form of it. His symptoms were even worse than those of Woerishoffer, by whom he was smitten, a peculiarity that very often occurs in the recipient of this financial malady.

Like Woerishoffer, Smith fought the market with desperation on every advance. He adhered steadily to the policy of attacking prices on every rally during the summer of 1885, while values were constantly advancing, with occasional healthy reactions. When his own money was exhausted he began to incur cumulative liabilities with the house of Wm. Heath & Co., until that famous firm had become almost depleted of its available resources in replacing margins as fast as they were wiped out by the persistent tide of advancing prices in speculation.

Thus Mr. Smith proceeded, in obedience to the spirit of bearish fanaticism, until his loss became so great that he not only had to pay out all his own money, but was in debt to the firm of Wm. Heath & Co. in a million dollars, which was the cause of their failure, and which crippled or caused to collapse several smaller houses.

When Mr. Smith appeared before the Governing Committee of the Stock Exchange to make application for the extension of time on his seat, he made the following extraordinary statement: "On January 1, 1885, I was worth $1,400,000. I had $1,100,000 in money, and the balance, $300,000, in good real estate. On the following January I had lost the whole amount, and was $1,200,000 in debt, a million of which I owed to Wm. Heath & Co."

Many people were surprised that Mr. Smith was enabled to obtain such an enormous and unlimited amount of credit in one house. I took the ground at the time, and I am still of the same opinion, that the animal magnetism or psychologic power of Henry N. Smith over the elder Heath was the real cause of all the trouble.

Mr. Heath had been in bad health for some time, consequently he left the general management of the business to Mr. McCanless, the head clerk and general manager of the firm, through whom the orders of Mr. Heath were strictly executed.

Mr. Heath being weak in both body and mind, yielded his opinions to those of Mr. Smith, by virtue of the superior mental force of the latter.

In conducting a large Wall Street business it is necessary that a man should have the mental stamina to say "no" firmly, and stand to it. In order to be able to do this he must be backed up by a vigorous, healthy physique.

The power to utter a negative in a determined manner requires, generally, a fair degree of physical force, and it is absolutely necessary to the success of a Wall Street broker that he should be able to do it when occasion requires. A deficiency either in will power or physical force to pronounce this small negative distinctly and firmly may result in financial ruin, as it did in the case of Wm. Heath & Co.

Henry Nelson Smith made many successful turns in speculation during the Tweed regime, owing to the facilities which the municipal bankers belonging to that famous coterie afforded him for manipulating the money market.

There were great fluctuations in stocks while William Marcy Tweed was the power behind the throne in the government of the city of New York. Mr. Tweed contributed largely towards these fluctuations. He and his trusty companions pulled the wires at the City Hall while the puppets in several of the brokers' offices in the vicinity of Wall Street danced to the sweet will of the managers in the municipal building.

One of Tweed's three famous maxims was, "The way to have power is to take it." The other two were, "He is human," and "What are you going to do about it?" In conformity with the first maxim, Mr. Tweed took control of the city funds, besides a number of the city savings banks, and other financial institutions, which he had organized through special charters from the Legislature, which he also owned during the period of his Boss-ship.

These funds were so managed that a very tight squeeze could, at almost any time, be effected in the money market. The city funds on hand were, at that time, usually about from six to eight millions of dollars, and were deposited in the banking institutions of the "Boss." They were ostensibly under the control of the City Chamberlain, who was under the control of Tweed.

Henry N. Smith and a few other favorite members of the syndicate would draw their balances from these banks, making money scarce to the general public, and the money market would suffer a sudden squeeze, and consequently the stock market would break, sometimes with such rapidity as to produce disastrous results to a number of brokers, business houses and other financial concerns outside the Tweed Ring.

On one of these occasions Mr. Smith drove up to the Tenth National Bank, the Black Friday ring institution, in a cab, and drew his balance therefrom, amounting to $4,100,000. He took it home and kept it there several days under lock and key. In the meantime Mr. Tweed and his companions withdrew from circulation the greater portion of the amount under their immediate control, making a tie-up, on the whole, of nearly twenty millions of dollars. At that time this was an amount sufficient to make a very stringent money market, and cause Wall Street operators to feel very uncomfortable. It was then a mighty power to be wielded by a few unscrupulous men. At that time Mr. Smith considered himself worth at least five million dollars. He lost most of this in the panic of 1873, largely in Western Union stock, as above stated, into which Commodore Vanderbilt had kindly put him.

I have referred to the prominent part which Mr. Smith played in the great speculative drama of Black Friday, in the scenes and incidents of my chapter on that ever-to-be-remembered day in Wall Street.

I shall, in another chapter, briefly review some of the methods to which the Tweed Ring resorted to make speculation and politics play into each other's hands, and show how a bold attempt was made to add the control of the National Treasury to that of New York.

CHAPTER 29

CHARLES F. WOERISHOFFER

THE CAREER OF CHARLES F. WOERISHOFFER, AND THE
RESULTANT EFFECT UPON SUCCEEDING GENERATIONS. —
THE PECULIAR POWER OF THE GREAT LEADER OF THE
BEAR ELEMENT IN WALL STREET. — HIS METHODS AS
COMPARED WITH THOSE OTHER WRECKERS OF VALUES. — A
BISMARCK IDEA OF AGGRESSIVENESS THE RULING ELEMENT
OF HIS BUSINESS LIFE. — HIS GRAND ATTACK ON THE
VILLARD PROPERTIES, AND THE CONSEQUENCE THEREOF. —
HIS BENEFACTIONS TO FAITHFUL FRIENDS.

BY the death of Charles F. Woerishoffer, Wall Street lost
one of the most prominent figures which has ever shown
up here. Mr. Woerishoffer died May 9, 1886. His career is
one worthy of study by watchers of the course of speculation
in this or any other country. The results of his life-work show
what can be accomplished by any man who sets himself at
work upon an idea, and who devotes himself steadily and persistently to a course of action for the development and perfection of the principle which actuates his life. Mr. Woerishoffer
possessed peculiar personal qualities which are denied to
most men and to all women. He had the magnetic power of
impressing people with confidence in the schemes which he
inaugurated; that is to say, he had the power of organization—the same power has made other men great, and will
continue to make men great who possess it in all walks of

345

life. Notable instances may be cited in the cases of Bismarck, Gladstone, Napoleon, Grant, and—coming down to Wall Street proper—Gould, Daniel Drew, old Jacob Little and the Vanderbilts, especially the Commodore, in his superior power of aggressiveness.

It has been said of Mr. Woerishoffer that he was fortunate. He was indeed. He was fortunate in the possession of natural ability, and he had the aptitude to take advantage of events, and associate circumstances and the strength of purpose, and to direct, instead of following, the operations with which he became connected. He was the leader of the bear element of the Street—at least he was such during the period which marks his successful operations here. There is no doubt that the death of Mr. Woerishoffer was hastened because of the great strain of mind growing out of his business transactions. There is one point in this connection which has been over-looked by his biographers, namely, that his boldness in the magnitude of his dealings was resultant from a careless or non-calculative mind. I do not believe that Mr. Woerishoffer ever undertook a speculation of any sort until he had care-fully calculated all the chances pro and con, and his success, remarkable as it was, was largely due to the combination of calculation and the natural development of business condi-tions, of which he was a close student.

Mr. Woerishoffer's conception of business principles was iconoclastic to an intense degree. As a broker, as a business man, as an operator in stocks, he "believed in nothing;" that is to say, he was a believer in the failures of men, and had no faith in the corporations and enterprises which were organized for the purpose of the development of the best interests of the country in which he lived. There is another view, or another statement of this peculiar feature, of the character of this man which may be given in description, and this is illustrative of the careful study he made of everything passing along in the lines of life with which he was con-nected. It is this: That Mr. Woerishoffer, by his intimate study of the prospects and probabilities of the projected plans of enterprising Americans, had come to the conclusion that the majority of them must fail, and that the first flush of enterprise would be changed to a darker shade as time progressed. That is to say, he saw and knew a great deal of the organization of the railroad schemes which have marked the growth of our rapid development in a business way, and he judged that the inflated ideas of the projectors must meet with a check as developments were made, and that the earning capacity of the roads would not equal expectations. Hence he sold the stocks, and sold them right and left from the start, and with his followers reaped the profits. Woerishoffer never indulged in the *finesse* of Gould or Henry N. Smith. He had the German ideas of open fight, and he attacked everything indiscriminately, losing money sometimes, but making money at other times, and by his open dash and persistency carried his point.

There is no doubt that the successful career of a man of this sort has a deleterious effect upon those who follow him in succeeding generations. It does not matter how successful the development of the business industries of this country may be hereafter, there will always be found men who will speculate upon the ruination rather than the success of the best interests of the country merely because Charles F. Woerishoffer lived and made a fortune by his disbelief and his disregard of the growth of the institutions of the country which gave him a home.

Woerishoffer was a wonderful example of the sudden rise and steady and rapid progress of a man of strong and tenacious purpose, who adheres with firmness to one line of action or business. He was born in Germany. Woerishoffer's Wall Street career was begun in the office of August Rutten, afterwards of the firm of Rutten & Bond, in which Woerishoffer subsequently became Cashier. He left this firm in 1867, and joined M.C. Klingenfeldt. Mr. Budge, of the firm of Budge, Schutze & Co., in 1868, bought him a seat in the Stock Exchange. Some time after he entered the Board he became acquainted with Mr. Plaat, of the well-known banking firm of L. Von Hoffman & Co. Mr. Woerishoffer was entrusted with the execution of large orders, especially in gold and Government bonds. At that time the trading in these securities was very large. Afterwards Plaat became an operator himself, and

Woerishoffer followed in his footsteps as an apt pupil. Eventually he formed the firm of Woerishoffer & Co., his first partners being Messrs. Schromberg and Schuyler, who made fortunes and retired.

Woerishoffer was connected in enormous operations with some of the magnates of the street; for instance, James R. Keene, Henry N. Smith, D. P. Morgan, Henry Villard, Charles J. Osborn, S. V. White, Addison Cammack, and last, though not least, Jay Gould. He was especially on intimate terms with his great brother bear, Addison Cammack, both speculatively and socially. Besides being a bold operator in the street, Woerishoffer was associated with large railroad schemes, which gave him the inside track in speculation. He was connected with the North River Construction Company, the Northern Pacific, Ontario & Western, West Shore, Denver & Rio Grande, Mexican National, several of the St. Louis Companies, and Oregon Transcontinental. He was originally a rampant bull on these properties until they began to get into trouble, and then he became a furious and unrelenting bear. He smashed and hammered them down right and left. He soon covered his losses, and began to make enormous profits on the short side of the market. On the bonds and stock of the Kansas Pacific, when it became merged in the Union Pacific, it is supposed that Woerishoffer cleared over a million dollars.

Woerishoffer, it seems, was one of the first to propose the building of the Denver & Rio Grande Railroad. On this enterprise he realized immense profits for himself and his friends. The stock rose until it reached 110, and was "puffed" up for higher figures. The public was attracted by the brilliant prospects of immense profits on the long side. Mr. Woerishoffer and friends held large quantities of long stock, but sold out, and afterwards put out a large line of shorts. The bear campaign had Woerishoffer as leader, and, it is said, he succeeded in covering as far down as 40, and some even lower. In 1878, when the market began its great boom on account of the resumption of specie payment and the general prosperity of the country, he organized a combination which bought stocks largely and sold wheat short. On this deal he made large profits, and began to develope into a pretty strong millionaire. He took advantage of the shooting of President Garfield, in 1881, together with his colleagues, Cammack and Smith, to organize a bear raid on a large scale, which was probably one of the chief, although somewhat remote, causes of bringing about the panic of 1884.

The great perspicacity which he had in the deals enumerated failed him in 1885. He thought, as the wheat crop was small, that wheat would go up and stocks would go down, but the very reverse occurred. The disappointment and depression, very probably, resulting from this brought on the aneurism of the heart, which killed the great bear operator, and his death was a fortunate event for Wall Street.

One of the many things which gave Woerishoffer great reputation as a speculator, both here and in Germany and England, was the bold stand be took in the fight for the control of Kansas Pacific against Jay Gould, Russell Sage, and other capitalists, railroad magnates and financiers in 1879. He represented the Frankfort investors, and had engaged to sell a large quantity of Denver extension bonds at 80, to the Gould-Sage syndicate. The syndicate, however, knowing that they had the controlling influence, declared the contract for 80 off, and "came to the conclusion, after examining the road-bed, that the bonds were not worth more than 70," and they would not take them at a higher figure. Woerishoffer then made a grand flank movement on the little Napoleon of finance and his able lieutenants. He seemed to be greatly put out that they had broken their contract, but did not complain very bitterly. He immediately cabled to the English and German bondholders, and soon secured a majority of the bonds which the syndicate wanted, and deposited them in the United States Trust Company. He then informed the syndicate that they could not obtain a single bond under par to carry out their great foreclosure scheme. It was this circumstance that caused Frankfort speculators and investors to come so largely into the New York stock market, and that also made English capital flow in freely, speculators throwing off their former timidity. The amount involved in the Gould-Sage syndicate deal was about $6,000,000 of bonds, thus netting

Woerishoffer considerably over a million. This deal at once gave him an international reputation as a far-sighted speculator, and this reputation was gained at the expense of Gould and Sage, owing to their disregard of the contract which had been entered into.

Woerishoffer showed great sagacity as a speculator when Henry Villard put forward his immense bubble scheme in Northern Pacific and the Oregons. Although invited to go into the big deal with other millionaire speculators who had taken the Villard bait so freely, Woerishoffer kept prudently aloof, and looked on the players at the Villard checkerboard with equanimity and at a safe distance. He was not then considered of very much account by the men of ample means who so freely subscribed $20,000,000 to the Villard bubble. At the moment when these subscribers were so highly elated with the idea that the Villard fancies were going far up into the hundreds and, perhaps, the thousands, like the bonanzas during the California craze, Woerishoffer boldly sold the whole line "short." This was a similar stroke of daring to that which James R. Keene had perpetrated on the bonanza kings in the height of their greatest power and anticipations. The Villard syndicate determined to squeeze Woerishoffer out entirely, and for this purpose a syndicate was formed to buy 100,000 shares of stock. There were various millionaires and prominent financiers included in the syndicate. These were the financial powers with which Woerishoffer, small in comparison, had to contend single-handed. The feat that Napoleon performed at Lodi, with his five generals behind him, spiking the Austrian guns which were defended by several regiments, was but a moderate effort in war compared with that which Woerishoffer was called upon to achieve in speculation. He took things very coolly, and with evident unconcern watched the actions of the syndicate. The latter went to work vigorously, and soon obtained 20,000 shares of the stock which they required. It still kept climbing rapidly, and so elated was this speculative syndicate with the success of its plans that it clamored for the additional 80,000 shares, according to the resolution. The speculators thought they were now in the fair way of crushing Woerishoffer, and with a hurrah obtained the 80,000 shares required, but Woerishoffer's brokers were the men who sold them to the big syndicate. It was not long afterwards that the syndicate felt as if it had been struck by lightning. In a short time the Villard fancies began to tumble. The syndicate was in a quandary, but nothing could be done. It had tried to crush Woerishoffer. He owed it no mercy. The inevitable laws of speculation had to take their course, and the great little bear netted millions of dollars. These events occurred in 1883.

After the Villard disruption, Mr. Woerishoffer became conservative for some time, and was a bull or a bear just as he saw the opportunity to make money. When the West Shore settlement took place he watched the course of events with a keen eye, and was one of the most prominent figures in pushing the upward movement upon the strength of that settlement. His profits on the bull side then were immense. After this he became a chronic and most destructive bear. The reason he assigned for his conversion and change of base was that the net earnings of the railroads were decreasing, and did not justify an advance in prices. He pushed his theory to an extreme, making little or no allowance for the recuperative powers of the country, and the large bear contingent, which he successfully led, seemed to be inspired with his opinions. These opinions, pushed to the extreme, as they were, had a very demoralizing effect upon the stock market, and constituted a potent factor in the depreciation of all values, throwing a depressing influence on speculation, from which it did not recover until many months after Mr. Woerishoffer's death. The great bear had wonderful skill in putting other operators off the track of his operations by employing a large number of brokers, and by changing his brokers and his base of action so often that speculators were all at sea regarding what he was going to do, and waiting in anxiety for the next move. It was considered remarkable at the time that his death had not a greater influence on the stock market than this result proved. If he had died a week sooner, his death might have created a panic, for he was then short of 200,000 shares of stock. His short accounts had all been covered before the announcement of his death on the Stock Exchange.

Woerishoffer was almost as famous for his generosity as James R. Keene. It is said that he made presents to faithful brokers of over twenty seats, of the value of $25,000 each, in the Stock Exchange. He made a present of a $500 horse to the cabman who drove him daily to and from his office. He was exceedingly generous with his employes. A short time before his death, feeling that the strain from over-mental exertion was beginning to tell on his constitution, he had resolved to visit Europe for the purpose of recuperating, but, like most of our great operators, he had stretched the mental cords too far before making this prudent resolve and he died at the early age of 43. How many valuable lives would be prolonged if they would take needful rest in time! The death of Woerishoffer should be a solemn warning to Wall Street men who are anxious to heap up wealth too rapidly. His fortune has been variously estimated at from $1,000,000 to $4,000,000. He left a widow and two little daughters.

Woerishoffer had simply the genius for speculation which is uncontrollable, irrespective of consequences to others. He had no intention of hurting anybody, but his methods had the effect of bringing others to ruin all the same. He merely followed the bent of his genius by making money within the limits of the law, and did not care who suffered through his operations. All speculation on the bear side involves the same principle. If there is any difference among speculators, it only consists in degree. Large transactions, like those in which Woerishoffer was engaged, are more severely felt by those who have the misfortune to get "squeezed;" but it all resolves itself into a question of the survival of the fittest

Woerishoffer's success in this country seems strange to Americans, but how much stranger it must have seemed to the people of his native town of Henau Hesse-Nassau, where he was born in 1843, in comparative poverty. John Jacob Astor was one of the first of a considerable number of Germans to find this country a veritable new El Dorado, where peasants' sons, as if my magic, became far wealthier than many of the nobility whom they had, as boys, gazed upon with awe. Who could have foreseen such a career for the poor young German, who came to New York in 1864?

He was then in his twenty-first year. He had had some experience in the brokerage business in Frankfort and Paris, but he came here poor. Addison Cammack, who was to become his ally in many a gigantic speculation, was then prominent in the South, where he had favored the cause of the people of his State during the war, and had made a fortune. D. P. Morgan, who was to be another of his speculative associates, had already won a fortune by speculating in cotton in London. Russell Sage counted his wealth by the millions. Jay Gould and Henry N. Smith had gone through the feverish excitement of a Black Friday, and either, in common parlance, could have "bought or sold" the poor young German. Nevertheless, by strange turns in the wheel of fortune, he acquired a financial prestige that enabled him to beard the lion in his den, and snap his fingers at powerful combinations that sought to ruin him. When Henry Villard demanded his resignation as a director in the Oregon Transcontinental Company, on the ground that he had been selling the Villard properties short, the "Baron" (as Woerishoffer was often called) tendered it at once, and flung down the gage of battle in the announcement that he would ruin the head of the Villard system.

Chas. F. Woerishoffer was slightly built, had a light complexion, was under the medium height, and, on the street, might have been taken for a bank clerk. He showed his inborn love of gaming in many ways. He is said to have broken a faro bank at Long Branch twice; he would play at roulette and poker for large stakes. He was kind-hearted and charitable. At Christmas his benefactions to clerks and messenger boys were notable. In the height of a great speculation he sometimes showed extreme nervousness, but during the memorable contest with the Villard party he exhibited the greatest coolness and composure. He was a curious compound of German phlegm and American nervousness. One of the fortunate events in his career was his marriage, in 1875, with Miss Annie Uhl, the step-daughter of Oswald Ottendorfer, the editor and proprietor of the great German organ of New York, the *Staats Zeitung,* who brought him, it was understood, a fortune of about three hundred thousand dollars.

The following circular to my customers, which I published May 13th, 1886, with special reference to the death of Woerishoffer, and its consequences, I think is worthy of reproduction here:

The future of the market is going to be a natural one, and will go up and down from natural causes; when this is fully realized there will be no lack of the public taking a hand in it. That element has been crowded out of Wall Street for a long time past, largely due to the fact that its judgment to predicate operations has been sat on by brute force. It has been, therefore, made to feel that the market was not one where it was safe to venture. This brute force power came from Woerishoffer, who has for a long time past been the head and front as a leader on the bear side, and was a gigantic wrecker of values. His method was to destroy confidence and hammer the vitality out of every stock on the list which showed symptoms of life, and his power was the more potential, as all the room traders were converted to believe in him and were his followers. His decease leaves, therefore, the entire bear fraternity without any head, and consequently in a state of demoralization, and in a condition not unlike a ship at sea without a rudder. Mr. Woerishoffer was a genial, hospitable man, lovely in character at his own home, true to his friends and generous to a fault, and will, therefore, be a great loss as a gentleman; but so far as the prosperity of the country goes, his death will be the country's gain. To the fact that Mr. Woerishoffer's power and influence are no longer felt on the market is almost entirely due the change of front of the situation, which is now one of hopefulness. While he lived the public and half the members of the Board were completely terrorized by the fear of him, and were kept in check from being buyers, however much the position of affairs warranted going on the long side. The bull side of the market has had for a long time past to contend with the bold and ferocious attitude of Mr. Woerishoffer. When the bulls felt justified in making a rally and forcing the market to go their way, when it looked most encouraging, as a result of their efforts, Mr. Woerishoffer would strike their specialty a sledge hammer blow on the head; he would repeat that on every attempt that was made, which finally resulted in discouragement. If ten thousand shares were not ample for that purpose, he would quadruple the quantity; in fact, he has often been known to have outstanding contracts on the short side of the market amounting to 200,000 shares of stock at least. As an operator he seemed to be so peculiarly constituted as to know no fear, and would often turn apparent defeat to success possessing that trait of character. It will be a long time before another such determined and desperate man will appear on the stage to take his place; in the meantime, it will be plainer sailing in Wall Street, besides safer for operators. Mr. Woerishoffer, as an operator, was full of expedients. He put his whole soul into his operations, and not only would he attack the stock market with voraciousness, but he would manipulate every quarter where it would aid him; sometimes it would be in the grain market, sometimes by shipping gold, and sometimes by the manipulation of the London market. He had all the facilities for operation at his fingers' ends, in fact he commanded the situation to such an extent as to make his power felt. Mr. Cammack, Mr. Woerishoffer's associate, while usually a bear, is a very different man and not to be feared, for that gentleman usually sells stocks short only on reliable information, and always to a limited extent. If he finds that the market does not go down by the weight of sales, he soon extricates himself at the first loss. In this method of doing business lies his safety. In this way he will sell often 10, 20 or 30 thousand shares and make the turn, but will not, like his late friend Woerishoffer, take a position and stand by it through thick and thin, and browbeat the market indefinitely until it finally goes his way. At the present time, therefore, the bulls have no great power to fear whenever they have merit upon which to predicate their operations. The future will be brighter for Wall Street speculators and investors than it has been for a long period, and with the public who may be expected to come again to the front, greatly increased activity should be the result.

CHAPTER 30

WHY I AM AN AMERICAN

I came to this country from England over fifty years ago, expecting to stay for merely a short visit. I had barely learned the localities of the public buildings and the principal streets, when I began to perceive the possibilities that presented themselves to a young man, who had the courage to push, to compete for a place in the race for wealth and position. I liked the hustle and the bustle that contrasted so vividly with the slow and easy style which prevailed in my native country. I could not escape being drawn into the spirit which surrounded me, and I made up my mind that I would make my stand in life in New York, and I sought and found employment. Fortunately I had letters of introduction to people of culture and refinement, so my social surroundings were both attractive and beneficial. In a few years the Civil War broke out and the leaven was thereby added to the liking I had for the flag which floats for freedom, and I became a more ardent American than though this had been my native soil. I had the good fortune to meet the great men of those days and they whetted my appetite to rise to their level, and much of my success is due to the quiet influence they exerted upon my young mind. When I landed in New York, most of what is now the great West, was boundless prairie or dense forest, but even then the indomitable spirit of people around me yearned to subdue this wilderness and make it blossom and bear fruit. Millionaires were few in those days and truthfulness and honesty, combined with a willingness to work, were the necessary requisites to enable a young fellow to succeed. The fact that this was a government for the people, and by the people, did much to determine me that here

I had found the promised land. No aristocracy to contend with but the aristocracy of brains and courage; no traditions of centuries to hang between you and your right to toe the scratch with any man. The country was growing beyond its population and immigration was invited in such an attractive way that the desirable classes from all over Europe were drawn to our shores. The fact that men born in humble life had become some of the world's leaders proved the possibilities that might come to any one who cared to try and who had the courage not to know when he was beaten. In this country Congress has always made, and is still making, laws that benefit all kinds and conditions of men who behave themselves. Before the law neither blue blood nor family tree protects any man who violates the statutes, for all are free and equal. This nation has never fought for conquest of territory and wherever our flag floats it has a moral and undisputed right to do so.

The foregoing is but a summary of the volumes I might add to the reasons why I am an American. One more is that I cannot help being an American and I don't want to.

                                        HENRY CLEWS.